POLITICAL LEADERSHIP IN AN ERA OF DECOLONISATION

What is leadership, and why is it so important? In what ways does it look very different in different contexts, and in what ways does it look the same? Malcolm Murfett brings together a range of emerging and established scholars to examine these questions in light of some of the mid-twentieth century's most intriguing national leaders.

In a series of striking biographical chapters, lessons are drawn from the apartheid era in South Africa, Lee's remarkable socio-economic transformation of Singapore, Castro's revolutionary overhauling of Cuba, and the playing out of Bandaranaike's populist agenda in Sri Lanka. The book illuminates what Brezhnev and Nixon were looking for in the Cold War and what happened when the people turned against Nyerere in Tanzania, the Shah in Iran, and Ceaușescu in Romania. These case studies address what leadership meant for the individuals whose record in power is being examined. These are not idealised portraits of 'how to do leadership' but warts-and-all portrayals of exceptional individuals who scrabbled their way to the top and stayed there for several years during a period of great change.

Business schools have long studied the theoretical axioms of corporate leadership. What this book does, however, is to move beyond the theory into the practical realm of politics and statecraft. This is a fascinating book on leadership that will be of interest for students, researchers, and practitioners studying leadership in business and politics, as well as for students of global history, decolonisation, and the Cold War.

Malcolm Murfett is Visiting Professor in the Department of War Studies at King's College London. A historian of the contemporary world with over a dozen books to his name, Malcolm is also Associate Editor of the Oxford Dictionary of National Biography and the Series Editor of Cold War in Asia.

POLITICAL LEADERSHIP IN AN ERA OF DECOLONISATION

Case Studies from Across the Globe

Edited by Malcolm Murfett

LONDON AND NEW YORK

Designed cover image: Getty

First published 2024
by Routledge
4 Park Square, Milton Park, Abingdon, Oxon OX14 4RN

and by Routledge
605 Third Avenue, New York, NY 10158

Routledge is an imprint of the Taylor & Francis Group, an informa business

© 2024 selection and editorial matter, Malcolm Murfett; individual chapters, the contributors

The right of Malcolm Murfett to be identified as the author of the editorial material, and of the authors for their individual chapters, has been asserted in accordance with sections 77 and 78 of the Copyright, Designs and Patents Act 1988.

All rights reserved. No part of this book may be reprinted or reproduced or utilised in any form or by any electronic, mechanical, or other means, now known or hereafter invented, including photocopying and recording, or in any information storage or retrieval system, without permission in writing from the publishers.

Trademark notice: Product or corporate names may be trademarks or registered trademarks, and are used only for identification and explanation without intent to infringe.

British Library Cataloguing-in-Publication Data
A catalogue record for this book is available from the British Library

ISBN: 978-1-032-54689-6 (hbk)
ISBN: 978-1-032-54688-9 (pbk)
ISBN: 978-1-003-42616-5 (ebk)

DOI: 10.4324/9781003426165

Typeset in Times New Roman
by Apex CoVantage, LLC

For Professor J.E. Spence

A gentleman scholar of integrity and wisdom. A true example to us all.

CONTENTS

List of Contributors	*ix*
Foreword	*xiii*
Acknowledgements	*xx*

1 Leadership in apartheid South Africa: the impact
of Hendrik Verwoerd and B.J. Vorster   1
J.E. Spence

2 Lee Kuan Yew: from political insurgent to national manager   24
Michael D. Barr

3 Fidel Castro: the eternal leader of a revolution or the leader
of an eternal revolution?   50
Vinicius Mariano de Carvalho

4 The unlikely prime minister: rethinking Sirimavo
Bandaranaike's leadership in a bipolar nation and world   62
Darinee Alagirisamy

5 Julius Nyerere: African leadership as a moral project   81
Sara Lorenzini

6 Leonid Brezhnev: rule through trust and care   100
Susanne Schattenberg

viii Contents

7 Nicolae Ceaușescu: interpreting a national-Stalinist   125
  Francesco Magno

8 The rise and fall of Richard Nixon as a global leader   146
  Umberto Tulli

9 Mohammad Reza Shah Pahlavi: a moderniser challenged
  by Islamists and Leftists   164
  Pejman Abdolmohammadi

  Coda   184
  Malcolm Murfett

Index   *191*

CONTRIBUTORS

Dr Pejman Abdolmohammadi (University of Trento)

Dr Darinee Alagirisamy (National University of Singapore)

Professor Michael D. Barr (Flinders University)

Dr Vinicius Mariano de Carvalho (King's College London)

Professor Sara Lorenzini (University of Trento)

Dr Francesco Magno (University of Messina)

Professor Malcolm Murfett (King's College London)

Professor Susanne Schattenberg (University of Bremen)

Professor J.E. Spence (King's College London)

Dr Umberto Tulli (University of Trento)

Biography of editor

Professor Malcolm Murfett is Visiting Professor of Contemporary History in the Department of War Studies at King's College London. An Oxford Blue and a double international, Malcolm has taught at universities in Australia, Canada, Italy, Singapore, and the United Kingdom, winning teaching awards at each of the

x Contributors

institutions he has represented. He has written and edited over a dozen books on a range of military, strategic, and political themes and was elected a Fellow of the Royal Historical Society in 1991 and became Associate Editor of the *Oxford Dictionary of National Biography* in 1997. His *Naval Warfare 1919–1945* is widely recognised as a pathbreaking book since it brings the element of simultaneity of action and decision-making to bear in each theatre across the globe and with every naval combatant involved in the process. Known for his experience in Asia, Malcolm was invited in 2017 to become the series editor for Routledge's new series of publications titled 'Cold War in Asia.' A management consultant for over 30 years and advising a number of multinational companies in both Asia and Europe, he has extensive broadcasting experience with both terrestrial and cable TV and has often been an advisor on European affairs for Channel NewsAsia and for the History Channel.

Biographies of contributors

Pejman Abdolmohammadi is Associate Professor of Middle Eastern Studies at the University of Trento's School of International Studies and Associate Research Fellow at the Italian Institute for International Political Studies in Milan (ISPI). He was formerly Lecturer in Political Science and Middle Eastern Studies at the American University 'John Cabot' in Rome (2013–2015) and Resident Visiting Research Fellow at the London School of Economics – Middle East Centre (2015–2018). His latest book titled *The Domestic and Foreign Policy of Modern Iran* was published by Palgrave-Macmillan in 2020.

Darinee Alagirisamy is Lecturer in the South Asian Studies Programme of the National University of Singapore. A historian whose research interests straddle colonialism, gender, and cultural studies, her current book project traces the history of alcohol prohibition in India. Alagirisamy's previous research has been published in *Modern Asian Studies* and *The Indian Economic and Social History Review*. Titled 'The Unlikely Prime Minister,' Alagirisamy's chapter in this volume proposes a new approach to thinking about Sirimavo Bandaranaike's premiership. From being dismissed as a clueless housewife who had fumbled her way into politics, to being termed the only man in her cabinet, it shows how Mrs Bandaranaike's career remains a compelling study: not just of female political leadership in the Asia Pacific region, but of leadership in general in a bipolar world.

Michael D. Barr is Associate Professor of International Relations at Flinders University (Australia) and Fellow of the Australian Academy of the Humanities. He has written or edited seven books on aspects of Singapore politics and history, beginning with his groundbreaking *Lee Kuan Yew: The Beliefs behind the Man*, which is currently in its third edition. His most recent books are *Singapore: A Modern History* (2019 and 2020) and *The Limits of Authoritarian Governance in Singapore's*

Developmental State (2019; co-edited with Lily Zubaidah Rahim). He regularly comments on Singapore politics and history through news media outlets including *The Financial Times, Australian Financial Review*, ABC (Australia), *The Wall Street Journal, The Economist, Nikkei Asia*, the BBC, and CNN.

Vinicius Mariano de Carvalho is Reader in the Department of War Studies at King's College London. Born in Barra Mansa, Brazil, he received his PhD from the University of Passau, Germany, and his undergraduate and MA degrees from the Federal University of Juiz de Fora, Brazil. Vinicius was a lieutenant in the Brazilian Army (2007–2008), serving in the Military Technical Corps. Before joining King's in 2014, he was Associate Professor of Brazilian Studies at Aarhus University (2008–2014), Denmark, where he was also Director of the Latin American Centre (2012–2014). At King's, Dr Carvalho has been Vice Dean (International) for the Faculty of Social Science and Public Policy, and between 2020 and 2022, he was Director of King's Brazil Institute. In the War Studies Department, he is the convener of the MA in Strategic Communications course and teaches undergraduate modules on Latin American issues. He is also Honorary Senior Research Fellow at the UCL Institute of the Americas.

Sara Lorenzini is Professor of Contemporary History at the School of International Studies, University of Trento (Italy). She has written extensively on Italian and German Foreign Policy and specialises in Cold War History, North–South relations, and the place of Europe in the world. She is known for her work on the history of development, including *Global Development: A Cold War History* (Princeton University Press, 2019). Her latest edited book is *The Human Rights Breakthrough of the 1970s. The European Community and International Relations*, with U. Tulli and I. Zamburlini (Bloomsbury, 2021).

Francesco Magno (Messina, 1992) is Adjunct Professor of Eastern European History at the University of Messina. In 2021, he obtained his PhD from the University of Trento, where he subsequently worked as a postdoctoral research fellow. His research interests focus on Romanian Nationalism, Institutional and Legal History of South-Eastern Europe, and Imperial Legacies in the Successor States of the Habsburg, Russian, and Ottoman Empires. Currently, he is working on a new project focusing on the history of Islamic law in Romania and Bulgaria after the end of Ottoman rule.

Susanne Schattenberg is Director of the Research Centre for East European Studies and teaches Russian and Soviet History at the University of Bremen, Germany. She is the author of *Brezhnev. The Making of a Statesman* (I.B. Tauris 2022) and *Die korrupte Provinz? Russische Beamte im 19. Jahrhundert* (V&R 2008). Her work on *Stalins Ingenieure: Lebenswelten zwischen Technik und Terror in den 1930er Jahren* (Oldenbourg, 2014) was first published in Russian

xii Contributors

(ROSSPEN, 2011). Currently, she is working on the dissident Natalya Gorbanevskaya (1936–2013).

J.E. Spence (Jack) retired from the Department of War Studies at King's College, London in 2021. He had taught at a number of institutions in the United Kingdom and abroad as well as acting as Director of Studies at the Royal Institute of International Affairs between 1991 and 1997. His publications include books and articles on Southern African issues, as well as more general topics in international relations. His last major publication (with Drs Claire Yorke and Alastair Masser) was a two-volume study on the theory and practice of diplomacy in international relations.

Umberto Tulli is Lecturer in International and Contemporary History at the Department of Humanities and at the School of International Studies, University of Trento. His research interests include American foreign policy during the Cold War, European integration history, and the history of human rights. He is the author of several publications, including *A Precarious Equilibrium. Human Rights and Détente in Jimmy Carter's Foreign Policy* (Manchester University Press, 2020); 'Wielding the human rights weapon against the American empire: the second Russell Tribunal and human rights in transatlantic relations,' *Journal of Transatlantic Studies* (2021). With Sara Lorenzini and Ilaria Zamburlini, he has edited the volume *The Human Rights Breakthrough of the 1970s. The European Community and International Relations* (Bloomsbury, 2022).

FOREWORD

I got the idea for this book from a very popular undergraduate course on this subject that I conducted for five years at King's College London before Covid-19 struck. My students became very animated in our debates on a whole slew of fascinating topics related to what was happening around the world in the 1960s. Their enthusiasm for what we were accomplishing in our classes made me feel that a book on this subject would have a place at both the undergraduate and postgraduate levels given the heightened importance of leadership these days and what it takes to be successful in that role.

Business schools have long studied the theoretical axioms of corporate leadership. What this book does, however, is to move beyond the theory into the practical realm of politics and state craft. Not all national leaders will succeed in the art of statesmanship since there is a narrow but perilous gap between stunning success and inglorious failure. As such, it's rarely a foregone conclusion as to what will happen when leaders navigate that tricky path between the two.

Although every generation feels it's special and unique, the 'baby boomers' certainly wrought massive changes in the social and cultural fabric of the Western world by the 1960s. Their world was not that of their parents, many of whom couldn't understand the remarkable transition that had occurred from the mid-1950s onwards. My British parents, though wonderfully kind and warm people, were certainly 'out of it' and frankly had no desire to be 'in it' either. A kind of social revolution was taking place in their community, and it was wildly disconcerting to them. Fascinatingly, however, this radical climate of change didn't prevail to anything like the same extent in Africa and Asia where decolonisation was making its epoch-making presence felt.

It was with this sharp contrast in mind that I ran my course by looking at a number of political leaders drawn from around the globe who had managed to climb

xiv Foreword

'the greasy pole' to success in these years of political volatility. Our task was to try and see how they did it and what they made of their success once they were in power.

Why is leadership such an important concept given that one size evidently doesn't fit all? Some who get to lead fail to either inspire or succeed in their role whatever the organisation is. Why are some more successful in their role than others? Is it down to initiative, talent, luck, unscrupulousness on their part, or multiple other factors? We can find different clues from studying those who have somehow got to the top and gone onto lead a state for several years.

This book will try and do justice to those aims. I began by asking a mix of nine established and emerging academics to look at some of the world leaders who were in power in these years. I didn't impose a strict methodology upon them, but knowing their work in the past I felt confident from the outset that they would be able to provide our readers with a reflective chapter on leadership and in some cases even from a personal perspective. I didn't adopt a 'same old, same old' approach in my course at King's and wanted this volume to reflect that approach too. For that reason, I chose not to have all of the usual suspects (Brandt, de Gaulle, Gandhi, Kennedy, Johnson, Kenyatta, Khrushchev, Mao, Nkrumah, Wilson) but instead went for an admittedly eclectic mix of individuals containing some obvious stalwarts of the period (Brezhnev, Castro, Lee Kuan Yew, Nixon) and also a few who could easily be overlooked when compiling a list of their arguably more illustrious peer group (Bandaranaike, Ceaușescu, Nyerere, the Shah, and Verwoerd/Vorster).

I began by inviting Professor J.E. Spence (King's College London) who grew up in South Africa and lived in the Republic under the apartheid regimes of Verwoerd and Vorster to give his insights on them in the opening chapter. Spence was always deeply uncomfortable growing up in a country dominated by a white minority government which cemented itself in power by denying the black majority equal rights in society. He will look at the bases of Verwoerd's rise to power and examine the measures he took to consolidate his hold over the country before his assassination in 1966. Verwoerd was determined not to let Macmillan's 'Winds of Change' speech become prophetical for his government. A stunningly bright intellectual, Verwoerd enjoyed the respect given to him by the Afrikaner community and felt incomparably superior to those around him. Arrogant, austere, and ruthless, he was totally committed to the establishment of a Bantustan strategy – a kind of internal decolonisation – which he and others had devised to deal with the black majority indigenous population of South Africa. Whatever the humanitarian cost of this social experiment would be, he was convinced that the tribal homelands project would ultimately succeed and apartheid would continue to reign supreme in his country. His successor B.J. Vorster wasn't the intellectual force that Verwoerd had been, but as Spence remarks, he was a cunning individual and one whose political infighting and survival skills were marked. Almost certainly underestimated by his domestic opponents, Vorster knew how to cope with challenges to his authority within the Nationalist Party. While his regime was a little more pragmatic than that of his predecessor, as his foreign policy showed, he was far from being a liberal as the domestic legislation he oversaw clearly demonstrated.

Professor Michael D. Barr (Flinders University), who has written extensively on Singaporean contemporary history and politics, has examined Lee Kuan Yew's long career as Prime Minister of Singapore (1959–1990) and asserts that for a man who had little time for theories or abstract ideas and didn't believe leadership could be learnt, Lee spent a lot of time talking and theorising about it! It's clear Lee felt that intellectual leadership was critical in forging a vision that others could buy into and did much to ensure it would become a formula for success. Lee was ambitious and ultra-competitive, sensitive to criticism, and utterly ruthless and pragmatic. Barr's hard-hitting chapter looks at the early years after Lee reached the summit of power in 1959 and contrasts them with the 1980s, when he took that power for granted. Lee's search for the key to social progress led, as Barr explains, to 'a life-long obsession with the roles of cultural, genetic and environmental determinism as drivers of societal and even civilisational success.' He had no doubts that leaders led while followers lay at the bottom of the pyramidal structure with executives wedged in between the two segments of the social hierarchy. As far as he was concerned, therefore, the individual was no more than a digit in a collective whole. In taking this view, he wasn't squeamish about the effects that his policies would have upon the Singaporean public. Pessimistic by nature, he was always on the lookout for failure and determined to address it before it became a destructive force. People either bought into his view, or they were ousted. There was no middle ground with him. Domestic opponents were undermined and thwarted wherever possible or humiliated and financially ruined if need be. Benign was not a part of his lexicon. While he took no prisoners, Lee's achievements in office were nonetheless astounding. On his watch, Singapore became a phenomenally successful multiethnic, multireligious city state with a booming economy and personal incomes to match. An entrepôt to envy and a restless rival to Hong Kong.

Dr Vinicius Mariano de Carvalho (King's College London) grew up in Brazil after Fidel Castro's rise to power, and in his chapter he explains that the Cuban revolution exerted a powerful attraction upon him and a much wider audience in Latin America than perhaps is usually acknowledged. Unquestionably, the legacy of a long presidential career such as that achieved by Fidel Castro is almost bound to be contested and oscillates between admiration and denunciation as Dr Carvalho indicates. Castro inspired both sets of opinions from those who knew him and with good reason. For those who saw the beneficial effects of the social revolution wrought by the Castro regime – a free education system that boasted adult and youth literacy rates of 100 per cent and provided opportunities for children born in the humblest of conditions to improve themselves; medical training that was the envy of the entire region, forged together with a genuinely progressive free health and welfare system – Cuba was a socialist success story with a more equitable distribution of income than in virtually any other country on the planet.

xvi Foreword

Despite these invaluable assets, however, another darker side of the story exists. Castro is accused of being a totalitarian despot; an opponent of free speech and the liberties of the subject if these posed a threat to his regime. Opponents weren't tolerated. Social harmony might have been an expressed aim, but his antagonism to the LGBTQ+ community was profound and cruel. He saw any form of homosexuality as an example of bourgeois decadence and regarded the entire LGBTQ+ community as a bunch of social deviants who could be subjected to imprisonment without charge or trial and/or confined to forced labour camps. Even those who admired Castro came to acknowledge that his halo may have slipped in his final years in power while those who hated him for his policies felt their enmity towards him was justified by his actions. In essence, therefore, Castro was a complex, passionate man; a mix of good and bad and one who was difficult to ignore in the region and beyond.

Sirimavo Bandaranaike became a strident force in Ceylonese (Sri Lankan) politics from the time she assumed the premiership after the assassination of her husband Solomon at the hands of a Buddhist monk in 1959. Although claiming to know nothing about being a leader before she accepted the role, Mrs Bandaranaike learnt fast, as Darinee Alagirisamy (National University of Singapore) points out in her revealing chapter on this controversial individual. Darinee points out that while the 'weeping widow' was underestimated by her patriarchal rivals both within the party and outside it, she was far more adept and astute than her opponents imagined she was. Determined to survive, she surrounded herself with family members whom she could trust and successfully made herself the 'Mother of the People' by promoting women and children's welfare. Although ethnic tensions were in play before she inherited the premiership, she made them much worse by playing the partisan political card strongly favouring the Sinhalese majority over the Tamil minority and Buddhism over the Hindu religion and Christianity. Populist policies of this nature were electoral assets, but they exacerbated the already-deep divisions among the people and led to a further breakdown in relations between the Tamils on the Jaffna peninsula and the Sinhalese elsewhere. Nationalisation wasn't the answer and neither was corruption, but both figured prominently in her later years at the top. On the foreign field, her championship of the Non-Aligned Movement became a double-edged sword. It gave her international prominence and burnished her ego but caused ructions with both the Americans and the British with negative knock-on effects to the Sri Lankan economy particularly in the wake of the Yom Kippur War of 1973.

Julius Nyerere may not have had the charismatic quality of Kwame Nkrumah or Jomo Kenyatta, but his longevity in power was much greater than those of either the Ghanaian or Kenyan leaders. Professor Sara Lorenzini (University of Trento) shows the steps he took in becoming the acclaimed father of the Tanzanian nation. But the mild-mannered and dignified Nyerere became a much tougher figure after the coup in Zanzibar in January 1964, and his attitude to what he saw as interference by the British, Americans, and West Germans did much to change his outlook

Foreword **xvii**

thereafter. What he perceived as Western arrogance touched a raw nerve in him, and he became far more hostile and independent of the power nexus exercised by Washington, London, and Bonn. As a result, he sought another way through African unity and the promotion of pan-Africanism. A more radical, nationalistic Nyerere sought to impose *Ujamaa* upon the Tanzanians as the integral ideological building block for a more harmonious socialist state based on self-reliance. It was a dream that didn't materialise in either economic autarchy or social harmony. In fact, contrary to his confident expectations, it produced quite the opposite results. Although his moral integrity was rarely in doubt, opposition to his ideas was no longer tolerated or overlooked as they once might have been. Ultimately, frustration on his part led to the exercise of more authoritarian rule at home in what became, sadly, a police state. Nyerere's radicalism was also seen on the foreign stage with his trenchant support for Third-Worldism as an economic antidote to the oppressive domination of the Global North.

Leonid Brezhnev rarely gets a good press internationally even to this day, and yet here was a man who sought to be radically different from both Stalin and Khrushchev – his predecessors as general secretary – and who could claim to have been more successful domestically than both of them. As Professor Susanne Schattenberg (Universität Bremen) points out in her rebuttal of much of the conventional wisdom about him, Brezhnev was far more successful than his critics would have us believe. Marked by his awful experiences in the terror and the war, by purges and the violent upheaval of Soviet society, Brezhnev found himself propelled to the upper levels of the party neither through ideological ruthlessness nor by skilled plotting but more by a combination of luck and the patronage of Nikita Khrushchev. Opportunities opened up for him in an inviting way, and he made the most of them. Brezhnev's aim was to improve the living standards for all within the Soviet Union. He wanted Soviet citizens to live without the fear and instability that had accompanied so much of the storied and lurid past. For him decisions by consensus rather than by dictatorial edict were the way forward. Unlike Stalin and Khrushchev, Brezhnev listened to others and treated his interlocutors with respect. Although he hated war and confrontation, he ironically found himself remembered for both the Afghanistan debacle and the dramatic ending of the Prague Spring. By the mid-1970s, ill health and the drugs he took to relieve his symptoms and overcome sleeplessness combined to reduce him to a physical wreck, blurring his mental acuity and leaving him listless and no longer in control.

Nicolae Ceauşescu was 47 when he took over as *conducător* (leader) of the *Partidul Comunist Român* (Romanian Communist Party), after the death of his patron Gheorghe Gheorghiu-Dej in March 1965. His background, particularly the years he had spent in prison alongside Dej and the other prominent Romanian communist leaders, conditioned his attitude and the policies he pursued thereafter. Much is usually made by academics of the radical, almost schizophrenic, change in his policies from the time he inherited his position in 1965 to his public hanging on Christmas Day 1989. In the first phase, as Francesco Magno (University of Messina)

xviii Foreword

illustrates, between 1965 and the first half of the 1970s, he was noticeably less inhibited by Cold War politics than the other communist leaders of eastern Europe and rejoiced in his maverick status and engagement with the West. Whereas, in the second phase lasting until his overthrow in late 1989, he became more embittered and suspicious as he grew older relying upon the secret police (the infamous *Securitate*), nationalist rhetoric, a gargantuan personality cult, and absurd economic and social policies to maintain his control over the people. What should we make of this contradiction? Magno believes that it was more than personal megalomania but the result of a complex mix of cultural influences and political contingencies, which were present in Romanian history and surfaced repeatedly throughout his rule.

Richard Nixon was one of those statesmen who it is difficult to be neutral about. From his activities on the House Un-American Activities Committee (1948–50) and particularly his hostile interrogation of Alger Hiss, Nixon stood out as a zealous anti-communist much in the mould of Joseph McCarthy. It did him no harm with the Republican Party across the country as could be seen when Eisenhower chose him as his running mate for the 1952 presidential election. Nixon's ambition had a ruthlessness that often crossed the line ethically, but he survived politically and did enough as vice-president to secure the Republican presidential nomination in 1960. Beaten narrowly by Kennedy in the November election and more handsomely by Pat Brown for the governorship of California in 1962, Nixon's political stock rose after the Barry Goldwater presidential fiasco of 1964. Increasingly seen as relatively moderate in comparison with the erstwhile senator from Arizona, Nixon's forte lay in the realm of foreign policy rather than domestic affairs. Building a coalition across the aisle with Southern conservatives, Nixon won the ensuing presidential election in the tumultuous year of 1968. Umberto Tulli (University of Trento) closely examines his record as President and shows that economic problems and social unrest could not be left unaddressed, and far more was done to tackle both than many of his critics expected beforehand. On the foreign stage, however, Nixon and his National Security Advisor Henry Kissinger achieved their greatest successes in reaching out to China and in negotiating the Paris Peace Accord, in January 1973, which brought an immediate ceasefire to the Vietnam War. His policies elsewhere, however, were not so sure-footed. Rejected in the Middle East by all and sundry, they became infamous in Chile for their covert participation in the undermining of the legitimate government of the Marxist President Salvador Allende and in supporting the military coup that led to his overthrow in September 1973. Although his record as President was mixed, Nixon wasn't undone by failure on the big questions of the day but by the botched break-in of the Watergate complex. Utterly unnecessary as it was, but fed by insecurity and the exquisite lure of discovering what his political opponents were plotting, Nixon deviously crossed the line once again in his quest for strategic intel. This time he failed to cover his tracks but not for want of trying as the world soon discovered.

Mohammad Reza Shah Pahlavi is yet another leader who inspires intense controversy from those who study his long reign as the ruling monarch of Iran. For some, of course, he is the epitome of evil, for others a wholly more acceptable leader than those who took his place as the force of the Islamic Revolution broke over the nation in 1979. Dr Pejman Abdolmohammadi (University of Trento) looks at the Shah's long and contentious reign (1941–1979) contrasting both the remarkable social and economic reforms he launched in the so-called White Revolution and the accompanying rapid modernisation of his country that resulted from it with the glaring political failures he made in running the country according to his personal whims. His complicity in the coup to remove his premier Mosaddeq and to stifle the National Front government he led in 1953 was to have enormous consequences for both the Shah and Iran. Dr Pejman believes that had Mosaddeq's government continued in office there would have been no Khomeinism and therefore no Islamic Revolution. It's a bold contention – unprovable of course – but fascinating nonetheless. Any revolution brings about winners and losers and while the Shah's reforms were intended to help all classes of society, none did as well from them as the middle classes. Not surprisingly, therefore, this became an active bone of contention with those who felt that the benefits of these transformational changes had not gone to them. Of all the groups who were most dissatisfied by the Shah's reforms none came close to the objections of the Shia clergy and in particular, Ayatollah Ruhollah Khomeini from the holy city of Qom who became a persistent thorn in the flesh of the Shah from the mid-1960s onwards. It's clear that the increasingly autocratic Shah didn't take kindly to opposition and had no compunction about using the SAVAK to keep his enemies at bay. But senseless brutality, which was often the trademark of the secret police, only served to alienate a growing body of Iranian people and others with a liberal conscience around the world. Khomeini, whether in the country or in exile, exploited this growing resentment almost faultlessly and the Shah, suffering from terminal leukaemia, was in no physical or mental state to counter the insurgency against him.

My task at the end of this volume is to offer some concluding remarks about the subject of leadership, which is as vital now as it ever was.

Malcolm Murfett

ACKNOWLEDGEMENTS

Covid-19 did much to delay this project by two to three years, but it did not derail the process altogether. Avoiding that fate comes down to my nine contributors who did not give up hope that their work would finally see the light of day. My gratitude to them is immense.

By the same token so is my appreciation for the support of Simon Bates, the commissioning editor at Routledge for many years, who saw value in this work from the outset and his two assistants Khin Thazin and Chelsea Low, who have managed to get it over the technical finishing line with great elan.

I would also like to record a special note of thanks to Caroline Clarke and Rachel Spence for their critical support in ways that go beyond the norm and to my old friend Richard Campbell for his design suggestions.

Friends of mine from an array of different fields and whose judgement I value have also offered ideas and scrutiny, and I am indebted especially to John Bittleston, Professor Jeremy Black, Professor Vernon Bogdanor, Professor Robert Bresler, Dr James Ellison, Michael Emery, Alice Evans, Aamir Farooqi, Dr Alan James, Liz Jones, Stuart MacAlpine, Vicky Münzer-Jones, Ambassador Anita Nergaard, and my wife Ulrike for their helpful suggestions.

And finally I want to go on record and thank all my former students at King's College London who tackled the Political Leadership course with me from 2015 to 2020 and who made going to class every week a tremendously enjoyable experience for me personally (and hopefully for them too!). Their enthusiasm convinced me that a book on this subject was long overdue. I hope they will like what they read.

In the last analysis, of course, if any mistakes are to be found in this volume after it has gone into production the fault will lie with me alone, and I apologise in advance if that is the case.

Malcolm Murfett
King's College London
23 April 2023

1

LEADERSHIP IN APARTHEID SOUTH AFRICA

The impact of Hendrik Verwoerd and B.J. Vorster

J.E. Spence

The assiduous student of South African politics during the long unbroken rule of the Afrikaner National Party (NP 1948–1989) will quickly become aware of the country's history as a nursery of several generations of leaders, all of whom were white Afrikaners whether in office, opposition, or coalition.

This chapter will concentrate on the role of two key NP leaders – Dr Hendrik Verwoerd and B.J. Vorster both of whom held high office: the first as prime minister (1958–1966) and the second in the same role from 1966 to 1978. Both played crucial roles in the history and application of apartheid legislation: Verwoerd presided over the elaboration of the policy into its Bantustan or homeland version while Vorster began a somewhat haphazard programme for reform until illness forced him from office to be succeeded by P.W. Botha (Prime Minister: 1978–1983 and State President: 1983–1989).

To fully understand the impact of these two leaders, some attention must be paid to both the domestic and international contexts in which they operated. What is striking about South Africa's role in international politics is its drastic fall in stature following the end of the Second World War. It is, I believe, fair to say that Prime Minister Jan Smuts – whether in government, opposition, or coalition – was a major and certainly at times dominant figure in the country's politics until his death in 1950.

His career was quite extraordinary: an outstanding guerrilla fighter in the Anglo-Boer War (1899–1902), an eager and successful participant in both world wars, the confidante of Churchill, and the survivor of both conflicts. As a politician, he was deeply attached to the idea of the British Commonwealth and South Africa's role in it; he saw the latter as a powerful mechanism for promoting unity between the two communities – English and Afrikaner – into a coherent and sustainable common source of nationhood. Hence his key role in the negotiation of the 1910

DOI: 10.4324/9781003426165-1

2 J.E. Spence

constitution, which unified the four provinces of South Africa into a Union which ensured respectability and reputation as a reliable ally in peace and war and a source of valuable trade and investment for the United Kingdom.

Thus, for many in the outside world Smuts, through sheer force of personality, political skill of a high order, and surviving many decades of international exposure, was a trusty partner and participant in global affairs, especially those relating to the Commonwealth. In effect, he gave his country a degree of visibility and influence out of all proportion to its weight as a relatively small to middle power. But this favourable image was bound to change as the world changed after 1939. Nonetheless, he died in 1950 with his reputation still intact although changes both at home and abroad were to have an impact in the context of domestic politics.

Its leaders – as we shall see – had to fight off and defend as best they could the cumulative weight of mounting criticism of the apartheid policy. This emanated from many Third World, newly established external actors at the United Nations in particular and elsewhere but also from a host of pressure groups, which coalesced under the banner of what developed into a global anti-apartheid movement strongly supportive of the banned and exiled African National Congress (ANC). This organisation, in particular, benefitted from the new structures and values that underpinned their day-to-day diplomacy.

We shall now briefly rehearse the impact of the outcome of the Second World War and its aftermath in ideological terms on South Africa's standing and that of the plight of the black opposition within its borders.

By 1939, politics had become ideological with a vengeance, and events thereafter conspired to weaken and undermine South Africa's hitherto good standing in the international realm. This process was gradual to begin with, but the global reaction to apartheid gathered strength in due course and was especially – as we shall see – heavily reflected in the General Assembly of the United Nations and on occasion (e.g. after the Sharpeville shootings of 1960 and the Soweto Revolt of the Black Young in 1976) in the Security Council and a host of other political organisations with standing and influence in global affairs.

This ideological discord affected the way the Second World War was fought, the terms on which it was ended, and the new values that emerged in its aftermath. Hence, the insistence on unconditional surrender, the establishment of new democratic regimes on the ruins of Fascist tyranny, the punishment of war criminals for crimes against humanity, and, in particular, the barbarous treatment of European Jewry. All these developments represented radical departures from the principle of non-interference in the domestic affairs of states, representing at one level, at least, an erosion of the sanctity of domestic jurisdiction – a cardinal principle of the old European state order and one in which successive South African governments had asserted time and time again in their diplomatic attempts to defend apartheid in international forums. I cannot overemphasise the impact made by the belated discovery of Nazi racist genocide on the post-war value system. The result was that human rights became a central issue in interstate relations. In particular, racial equality became a human right which acquired, over time, a status qualitatively different from other such rights, and in this particular context South Africa was especially vulnerable to external hostility.

Another human right to acquire global significance was that of self-determination. Its standing was reinforced by the Atlantic Charter of 1941 with its emphasis 'on the right of all peoples to choose the form of governments under which they live.' Now this right had particular significance, as we shall see, for the anti-colonial struggle of the post-war period. And again, the events of the Second World War did much to give this particular right salience in the international system. The defeat of the British, Dutch, and French colonial empires in Asia during the war by Japan, a non-European power, convinced Asian and African nationalists that white men were not morally, psychologically, or technologically superior simply by virtue of being white.

Both these demands for racial equality and national self-determination were pressed in an international climate where the victorious Second World War powers had lost the will, and perhaps the capability, to maintain imperial rule. Thus, the United Kingdom set the example by giving independence to India and Pakistan. That precedent, once admitted, could hardly be denied or resisted with respect to colonial empires in Africa, elsewhere in Asia, or the Caribbean. Of course, the criteria for granting independence changed. No longer did governments in the 1950s and the 1960s insist on political and economic viability, as they had done in the 1940s.

Thus, by 1945, the stage was set for a fundamental change in the structure (the numbers of states entering the system), in the process, and in the values of the international society of states. The state, nonetheless – the dominant unit in both the theory and practice of international politics – survived as African and Asian nationalists opted to express their demands for freedom through the medium of the state. There were, of course, attempts to establish federal or conferral systems: the West Indies and the Central African Federation are cases in point, but these proved abortive.

Nationalist movements were, therefore, conservative insofar as they accepted a Western definition of statehood, symbolised very clearly in the Charter of the Organisation of African Unity (OAU). Here the emphasis was placed on sovereign equality, the inviolability of existing frontiers and the principle of non-intervention. But if African and Asian nationalist elites were conservative in their choice of mechanism through which to express their aspirations, they were revolutionary in terms of the demands they made upon the international system as a whole.

There were three in particular: first, the aspiration to remove the inequality in wealth and resources between the First and Third Worlds; second, they pressed for an end to colonialism; third, they demanded the recognition and implementation of the principle of racial equality between and within states. These aspirations fused

4 J.E. Spence

together to produce a new value system – an ideology, if you like – namely, anti-colonialism. And like all such ideologies, it had an inherent dynamism because it had the capacity to explain the past – the colonial past – to analyse present discontents and offer a vision of the future. The key value at the heart of that ideology was that of justice – not simply within states but between states as well. And under attack was the notion of 'unjust enrichment' by which colonial powers had allegedly exploited their colonies.

This ideology was important in providing coherence for some 150 or so new states – states which otherwise might have had little in common in terms of culture and traditional and political complexion. And it is the common experience of economic deprivation and racial stigma which divides the Third from the First and Second Worlds and finds concrete expression in the United Nations and in its specialised agencies. For the First World, security has always been the most important function of the United Nations. That was why it was set up originally.

For the Third World, by contrast, the United Nations became a forum for asserting an anti-colonial ideology. The Charter of the United Nations has been described by Professor Ali Mazrui as a global 'Bill of Rights' and the United Nations was, therefore, seen as an instrument of the collective legitimisation of new states as they entered the international system. It's also been seen as a forum for asserting the demand for economic and racial equality. And the United Nations again, by receiving petitions, by offering a platform to liberation movements internationalised the indigenous struggle for independence, especially in the 1950s and 1960s. In effect, what the United Nations did was to legitimise the ideology of anti-colonialism both as ideology and as strategy. And in the process, it elevated racial equality and national self-determination to the status of norms by which the actions of states in both domestic and foreign policy could be judged. As my old teacher, Geoffrey Goodwin, once perceptively remarked, the United Nations 'has become a mechanism through which race relations are apt to be transformed into international relations.'[1]

The scope and substance of international law have also undergone a transformation in the post-war period, and again, this has been largely through the mechanism of the United Nations. Initially, 25 years earlier in 1919, the Japanese delegation – members of a state in good standing – failed to get the designers of the Covenant of the League of Nations to insert a clause asserting racial equality.

Yet, by contrast, the Charter, in 1945, made clear references to fundamental freedoms without distinction as to face, sex, language, and religion. In the United Nations, over the next 50 years, a series of declarations and covenants was passed, largely the work of the Third World majority, affirming the sanctity of human rights and legitimising resolutions for obtaining those rights. There were many, but I will mention only three: the Declaration of Human Rights of 1948; the Declaration on the Granting of Independence to Colonial Peoples of 1966; the 1965 Convention on the elimination of all forms of racial discrimination.

These covenants and declarations have been interpreted by an influential school of legal theorists as a source of customary international law, binding on all states. Professor Rosalyn Higgins, for example, argues that:

> Human rights have long since passed . . . into that realm which is of legitimate international interest . . . that specific resolutions directed at individual states have been widely tolerated as a legitimate method of bringing pressure upon a state and yet, not falling foul of the prohibition against intervention in Article 2, Paragraph 7.
>
> *(Domestic jurisdiction clause of the UN Charter)*[2]

This is a considerable achievement: over a 40-year period Third World states have succeeded in injecting new legal norms and new moral values into the international system, and the implications have been far-reaching. It is no longer possible to defend the proposition that what happens inside a state should be a matter of indifference to the international community. To this extent, a traditional value of international politics – the doctrine of domestic jurisdiction – has been considerably weakened and South Africa, correspondingly, became an object of intense international concern.

The mass media and human rights

There have, of course, been other changes in international society besides those in structure and values. I refer to one in particular which does have importance and about which white South Africans have felt strongly – the technological revolution in mass communication. The role of the media in promoting consensus on the new values which have been articulated in international society over the last 40 years has been crucially important. The late Raymond Aron, the distinguished French sociologist, argues that:

> The diplomatic universe is like an echo chamber: the noises of men and events are amplified and reverberated to infinity. The disturbance occurring at one point of the planet communicates itself, step by step, to opposite sides of the globe.[3]

Of course, media presentation is highly and inevitably selective. The tone of the Western media in the post-war period has been predominantly liberal, reflecting, indeed reinforcing, post-war consensus on such issues as racial discrimination and social and economic deprivation. Equally, the media have been important in reflecting that consensus which stresses the state's responsibility to remedy the evils of deprivation and inequality; that the rich and powerful have an obligation to help the poor and the weak. After all, would Bob Geldof have succeeded quite so magnificently in articulating that sense of moral outrage and moral obligation

6 J.E. Spence

unless the technology had been available? And it's been very difficult, understandably, for Western conservatives to argue against this consensus. Few can be found to defend racial discrimination or economic injustice.

I would also draw your attention to the impact of the media on the tone and the quality of decision-making. One effect of the technology available to media coverage is that crises are exposed very quickly. There is immense pressure on politicians, as a result, to make quick, often hasty and ill-considered decisions. It is difficult for decision-makers to be indifferent, to appear callous in the face of what appears to be harsh repression of human rights. A decision-maker facing a battery of cameras has to give an impression of control, of capacity to influence events. He/she cannot admit to weakness. He/she cannot adopt the traditional conservative view that there is no easy solution, if one at all, to many of the problems that confront governments in international politics – whether in South Africa or elsewhere. That may be true in theory, but it's a difficult admission to make in state practice.

In other words, the politician faced with the kind of pressure articulated by the post-war consensus via media technology has to assume that solutions **are** possible. Lack of time when crises break and the pressure of the media mean that he/she has to make a statement or issue a communique. The statement itself becomes news, and that in turn influences events. The media, therefore, has a significant political role, as well as the more orthodox one of distributing news and information. And bear in mind that the international media are the prime source of news and debate about the rights and wrongs of international politics.

It might be appropriate in discussion of the role of the media – especially the English-speaking press and its counterparts elsewhere in the Western world – in offering a regular critique of the worst excesses of the apartheid regime and by so doing providing an important stimulus to opposition at home and abroad. Thus, both Verwoerd and Vorster had to devote considerable time and energy to counter extensive media hostility to their policies while correspondingly, the exiled ANC was provided with valuable commentary for use in lobbying governments and the public abroad for action against apartheid.

Furthermore, there was a commitment to the rule of law however battered it was during the apartheid years, and this important concept was one that could be asserted and defended in courtroom battles during the various states of emergency characteristic of the apartheid era whenever there were major episodes of black resistance such as Sharpeville (1960), the Soweto Uprising (1976), and the dislocation that punctuated the 1980s before the emergence of the de Klerk regime and the beginnings of a fundamental reform of South Africa's political system in the later part of that decade.

Finally, the remaining advantage enjoyed by the exiled ANC was the existence in the Republic of a vigorous civil society, which never completely lost its voice and capacity for critical scrutiny of the apartheid government's policy.

Leadership in apartheid South Africa **7**

All these factors taken together help explain the survival capacity of the ANC over the 30-year period from 1960 onwards. As Graham Evans has explained:

> Indeed, the past four decades both supporters of the ancient regime and opponents of it were united in regarding the external world as essentially contested territory in the sense that a vital strategic component of the foreign policies of the government and of the ANC's International Department was to secure international recognition, legitimisation and support. And until February 1990 when de Klerk began the transition process away from apartheid, there is little doubt that of the two mutually competing sets of foreign policies, that of the ANC was the more successful, in that it succeeded in mobilising near-universal support for the imposition by the UN of mandatory sanctions against Pretoria.[4]

This was achieved by a variety of means: maintaining the armed struggle both at home and in the southern African region forcing the South African state to embark on repressive measures, which singularly failed to win 'hearts and minds' in the conventional method of counter-insurgency strategy. True, the so-called war of liberation never had much prospect of toppling the South African state, but it did succeed in maintaining a perception among many blacks that the organisation had a serious purpose, and its reputation correspondingly rose. Equally, the liberation campaign and the government's counter-response of destabilising South Africa's neighbours for harbouring ANC insurgents in the 1980s enhanced the salience abroad of the ANC's claims to have just cause for its military campaign.

These factors clearly impacted on the Verwoerd/Vorster leadership roles in the years between 1958 and 1979, a detailed consideration of which now follows. By way of introduction to this theme, it would, I believe, be helpful to preface my argument with the persuasive distinction cited by Alexander Johnston in his recent volume on political leadership in post-Mandela South Africa. Thus he refers, with reservations, to Robert Rotberg's definition of a 'transformational leader' personified by Nelson Mandela as a 'supreme motivator . . . They challenge settled expectations and demand new, higher levels of national and governmental performance. . . . They drive a nation forward to new achievements, and to new views of itself.'[5] By contrast:

> Transactional leaders might govern well, but only from a limited repertoire. They are incrementalists, 'business-as-usual' politicians focusing on the mechanics of statecraft and perpetuating themselves and their parties on office. They exchange mutual self-interests with their followers and hence are primarily engaged in transactions.[6]

Verwoerd could be regarded as an example of the former trend with this qualification that his 'political skills did not lead to good leadership outcomes.'[7]

8 J.E. Spence

By contrast, it could be argued invoking this distinction that B.J. Vorster's premiership falls into the transactional category.

Turning now to the international realm, the ANC, according to Scott Thomas,

> exaggerated expectations of what the United Nations could accomplish. The ANC and many Afro-Asian states wanted the United Nations, quite beyond its capacity (and arguably, contrary to the Charter's principles), to become an instrument of coercion, to force the Western powers to implement economic sanctions by setting the General Assembly against the Security Council. Even after the Special Committee on Apartheid was formed with this implicit role, the UN's ineffectiveness became apparent because it was unable to force member states to implement General Assembly resolutions, which is why the ANC became disillusioned with the UN.[8]

Nonetheless, the organisation played an important role in isolating South Africa from the mainstream of international relations. True, it proved impossible to translate the widespread hostility expressed in countless anti-apartheid resolutions in the General Assembly into meaningful and sustained practical measures against the South African state. One exception was the voluntary arms embargo of 1963, which the Security Council made mandatory on member states in 1978. This, however, had unexpected consequences; it hastened the development of the local arms industry to the extent that by the late 1980s South Africa was the world's twelfth-largest arms exporter.

But the real value of the United Nations for the anti-apartheid struggle was its success as a form for mobilising support against apartheid from the Afro-Asian bloc (as noted earlier), which dominated the General Assembly for much of the post-war period. Many of the states – in Africa in particular – were small, poor, and lacking in international visibility once the heady moment of independence had passed. Yet membership of the United Nations offered the Afro-Asian bloc an opportunity to unite behind an anti-colonial ideology, which identified South Africa as a prime target for condemnation. This strategy was strengthened by the absence of any conflict of political and economic interest over the South African issue. In general, the states perceived themselves as 'revolutionary' – that is as a dissatisfied group determined to change an international status quo which, in their view, had been profoundly biased against *their* interests.

As R.B. Ballinger argued the matter,

> [T]he dispute over South West Africa and the Union's racial policy are now so closely interwoven that they react one upon the other in ways which, if not easy to define, nevertheless inflame the atmosphere in which either is considered.[9]

Faced with this barrage of criticism, South African delegates to the General Assembly initially invoked Article 2:7 – the domestic jurisdiction clause of the

UN Charter claiming that the international community had no right to intervene in the internal affairs of a member state. After all, apartheid did not constitute 'a threat to international peace and security,' but this defence made no real headway as resolutions criticising South Africa became an annual event at meetings of the General Assembly.

The erosion of human rights in South Africa

I do not propose to catalogue the depredation of apartheid into the rule of law and civil liberties in the Republic during the post-war period. Yet it is important to have some understanding of the historical record if we are to understand the reaction of South Africa's leadership especially in the Verwoerd/Vorster periods of government.

From 1948 onwards, the National Party government filled the statute book with legislation systematically designed to maintain white majority rule and prevent any legal, let alone effective, political challenge to institutionalised racial discrimination. Yet even in the worst days of the apartheid regime, the concept of the rule of law never quite disappeared from the lexicon of political debate: liberal concern for these matters surfaced in the campaigns of the South African Liberal Party, the Black Sash Women's Movement, and the exiled black political organisations.

Moreover, even diehard Afrikaner Nationalist legal theorists felt obliged to offer an alternative definition of the rule of law: hence the view of the Afrikaner academic, Pieter verLoren van Themaat that 'the rule of law was not a juridical concept but simply a pious expression of the wish that Parliament would not infringe on certain rights and liberties.'[10] Similarly, one judge, J.H. Snyman dismissed the rule of law as 'very much the tool of the politician and the politically minded lawyer.'[11] One major objection by Afrikaner Nationalists to Western doctrines of human rights was exemplified in the Universal Declaration of 1948 (which South Africa with Saudi Arabia and the Soviet bloc alone refused to sign and its so-called humanistic basis). Thus, Francois Venter concluded that 'the South African State is based on the sovereignty of God, which stands in radical opposition to the humanistic point of departure.'[12] As John Dugard emphasised, this meant that 'the rule of law, and for that matter any doctrine of human rights, has no place in South Africa.'[13]

Similarly, another objection to the Western concept was the belief that the 'rule of law is synonymous with rule by law'; as John Dugard critically interprets this view 'acts in terms of the law enacted in accordance with the correct constitutional procedure, are evil, repressive and discriminatory.'[14] There was, nonetheless, an acknowledgement of one important feature of Western rule of law doctrine. I quote from a 1968 publication by the South African Department of Foreign Affairs:

The rule of law may mean different things to different people, but there is general agreement that it requires that a person on trial be accused in open court; be

10   J.E. Spence

given an opportunity of denying the charge and of defending himself and that he be given the choice of counsel. These rights are at all times assured by the South African courts.[15]

Yet this recognition was more honoured in the breach periodically as even this limited acceptance of the rule of law was suspended by draconian legislation, which effectively gave the state – in terms of a state of emergency – the right to detain individuals for periods of up to 180 days without the right of *habeas corpus*.

Perhaps, the classic example of the South African government's refusal to acknowledge the supremacy of the law was the prolonged struggle in the 1950s to remove coloured voters in the Cape Province from the common roll – a right that had been recognised and given the protection of an entrenched clause (requiring a two-thirds majority for its deletion) in the 1910 constitution which established the Union of South Africa. Despite the Supreme Court's ruling that the government had no right to employ a simple majority, the state resorted to a variety of subterfuges, including packing the Senate and the Appellate Division of the Supreme Court with sympathetic supporters. The consequence was the loss of the Coloured franchise. Finally, in 1956, Parliament legislated to exclude the testing powers of the courts. What was interesting about this extraordinary episode was that government policy succeeded in uniting orthodox liberals and enlightened conservatives alike: the first group because the rule of law was being so vehemently denied; the second because government legislation was designed to remove existing rights vested in a constitution and – in a Burkean sense – hallowed by the passage of time and long-established constitutional principle and convention.

Yet by the decade of the 1980s there were clear signs of division among Afrikaner Nationalists especially in the intellectual class. The so-called *verligte* or enlightened Afrikaners began to agitate for the establishment of a bill of rights and this plea was occasionally echoed by politicians. Listen, for example, to the words of the State President, P.W. Botha, opening Parliament in 1986:

> *We believe in the sovereignty of the law as a basis for the protection of the fundamental rights of individuals as well as groups. We believe in the sanctity and indivisibility of law and the just application thereof. There can be no peace, freedom and democracy without law. Any future system must confirm with the requirements of a civilised legal order, and must ensure access to the courts and equality before the law. We believe that human dignity, life, liberty and property of all must be protected, regardless of colour, race, creed or religion.*[16]

This change of heart was more apparent than real, though it was a reflection of the slow, haphazard reform process which the Botha government embarked upon in the late 1970s and early 1980s: a gradual recognition that black workers were entitled to trade union rights; the relaxation of so-called petty apartheid in the social and economic sphere are two obvious examples. These piecemeal steps at reform culminated in the botched attempt to restructure the constitution in 1984 with the establishment of the tricameral parliament for white, Indian, and Coloured representatives.

The entirely unintended consequences of that particular reform were the bitter anger on the part of the still-deprived black majority; a wave of protest; violent conflict between the black activists and the security forces; and the declaration of a state of emergency in July 1985, which effectively – as it now seems in retrospect – sounded the death knell of the Botha regime. One is irresistibly reminded of de Tocqueville's famous remark that the most dangerous moment for a bad government is when it embarks on a process of reform.

During the five-year period between 1985 and 1990, internal and external pressures mounted on South Africa: a combination of private and public sanctions imposed by giant corporations and international organisations hastened by the steep decline of the South African economy. There was too, in H.A.L. Fisher's well-known phrase, 'the play of the contingent and the unforeseen' – in particular, the forced removal of P.W. Botha through illness in September 1989 and the collapse of Communism in the Soviet Union and eastern Europe two months later. A new State President, F.W. de Klerk had at least this advantage that he could – almost casually it seemed – abandon his government's traditional deeply rooted belief in the notion of a total Communist onslaught against South Africa orchestrated from Moscow. At the same time and for the same reason, he downgraded the role of the military in decision-making, though their covert influence has been much harder to eliminate.

The Verwoerdian legacy

Hendrik Verwoerd was born in Holland and emigrated with his family to South Africa, becoming an influential academic (Professor at the University of Stellenbosch) and a leading Afrikaans newspaper editor. He has been described as apartheid's 'master builder' and was revered by his Afrikaner supporters generating respect from a community which had traditionally placed high value on those with impressive academic qualifications and a capacity for strong and unyielding leadership. Thus, he was an obvious candidate to succeed his predecessor J.G. Strijdon after the latter's death in August 1958. He was that *rara avis*, an intellectual in politics, one with a clear and entirely inflexible vision of his country's future and, in particular, the role of the 6.5 million Africans who – in the view of the influential Tomlinson Commission appointed in the late 1940s – it was assumed would remain in the so-called white urban areas of South Africa, well outnumbered by their black counterparts.

In the prime ministerial office, Verwoerd's zeal, dynamism, and intellectual ability gave him an authority that was unmatched by either his two predecessors or successors. He was never wracked by self-doubt and prided himself on being made of granite. He was also zealous in his oversight of cabinet colleagues and their

12 J.E. Spence

departments, especially those concerning African affairs to which he had appointed ideological acolytes. Verwoerd was also ruthless in dealing with those who stepped out of line, whether NP MPs, who differed publicly with policy, Dutch Reformed Church clergy whose faith in the immutable truths of apartheid showed signs of wavering, or think tanks like SABRA (the South African Bureau of Racial Affairs), a group of mostly Cape-based pro-Nationalist academics, who questioned official policy regarding the Coloured people. Even the doyen of Afrikaner entrepreneurs, Anton Rupert, was slapped down for daring to contemplate establishing a factory in which apartheid rules would not apply. Even his chosen Minister of Bantu Administration and Development M.D.C. de Wet Nel was given a (private) dressing down for suggesting that the targeted *annus mirabilis*, 1978, was unlikely to be achieved.

As noted, Verwoerd was not fazed by the demographic issue. He refuted the opposition argument that the economic integration of the races was so far advanced that separation was impossible. Apart from taunting the opposition with the argument that economic integration would in time be followed by political and social integration, he invoked a remarkable piece of intellectual legerdemain to show that they misunderstood what 'integration' actually amounted to. The following quotation gives the key to Verwoerd's ability to build logical constructions on the foundations of bogus premises:

> We say that when a Native drives a tractor on a [white] farm, he is not economically integrated. . . . Merely because he helps the farmer to produce, is such a Native who operates a tractor integrated into the farmer's life and community? Of course he is not, because the concept of integration relates to people, and here we do not have people whose activities are becoming interwoven. They will only become interwoven in this way if the other forms of integration, namely equal social and political rights, result from these activities.[17]

In other words, there was a fundamental difference between labour that was interchangeable and, hence, easily removable, and labour that was so interwoven with the white community that it could not be removed, even if the state wanted to do so.

Verwoerd's insistence that Africans in the 'white' areas not be permitted to rise 'above the level of certain forms of labour' dovetails with his views on what constituted 'integration.' The quotation also shows how fundamental to Verwoerd's thinking the perpetuation of inequality was, and also he insisted that there was no distinction between 'petty' and other forms of apartheid: the (absurd and hurtful) separate entrances, separate lifts, and myriad other forms of petty apartheid were deemed necessary because the cumulative effect of infractions could blunt racial perceptions and eventually bring the apartheid edifice down.

The second phase of apartheid is associated principally with Verwoerd's efforts to put a positive gloss on apartheid: reserves, now called homelands, would be prepared for self-government and even, it was eventually conceded, independence. The vision of freedoms awaiting Africans in their homelands had been part of the

Leadership in apartheid South Africa **13**

original policy laid down in 1947. Verwoerd sought to implement the new version of apartheid, now designated 'separate development.'

The foundations of policy had been laid in 1951, with the enactment of legislation that granted additional powers to chiefs or traditional leaders. In the Nationalists' view traditional authority structures were to be the basis of political development in the homeland. Chieftainship was to be the pivotal institution. Chiefs had long been recognised as minor cogs in the administration of rural areas: they were responsible for the administration of customary law, for the allocation of communal land, and settling minor disputes and other duties, subject to the oversight of the Native Commissioner. The Nationalists insisted that chieftainship embodied the essence of traditional democracy. There had been truth in this contention: traditionally, chiefs were not autocrats who could ignore the wishes of their people – as the Xhosa saying had it, 'Inkosi yinkosi ngabantu,' meaning that 'a chief is a chief by the people.' White rule and the alienation of much traditionally occupied land, however, had removed the basis for popular sanctions on the exercise of chiefly power; and chiefs were now more beholden to the white authorities than their people, though many sought to straddle potentially divergent interests.

The terms of the legislation, the Bantu Authorities Act, provided for a hierarchy of authorities – tribal, regional, and territorial. The principle of ethnic separation was to be rigorously enforced so that each of the initial eight territorial authorities established by 1970 encompassed a specific ethnic group. It was an article of faith among Nationalists that every African, apart from a few deracinated townspeople, owed their primary tie to one or other ethnic group: African nationalism was a fiction, encouraged by agitators.

The political aim underlying Bantu authorities was obvious: the socio-economic progress of Africans was possible only through the vehicle of traditional institutions. As Verwoerd explained in 1952:

> [I]t is clear that the key to the true progress of the Bantu community as a whole and to the avoidance of a struggle for equality in a joint territory or in common political living areas lies in the recognition of the tribal system as the springboard from which the Bantu in a natural way, by enlisting the help of the dynamic elements in it, can increasingly rise to a higher level of culture and self-government on a foundation suitable to his own inherent nature.[18]

In 1959, Verwoerd unveiled the first instalment of separate development, intended partly as an attempt to provide moral justification for his government's policies and partly to persuade increasingly hostile international opinion that South Africa was now embarking on a process of decolonisation and self-determination similar to that of other colonial powers in Africa. The Promotion of the Bantu Self-Government Act established the framework for the future constitutional development of the homelands. It also abolished the small parliamentary representation of Africans (by whites) as being inconsistent with the proposals for separate development

14 J.E. Spence

contained in the legislation. Verwoerd, however, rejected the Commission's proposals and in particular, the suggestion that white capital be permitted to invest in the reserve areas, that individual land tenure be instituted, and that 104 million pounds be spent on development over the next decade.

Verwoerd was an austere intellectual who dominated the National Party during his tenure of office and was totally committed to the Bantustan strategy, which he with others had devised as a solution to the so-called native problem. His response to the critics who pointed to the demographic deficit bordered on fantasy. It also foreshadowed a gigantic and inhumane exercise in social engineering. First, according to Verwoerd, of the 6.5 million Africans who would remain in the 'white' areas, some four million would be mostly on white-owned farms 'where the problem of apartheid presents no difficulty to us and where apartheid is maintained locally.' This meant that in the semi-feudal conditions on the farms racial inequality was firmly maintained. The comment underlined Verwoerd's conviction that the essence of apartheid was racial inequality.

Second, Verwoerd agreed that Africans in the 'white' areas would resemble *gastarbeiters*, who originated from the poorer parts of Europe and worked in western Europe, but retained citizenship of their home countries. It was obviously a disingenuous analogy. Third, Verwoerd argued that it was an incorrect assumption that the same Africans would be permanently domiciled in the 'white' areas, since it was his intention that the labour force would be migrant workers who oscillated between the reserves and their places of employment. In other words, the 6.5 million would be a constantly shifting mass of people, supposedly anchored in their respective reserves of origin.

Despite rejecting the Commission's recommendation that white capital be allowed to invest in the reserves, Verwoerd recommended that white-owned enterprises should be allowed on the borders of the reserves, enabling African employees to commute on a daily or weekly basis from their homes. Border industries would turn out to be a major strategy of apartheid's planners but also one that failed.

Verwoerd recognised that if apartheid were to have any credibility there must come a time when the flow of Africans from the reserves to the 'white' areas would be reversed. He believed that 1978 would be the *annus mirabilis* when it would begin. How this date was arrived at was never revealed: possibly it had been cooked up by Verwoerd and some of his equally zealous officials. Despite its basic improbability (and the scepticism of some of his colleagues), the ideological fiction was maintained throughout Verwoerd's premiership, being dropped only after his death.

Instead, in January 1959, Verwoerd announced his government plan 'to create separate independent black African states, or Bantustans, where blacks could exercise their political rights.' Some eight of the so-called new states 'were to be geographically based on the old tribal boundaries: North and South Sothu, Swazi, Tsongo, Tswana, Venda, Xhosa and Zulu.'[19] This elaborate scheme was justified on the spurious ground that it was similar in substance to the decolonisation process followed by the one-time imperial powers – the United Kingdom and France in particular – and was in part an attempt to ward off the mounting tide of external criticism engulfing government policy during the 1970s and 1980s. This policy of 'separate development' had intellectual antecedents in the work of Afrikaner intellectuals before the Second World War, but it was Verwoerd who gave the concept both local and international visibility in his academic writings and also in the policies he pursued during his premiership.

Vorster's reign

Verwoerd's premiership ended with his assassination in the House of Assembly in September 1966. His successor, John Vorster, had been Minister of Justice in Verwoerd's administration and had initiated draconian security laws. He was entirely different from Verwoerd in personality and style. Before and during the Second World War, he had supported Nazi Germany and was interned by the Smut's government. He was no intellectual, and his premiership would be substantially devoid of any creative response to the mounting crisis that was engulfing South Africa. But he was possessed of a certain native cunning and a capacity for political infighting. He was described by Sir de Villiers Graaff as 'the main inquisitor, local chief jaoler and lord high executioner.'[20] He was forced to resign as prime minister in September 1978 on 'health grounds' and again, as state president in January 1979. Nothing whatever suggested that he might deviate from the rigours of Verwoerdian orthodoxy. He was, unlike Verwoerd, less inclined to be vindictive and intolerant of internal critics. Moreover, also unlike Verwoerd who completely dominated his cabinet, Vorster gave his ministerial colleagues substantially more freedom of action, acting more, as has been said, like a 'chairman of the board' than an autocrat. While it is an exaggeration to describe the advent of Vorster as a 'Prague Spring,' his less hegemonic style would open the way for divisions inside the NP and within the wider Afrikaner nationalist movement. Under Verwoerd, Afrikaner nationalism had reached the zenith of its solidarity; under Vorster hairline cracks soon started to appear.

Verwoerd had created the template for apartheid, as well as bureaucratic leviathans, the departments of Bantu Administration and Development of Bantu Education, both headed by M.C. Botha, a wooden reactionary and an ideological acolyte of Verwoerd. The apartheid juggernaut appeared to have gained an unstoppable momentum. With the parliamentary opposition in disarray, increased English-speaking support for the NP, and the black opposition seemingly routed, there was every reason for the NP to feel confident. Moreover, the economy had recovered rapidly after Sharpeville, and GDP grew at an annual average of 5.7 per cent in the 1960s while both domestic and foreign fixed investments rose appreciably. Underneath the apparently calm water, however, currents that would later cause turbulence were beginning to swirl.

16 J.E. Spence

Another characteristic of Vorster was the absence of Verwoerd's diagnostic omniscience; in fact, he was showing signs of pragmatism, even flexibility, that would shock the ultra-right-wingers who were beginning to raise their heads above the parapet. Being conservative, he said of the NP, did not mean that it would stand still or stagnate; and he caused concern by saying to a group of NP MPs that separate development/apartheid was a method of maintaining Afrikaner identity and not an immutable dogma. It was interpreted as a sign by ultra-right-wingers, now called *verkramptes*, that Vorster was going soft on fundamental principles.

Cautious moves by Vorster to permit a multiracial rugby team from New Zealand to tour South Africa were negated by his refusal to allow Basil D'Oliveira, a Coloured exile from South Africa, to tour with the England cricket team in 1968. He had not been chosen for the original squad but was subsequently included when one of the team members dropped out due to illness. Vorster refused to allow this, saying that it was an attempt to make political capital out of sport. The England cricket authorities thereupon cancelled the tour and subsequently announced that no future tours would be undertaken until South African teams were chosen on merit. It was a major step in the sporting isolation of South Africa, which proved to be one of the most effective forms of international sanctions.

Vorster's so-called outward policy, initiated in 1967, sought to achieve détente with black Africa, much of which was implacably hostile to apartheid. His hope was that dialogue would achieve 'understanding' of South Africa's policies; but the few leaders of African states who were prepared to talk to Vorster hoped that dialogue would assist in breaking down apartheid. The hope of establishing diplomatic links with Africa yielded a poor harvest: only Malawi agreed. Even Botswana, Lesotho, and Swaziland, although essentially economic hostages to their powerful neighbour, declined to establish formal diplomatic ties. In short, apartheid was an unsaleable commodity.

One outcome of the outward policy caused further rumblings of discontent among *verkramptes*: they maintained that the arrival of African diplomats, who would be treated as diplomats from any other continent, violated South Africa's colour bar. In the event, only Malawi took the bait and established relations, but even this was enough to raise *verkrampte* hackles. It became an article of faith among them that even the smallest cracks in the colour bar would create momentum for more.

Vorster showed no signs of relenting on the main thrust of apartheid: there would be no more land allocated to homelands; there would be no political rights accorded to Africans in the 'white' areas – they could exercise their political rights in the respective homelands, regardless of where they actually lived; and, following Verwoerd's line of argument, the numbers of Africans in the 'white' areas were not the most important issue since what mattered was the maintenance of inequality. He did, however, refuse to be bound by the *annus mirabilis*, 1978, the date by which, according to Verwoerd's fantasy, the flow of Africans to 'white' areas would turn around.

Much of Vorster's emotional energy in the first few years of his premiership was expended on coping with divisions that had emerged in the NP. The focal point of the tension was the mobilisation of a seemingly strong *verkrampte* element centred on Albert Hertzog, a somewhat eccentric figure, who had been appointed Minister of Posts and Telegraphs and in that capacity had fought a battle to prevent the coming of television to South Africa. Hertzog, the son of a former prime minister, had long been associated with a shadowy Pretoria-based group, the *Afrikaner-Orde*, which represented ultra-right-wing sentiment. He had also been intimately involved with the Afrikaner trade union movement, notably the Mine Workers' Union, which he had 'rescued' from control by English-speaking workers. Vorster dropped him from the cabinet in August 1968.

The *verkramptes* claimed to be faithful to the ideological legacy of Verwoerd. Vorster, they alleged, was whittling away that legacy, by permitting 'mixed' sport, allowing black diplomats, welcoming Roman Catholic immigrants, and seeking a *toenadering* (rapprochement) with English-speakers. In a parliamentary speech, delivered on 14 April 1969, Hertzog declared that the culture of English-speakers was sated with liberalism and that only Calvinist Afrikaners could be trusted to save whites from obliteration.

Outside Parliament, the conflict was raging even more fiercely, notably in cultural and literary circles. The *verkramptes*, who were actively white-anting Afrikaner associations, alleged that much of the recent wave of Afrikaans literature reflected 'spiritual decay' and a weakening of Afrikaner defences against liberalising forces. Conflict in the ranks raised the ominous possibility of *skeuring*, a split in the NP and the wider Afrikaner nationalist movement. The Afrikaans press, or mostly that part of it owned by the Cape-based *Nasionale Pers*, and particularly the big Sunday newspaper, *Die Beeld*, devoted large amounts of space to the conflict, flushing out *verkrampte* activities wherever they could. The story was not only intrinsically newsworthy, but it also made for copy that was avidly read by Afrikaners.

The *verkramptes'* attacks on supposed policy adjustments were thinly veiled attacks on Vorster himself. They were not aiming at hiving off to establish a new party; the aim was rather to capture control of the NP and other spheres of Afrikaner nationalism. Vorster realised this and decided to smash the tendency comprehensively before it had time to establish itself as an organised force: four MPs were forced out of the NP. In October 1969, the dissidents, led by Hertzog, formed the *Herstigte Nasionale Party* (HNP, Reconstituted National Party) at a meeting in Pretoria.

Vorster responded by bringing forward the general election by a year to give the new party little time to establish itself. What followed was one of the most rancorous campaigns in South Africa's electoral history. The HNP contested 77 seats, mostly in the Transvaal and Orange Free State. Its candidates were pitted against the might of the NP's formidable machine and the full force of the powerful pro-NP press. It was not surprising that the HNP was decimated: only ten of the candidates

18 J.E. Spence

managed to win over 1,000 votes, mostly in smaller towns in the Northern Transvaal. Overall, their share of the votes cast countrywide was 3.5 per cent – it was a comment on the state of white thinking that the moderately liberal Progressive Party won slightly fewer votes, though the redoubtable Helen Suzman retained her seat in the Houghton constituency of Johannesburg to continue her lonely battle against the ravages of apartheid.

Vorster, anxious to wipe out the HNP, was equally anxious to see how much support it had among Afrikaners. It was less than ten per cent, small, but disquieting since it was apparent that many more Afrikaners had sympathy for the HNP, but its crude, street-fighting style had put them off. The spiritual leader of the *verkramptes* had not even joined the HNP. This was Dr Andries Treurnicht, whose record suggested that he was one of Afrikanerdom's golden sons: a provincial rugby player, a clergyman of the Nederduitse Gereformeerde Kerk and a former editor of its newspaper, and then editor of the Pretoria daily, *Hoofstad*. He had also risen in the ranks of the *Broederbond*, becoming a member of its executive council in 1963, deputy chairman in 1970, and was to become chairman in 1972.

The founders of the HNP had confidently anticipated that the urbane Treurnicht would join them, but, to their ire, he declined. He became an NP MP in 1971, easily defeating Jaap Marais, the HNP's deputy leader, in a by-election in Waterberg, a *verkrampte* stronghold. Treurnicht's stature ensured that his rise in the party hierarchy would be rapid: in a move with fatal consequences he was appointed Deputy Minister of Bantu Administration and Education early in 1976. His responsibilities included oversight of African education in the 'white' areas. He would be a key player in the blunders that led to the Soweto Uprising in June 1976.

The rise of the *verkrampte* movement had a wider significance than a relatively small split. It signified that underlying changes in the Afrikaner community were beginning to have political consequences. By the 1970s, some 80 per cent of Afrikaners were urban. High economic growth rates, especially in the 1960s, had largely wiped out remaining white poverty, diffused higher living standards, and accelerated the growth of thrusting Afrikaner entrepreneurs. Afrikaners were better educated and more widely travelled than ever before; in short, the process of *embourgeoisement* was under way. These developments also meant that the Afrikaner community was becoming internally more diversified – and less amenable to accommodation within a single nationalist movement. Class differences had always been a feature of Afrikaner society, but they had largely been contained under the rubric of ethnic solidarity. The virtual elimination of white unemployment and the diffusion of greater prosperity concealed the widening of the income gap among Afrikaners. It was no coincidence that *verkramptes* and their (puny) press inveighed against *die geldmag* (the money power) and pointed accusing fingers at leading Afrikaner tycoons, notably Anton Rupert, for allegedly reneging on apartheid aspirations.

There was some truth in the allegations: Rupert had never been an enthusiastic supporter of apartheid, despite being a true-blue Afrikaner; and a number of other leading members of the business community chafed against some of the restraints caused by apartheid, and limits on their markets caused identification with Afrikaner nationalism. But if there were differences within the government, they were taken up privately and discreetly.

At the other end of Afrikaner nationalism's internal spectrum were the *verligtes* (enlightened ones), a heterogeneous collection that included some MPs, a number of academic and other intellectuals, and various professional people. If there was any linking thread among them it was that, generally speaking, they were better educated than the *verkramptes*. Also, they enjoyed the support of much of the Afrikaans press. But there was no overarching association or movement uniting them. There were several *verligte* concerns: the slow pace of homeland development; the humiliation inflicted on black people in the name of petty apartheid; and the anomalous status of the Coloured people. They, too, believed that the most effective strategy was to work for change within the NP. Other Afrikaner intellectuals, so-called *oorbeligtes* (over-enlightened ones), scorned them, insisting that they had not rejected the apartheid paradigm and were concerned merely with cosmetic changes.

The question of fitting the Coloured and Indian categories into the apartheid scheme of things was problematic: they had no homelands, and the Coloured people were biologically and culturally akin to Afrikaners. In Verwoerd's time, the Coloureds had been deemed 'a nation in the making' – which was a nonsense. They were an intermediate category in the racial hierarchy, subject to racial discrimination that was severe (notably in the form of the Group Areas Act and myriad petty apartheid regulations), though not as severe as that imposed upon Africans. Their political rights in the Cape had been whittled away, culminating in the eventual removal in 1956 of their right to vote on the common voters' roll and its replacement by the right to elect two white representatives to the House of Assembly.

Historically, most Coloured political aspirations were directed at inclusion in the dominant category. Mohamed Adhikari writes:

> If the ultimate aim of much of Coloured political organization was acceptance into the dominant society, then most of the day-to-day politicking was a narrow concern with the advancement of Coloured interests. Thus, though there was an assertion of non-racial values and protest against discrimination, there was also an accommodation with the racist order and an attempt to manipulate it in favor of Coloured people.[21]

It is worth noting that many Coloured people held similar racist stereotypes of Africans to those held by whites.

There were small groups of radicals, mostly better-educated people, who joined the Communist Party, the South African Coloured People's Organisation (an ally of the ANC), and the Non-European Unity Movement.

20 J.E. Spence

In 1968, the Coloured Persons' Representative Council was established: 40 of its members were elected and 20 nominated by the government. Its powers were strictly limited, which meant that elections were poorly supported. It survived until 1983, when a new constitutional system, the Tricameral Parliament, came into existence – causing in the process a far more serious split in the ranks of the NP than that of 1969 (see later).

For the NP, the political accommodation of the Coloured and Indian minorities posed a problem. The abolition of Coloured voting rights was due solely to NP fears that Coloured voters represented an anti-NP voting bloc and, moreover, one whose size could grow. By the 1960s, *verkramptes*, including a few in the NP, were demanding a Coloured 'homeland,' also a nonsense since white and Coloured lived, subject to Group Areas, closely intermingled in towns and villages, as well as on farms. Coloured 'reserves' were few in number, scattered, and small in size and, consequently, wholly inadequate as a potential homeland.

In 1973, the government appointed a commission, chaired by Professor Erika Theron of Stellenbosch University – a staunch but by no means uncritical Nationalist – to enquire into all matters concerning the Coloured people. The Commission's membership of 20 included six Coloured people and a spread of political views. In 1976, it produced a voluminous report, whose key recommendation was that Coloured people be directly elected in the central government and other levels of authority. It concluded also that the Westminster system of government might have to be altered to meet the circumstances of South Africa's diversity. The government rejected the recommendation, as well as that proposing abolition of the Mixed Marriages and Immorality Acts. For the time being, the issue of accommodating the Coloured and Indian categories remained unresolved. It would be a major irony that precisely this issue would trigger a major split in Afrikaner nationalism in 1982, which played no small part in accelerating the erosion of Afrikaner nationalism.

By the early 1970s, more pressing matters confronted Vorster's government. The seeming quiescence of black opposition for much of the 1960s had given way to greater militance as the Black Consciousness movement made its presence felt. Of equal significance were the large-scale strikes of African workers that occurred in 1973, particularly in Natal. These were the harbingers of a powerful new focus of mobilisation, independent trade unions. Moreover, there were stirrings in nearby territories: the *coup* in Portugal in 1974 led quickly to the independence of its colonies, Angola and Mozambique; revolt against the illegal white regime in Rhodesia was intensifying; and from 1974, the South West Africa People's Organisation (SWAPO) stepped up its campaign against South African rule in South West Africa. All of these conflicts had reverberations among Africans in South Africa. For Vorster, the danger was that the *cordon sanitaire* separating South Africa from hostile black Africa was coming apart.

The South African government had not formally recognised the illegal Rhodesian Front regime of Ian Smith, but it had supported it materially, refusing to participate in the sanctions campaign and permitting its ports and rail links to be used by the Rhodesians. South African security personnel had also been deployed inside Rhodesia to assist the Rhodesian forces in their conflict with the guerrilla movements.

At a meeting in Cape Town on 16 February 1975, however, Vorster told a shocked Ian Smith, the Rhodesian leader, that South Africa's support would end. Although this did not mean that South Africa would assist in the enforcement of sanctions, its security personnel would be withdrawn. As much as anything it was a psychological blow to Smith, who believed that it was part of a campaign 'to pressurise us into coming to an accommodation with our terrorists.' Intriguingly, Smith claims to have been told by Vorster at an earlier meeting that apartheid was 'unworkable.'[22] Vorster, of course, would have denied saying anything of the kind, even if it were true. By the mid-1970s, it was clear to all who wished to see that apartheid was, indeed, unworkable.

Conclusion

What conclusions may we draw from this survey of South Africa's political leadership in the post-1945 period but, in particular, the 1960s and 1970s? We began with Smuts as his brooding presence dominated South Africa's political system. Throughout much of his lifetime he earned the trust of the white English-speaking community, content to leave the business of politics to him and sharing his belief in the enterprise of creating a South African nation uniting both language groups. This ambition founded on the powerful rise of an Afrikaner nationalism which made successful inroads into the latter support for Republican status and ultimate domination of the country's bureaucratic structures and the electoral system.

The truism that foreign policy begins at home is profoundly true of South Africa's position and status in the society of states. For much of the post-war period, the country's policymakers and their leaders in particular had to devote time, energy, and resources to defending its domestic arrangements. Any proposal for reform by opposition parties such as the Liberal Progressive Party (established in 1959) was bracketed as 'selling out' to national and international critics. Of course, time and circumstances played a role in making policy. Then what can be asserted with a degree of confidence is that South Africa was well-regarded unquestionably among the ranks of small-to-modern powers. Insofar as its leadership from Smuts onwards had to combine domestic and foreign policy into an unsuccessful and constraining structure where inevitably each strand of major decision-making interacted with its counterpart setting limits to operating in a constructive and openminded way. Thus, any major decision – whether on domestic or foreign policy – had to consider the impact of each strand of policy on its counterpart. This made for a defensive and, at times, resentful reaction to external powers' protest at the iniquities of apartheid. One deleterious consequence was the migration year on year of many well-qualified individuals to more hospitable and seemingly stable societies, which

22 J.E. Spence

offered freedom from torrents of criticism and little, if any, prospect of any deeply rooted community conflict leading to social and economic dislocation.

Indeed, it could be said that many South Africans – both white and black – who hoped for a massive spurt of development post-apartheid have been disappointed despite improvement in public housing, education, and social development. Whether a new generation of leaders replacing the old order of apartheid within the ANC will make a significant difference can only, at this stage, be a matter of speculation.

Notes

1 Geoffrey Goodwin, *Britain and the United Nations* (London: Oxford University Press, 1957), 259.
2 Rosalyn Higgins, *The Development of International Law Through the Political Organs of the United Nations* (London: Oxford University Press for the Royal Institute of International Affairs, 1963), 2.
3 Raymond Aron, *Peace and War: The Theory of International Relations* (New York: Doubleday, 1966), 373.
4 Graham Evans, "The International Community and the Transition to the New South Africa," *The Round Table* 83, no. 330 (1994): 177–79.
5 Alexander Johnston, *In the Shadow of Mandela – Political Leadership in South Africa* (London: I. B. Tauris and Bloomsbury, 2020), 29.
6 Ibid., 31.
7 Ibid.
8 Scott Thomas, *The Diploma of Liberation: The Foreign Relations of the ANC Since 1960* (London: I. B. Tauris, 1966), 236.
9 R. B. Ballinger, *South West Africa: The Case Against the Union* (Johannesburg: South African Institute for International Affairs, 1961), 178.
10 Pieter verLoren van Themaat, "The Rule of Law," cited in J. E. Spence and David Welsh, *Ending Apartheid* (London: Longman Pearson, 2011), 10.
11 J. H. Snyman, cited in Spence and Walsh, *Ending Apartheid*, 11.
12 Francois Venter, cited in Spence and Walsh, *Ending Apartheid*, 12.
13 John Dugard, cited in Spence and Welsh, *Ending Apartheid*, 13.
14 Ibid.
15 Ibid.
16 P. W. Botha, Parliamentary Open Address, January 1986, House of Assembly, Cape Town.
17 See Spence and Welsh, *Ending Apartheid*, 23–24.
18 Ibid.
19 Ibid.
20 Eileen Riley, *Major Political Events in South Africa 1948–1990* (Oxford: Facts of File, 1991), 236.
21 Spence and Welsh, *Ending Apartheid*, 37.
22 Ian Smith, *Bitter Harvest: The Great Betrayal* (Johannesburg: Jonathan Ball, 2000), 170.

Select Bibliography

Aron, Raymond. *Peace and War: The Theory of International Relations*. New York: Doubleday, 1996.
Ballinger, R. B. *Southwest Africa, the Case for Union*. Johannesburg: South African Institute for International Affairs, 1961.

Evans, Graham. "The International Community and the Transition to the New South Africa." *The Round Table* 83, no. 330 (1994): 175–87.

Goodwin, Geoffrey. *Britain and the United Nations*. London: Oxford University Press, 1957.

Higgins, Rosalyn. *The Development of International Law Through the Political Organs of the United Nations*. London: Oxford University Press for the Royal Institute of International Affairs, 1963.

Hill, Christopher. *Bantustans*. Oxford: Oxford University Press, 1965.

Johnston, Alexander. *In the Shadow of Mandela – Political Leadership in South Africa*. London: I. B. Tauris and Bloomsbury, 2020.

Riley, Eileen. *Major Political Events in South Africa 1948–1990*. Oxford: Facts of File, 1991.

Rotberg, Robert. *Transformational Political Leadership: Making a Difference in the Developing World*. Chicago: Chicago University Press, 2012.

Smith, Ian. *Bitter Harvest: The Great Betrayal*. Johannesburg: Jonathan Ball, 2000.

Spence, J. E., and David Welsh. *Ending Apartheid*. London: Longman Pearson Ltd., 2011.

2

LEE KUAN YEW

From political insurgent to national manager

Michael D. Barr

> I do not think you learn leadership. You learn about human beings in given cultural, social and economic contexts. You learn to get things done or get people to do things within these contexts. But this attribute called leadership is either in you or it is not.
>
> Lee Kuan Yew, *The Business Times*, 16 September 1978[1]

For someone who did not believe leadership could be learnt and who did not have much time for theories or abstract ideas, Lee Kuan Yew talked and theorised about leadership a lot. A perusal of his speeches and interviews spanning three decades as Prime Minister of Singapore (1959–1990) reveals a near-obsessive focus on leadership. Not that his musings were truly theoretical or abstract. Even as he was seemingly thinking aloud in front of a microphone, he was deploying two of his most powerful political assets – his intellect and his wordcraft – to both establish his own credentials as a leader and invite Singaporeans to join his team as partners-cum-followers.

Leadership was, in Lee's mind, a force of nature to be understood, harnessed, and deployed. It was both a wonderful mystery and the primary ingredient in a nation's cohesion and development, the other two being administrative capacity and what he called 'social discipline,' but which we might just as easily call 'followership.'[2] His vision of leadership was, in fact, intimately connected to his ultra-realist understanding of the nature of power.

By the early 1980s, Lee was at the peak of his political power, and only as he approached that point did he begin dialling down his public musings about leadership, presumably because the hard part was done. By the mid-1980s, he had so much power and authority – both in Cabinet and with the broader population – that

DOI: 10.4324/9781003426165-2

leadership could be, to some extent, taken for granted. Or so he thought. It is note-worthy, however, that when Lee started taking leadership for granted, he began losing his touch: his initiatives on such eclectic projects as eugenics, health policy, race, education, and language policy were so unpopular and/or poorly understood that Cabinet spent the second half of the 1980s reversing or softening them in the lead-up to Lee stepping down as prime minister in 1990.[3]

Hence, as we consider the nature of Lee's approach to leadership, it is the early decades of his public life that are the most edifying, when it was still a work in progress, and the prospect of failure was either a real-time fear or a recent memory. In the 1950s–1970s, we have the chance to view Lee Kuan Yew's bare-knuckle leadership techniques, operating without the crutch of having sufficient power to act on a whim. The period from the 1980s onwards is of diminishing value to a study of his leadership because during that time he was mostly deploying power rather than exercising leadership, whether as prime minister until 1990, as a semi-retired senior minister from 1991 to 2004, or as an octogenarian minister mentor from 2004 to 2011. Yet the post-1970s period is not totally devoid of interest because it provides opportunities to identify strands of continuity with the earlier period, which is a rewarding exercise because those strands are very strong: both periods of his leadership pivoted around his realist and structuralist understanding of power and depended heavily upon his personal energies and communication skills. The latter period also hosted Lee's experiment in trans-generational transfer of leadership, which provides further insight into his thinking. As Lee settled into the comfortable exercise of power, his idealised vision of the next generation of leaders gradually morphed into something bland, technocratic, and managerial, with a minimum of fanfare, rhetorical flourish, passion, and – at least in public view – distortions due to personal power. Oddly, this was the exact opposite of the techniques he personally employed in the decades when he was on the front line of political and national leadership.

Impatient, ruthless, brilliant: portrait of a young Lee Kuan Yew

Lee Kuan Yew's first political manifesto was effectively an ambit claim to political leadership in late- and post-colonial British Malaya. In 1950, while waiting to sit for his Bar examination in post-war London after finishing his law degree at Cambridge University, he gave a speech to one of the fortnightly meetings of the Malayan Forum, which was an informal group of Malayan and Singaporean university students living in London. He titled his contribution 'The Returned Student' and used it to scope out a central political role in post-war Malaya for himself and all those present.[4] They were, he maintained, Malaya's best, if not its only, hope for stability and progress, with the alternative being a country fraught by racial tensions or ruled by communists. It also revealed his understanding of political and social power as an inherently structural and hierarchical relationship between holders of power – both inside and outside government – and their constituents or subjects.

26 Michael D. Barr

The speech was not especially memorable to members of his audience,[5] but in hindsight we can identify in its content and context many of the enduring personal elements that came to make up Lee the leader, over and above his focus on practical outcomes and his obvious self-confidence. Those personal elements included his elitism (and a concomitant hierarchical view of society), impatience, intelligence, and a way with words that seemed to make his message sound like an undeniable truism. These elements were easily recognisable in the older Lee when he was a professional politician, but it is significant that they were present at this time. Indeed, many of these characteristics were visible when he was a schoolboy in colonial Singapore, as a young man in Japanese-occupied wartime Singapore and in British-ruled post-war Singapore, and as a law student at Cambridge University. Just as significant, from childhood he also displayed a strongly competitive ethic that in turn fostered an extraordinary capacity for hard work and a tendency towards being a loner who restricted friendships mostly to people he could dominate.[6]

His speech to the Malayan Forum effectively declared Lee's personal leadership ambition, but even though it provided some indication of the direction of his thinking, it was just an early step in a very long journey of learning in which he studied leadership and leaders with obsessive dedication. His speeches over the next couple of decades were littered with his observations of other leaders. Wang Gungwu remembers Lee's Malayan Forum friends being 'fascinated and intrigued by the fact that he had bought and was studying intently the whole set of Lawrence and Wishart's English translation of the *Selected Works of Mao Tse Tung*,' and Lee himself gave testimony to having read the prison diaries and other writings of Jawaharlal Nehru with considerable attention.[7]

He also read widely and spoke with a similar level of focus on grand narratives of sociology, history, and national-cum-civilisational development. He was not just interested in how leaders related to their followers and constituents but how the ingredients making up national, political, or social culture impacted on national outcomes, especially as it related to development. This line of thought was already prevalent in his social cognition when he travelled through post-war Europe as a young man, and it fell in naturally with his propensity to view the world through stereotypes as he constantly searched for the elusive 'X-factor' in development; hence he mused aloud about lazy Italians and disciplined Germans; lazy Malays and disciplined Chinese.[8]

His search for the key to social progress led to a lifelong obsession on the roles of cultural, genetic, and environmental determinism as drivers of societal and even civilisational success. His conclusions on such matters were remarkably fluid, but the element that stayed constant was the conceptualisation of nations as organic wholes functioning through the operation of an internal social hierarchy: leaders at the top, followers at the bottom, and executives in between. Such an organicist view of society lent itself to identifying simplistic, one-dimensional solutions to complex problems. This trait would have been a great disadvantage for an academic, but it was a boon for a professional politician. It gave him a disproportionate level of confidence in his own judgement and a simple style of messaging that enabled him to build a rapport with his constituency. Lee combined this organicist conception of society with an inherently modernist expectation of social progress, whereby for the early decades of his adult life (at least) he presumed that the world was moving inexorably towards a higher destiny. In this, he was echoing both the Whiggish British history he learnt in school and the socialism he learnt from reading Nehru and Mao.

The common and complementary element of Lee's social cognition was that it maintained his focus on people as collectives rather than people as individuals. This societal view freed Lee from squeamish concerns about ethics and from worrying overly much about the consequences of his policies on people as individuals – hence his propensity in the 1960s to refer to Singaporeans as 'digits.'[9]

Such progressivist views of history and society are commonly associated with optimism and 'progressive' politics. If Lee had embraced such an outlook, it is likely that his record as a national leader would have been fraught with missteps due to complacency, but optimism was not in Lee's nature. Ever the pessimist, Lee restricted his optimism to the future of global society as a whole while living with the constant fear that his little bit of the global society would fail or be left behind. In this, too, his social cognition was thoroughly collectivist, and it came fully provided with an intellectual rationale – this time via Arnold Toynbee's *A Study of History*, which conceived of history in civilisational collectives, going even beyond societies and nations.

Lee read Toynbee's ten-volume *History* (or more likely, the two- or one-volume summary) as extracurricular reading at Cambridge, and then he cited it explicitly in the very first Cabinet meeting after he formed government in 1959, focusing on Toynbee's theory about the role of crises in making and shaping leadership elites and in determining the rise and fall of civilisations.[10] Notwithstanding the leap of imagination required to downscale a civilisational landscape to one appropriate for Singapore, this theme of crisis-driven progress settled itself as the constant background in his leadership style, leaving him always looking for the next Toynbeean catalyst – a new national crisis – that would give the national leadership its edge and drive the nation onwards and upwards.[11] Toynbee's theories even contained the seeds of pessimism that Lee sought, since the civilisational leaders of his imagination – dubbed the 'creative minority' – were themselves always just one crisis away from catastrophic failure.

Lee was an elitist by nature, and his reading reinforced this inclination, as did the experience of living and studying in class-ridden post-war England. His natural preference was for an elite drawn from the intelligentsia, but truly, any elite would do. Hence, in speeches in the 1960s, he moved seamlessly from declaring his conviction that Mao could not have ruled China without the support of the intelligentsia, to eulogising the public school culture of England, even citing the trope about the Battle of Waterloo being won on the playing fields of Eton.[12]

28 Michael D. Barr

It should be apparent by now that Lee painted his ambition on an unusually grand social and historical canvas. Indeed, Lee had never seen himself merely as the leader of a political party or even of a government. Such limited ambition was never sufficient to satisfy his self-image. Hence, a perusal of the six decades of Lee's speeches, interviews, election campaigning, and published books reveals a persistent conflation of partisan interests and ambitions into national and even international projects. Most politicians like to present themselves as working for a higher, altruistic goal – social, ideological, or national – but Lee pursued this trajectory with pseudo-religious rigour. Lee's imagination refused to be stifled by talk of mere national interest; his analytical rhetoric routinely burst beyond Singapore's borders and onto a global stage of rival powers, ideas, and ideologies.

Lee's boundless vision and self-confidence, combined with his political skills, were wonderful drivers for his ambition and useful tools for his rhetoric in the early decades of his public life when he had to work hard to win and retain people's loyalty. They also proved to be a useful compass when the time came to transform himself from being a political insurgent to becoming the head of a stable and long-term government but not as useful as his more down-to-earth and intuitive understanding of institutional power. It was thanks mostly to this practical bent that he was able to successfully integrate his techniques as a rabble-rousing troublemaker into a new persona that made him both a statesman and a ruthlessly effective national manager.

During both phases of his career, he was beset with occasions of hubris and misjudgement that threatened his projects. Despite these very human shortcomings, he managed to survive and thrive as a leader until he could hand the reins of power on to a new generation led by his son. It remains to be seen how that multigenerational project runs into the future.

Into the fray

Lee returned to Singapore from the United Kingdom in 1950 and found employment with the law firm of one of the colony's leading conservative politicians, John Laycock.[13] At this stage, Lee had overt political ambitions with a radical, anticolonialist flavour, and the beginnings of a network of fellow 'returned students,' but no political base. Lee was at a loss to know what to do about that lack when, in March 1952, Laycock offered him a brief suited to a junior solicitor: a trade union in need of a legal advocate. Lee offered to work for free and soon found himself as the solicitor of choice for the colony's English-speaking militant union leaders, student radicals, and various left-wing and communist figures.[14]

This project began building steadily among English-speaking activists, but Lee, who spoke no Chinese language at this time, was conscious that he had not managed to reach out to Singapore's majority community – Chinese-educated, Chinese-speaking workers and students. Hence, when a delegation of Chinese school students arrived at his home seeking his help in 1954, he seized his chance.

He quickly reached past the school students and through them made contact with key Chinese-educated left-wing union leaders in the person of two very young men named Lim Chin Siong and Fong Swee Suan. Their spoken English was so poor that they brought a translator with them to talk to Lee, who assumed (correctly) that they were closely connected to the Malayan Communist Party (MCP). Lim and Fong introduced Lee to Singapore's vibrant world of radical and communist Chinese politics, which quickly became a new, critical partner in Lee's next political venture, the People's Action Party (PAP).[15]

The PAP at its outset thus comprised three distinct elements: a mainly Anglophone, highly educated intelligentsia comprising predominately, but not exclusively 'returned students'; Anglophone trade union and student leaders; and Chinese-educated student and union activists, the vast majority of whom were broadly in Lim Chin Siong's and the MCP's orbit of leadership. Significantly, both of the English-speaking groups contained a racial cross section of Singapore's population, with Malays, Indians, and Eurasians disproportionately represented, but the third group was entirely ethnic Chinese in composition. Anti-colonialism and socialism were unquestioned doctrines in every group, though without much agreement on what each term might mean in practice. The MCP had a presence in each group but was most powerful among the Chinese-educated activists.[16]

Lee's task was to convert this ungainly coalition into a political movement that he could control and which would suit his ends. In his structuralist view of society and power, this meant winning over, neutralising, or removing rival power holders. This was no small order, since the direct power exercised by his rivals – both at the grassroots and at the executive level – dwarfed Lee's own and continually risked leaving him as the public face of forces that were beyond his control.[17]

Since he had very little power in his own right, Lee needed a powerful ally and so set about cultivating a partnership with the single-most powerful force on the island: the colonial authorities, beginning with the police Special Branch and working his way up to the governor.

There is no evidence that Lee suffered any qualms about colluding with the colonial authorities at the expense of his allies. Rather, his choices illustrate his utterly realist approach to power and the relationship he saw between power and leadership. The most critical element of his structuralist vision of leadership was his understanding of power as an almost-tangible reality. Lee and his closest allies had little real power themselves until well after the PAP had won office in the 1959 elections – and arguably not until after Singapore became independent in 1965 – and so it was a very simple calculation that led him to the conclusion that he needed to co-opt someone else's power. Who held power in the 1950s? The answer is set out with crystal clarity in Lee's memoirs:

Power was in the hands of the governor, his colonial secretary and his attorney-general. They all lived in the Government House domain that symbolised it. The governor lived in the biggest building, Government House, the colonial secretary in the second biggest bungalow, the attorney-general in the third, and the undersecretary and private secretary to the governor in two other bungalows. The telephone exchange serving these five buildings was manned 24 hours a day. This was the real heart of government.[18]

His regular back-door contact with the colonial authorities began in 1952, soon after he began taking in unions as clients. One Sunday morning, an officer from Special Branch visited him at home to swap notes about persons of mutual interest.[19] By mid-1954 (even before the foundation of the PAP and at the height of activism by his Chinese-educated allies and clients), Lee was on such familiar terms with Special Branch officers that he felt comfortable seeking favours on behalf of his brother, Dennis, who was keen to join the legal service.[20] In March 1955, he surprised the colonial secretary for Chinese Affairs by presenting himself as the government's partner in its campaign against the communists.[21] By 1958, Lee had established a clear pattern of confiding with Governor Goode and other senior officials as if they were political partners who were essentially of the same mind – on one occasion even giving the governor the benefit of an hour-long 'homily' (Goode's word) on the political situation in Singapore.[22] Just before the elections that brought Lee to power in 1959, Lee boasted to Governor Goode of his 'cleverness' in purging the PAP of communists and sealing the party from further communist penetration.[23] In another meeting, he congratulated Goode on a recent police action against a trade union and urged him to maintain the pressure leading up to election day.[24]

It is indicative of the intimacy that existed between Lee's group and Special Branch that the British archives contain a long, written report on PAP members and activities written by Lee's closest personal ally at the time, Dr (and later Deputy Prime Minister) Goh Keng Swee.[25]

The personal touch

Beyond co-opting and deploying state power, Lee needed to exercise his natural talents to win his own political victories: winning allies and neutering rivals. He pursued this programme with remarkable success. With the advice and assistance of Special Branch, he personally 'turned' one important communist trade union leader (C.V. Devan Nair), who proved to be one of his key political allies throughout the 1960s and 1970s.[26] He also substantially reversed his power relationship with the MCP by convincing its local plenipotentiary (Fang Chuang Pi; known in Lee's accounts as the 'the Plen') to withdraw from its other 'open front' operations – most notably the Workers' Party – as a gesture of goodwill, thus leaving the MCP-linked leftists with no viable option but to work through the PAP.[27] (In the event, a group of independent-minded left-wing union leaders considered contesting the 1959 Legislative Assembly elections as independent candidates, but even this half-hearted break with the PAP came to nothing.)[28]

Lee also had his share of luck. In 1957, the colonial authorities detained Lim Chin Siong, all the left-wingers on the PAP Central Executive Committee (CEC), and a number of other leftists. This security sweep was conducted at the behest of colonial Singapore's vehemently anti-communist chief minister, Lim Yew Hock, without Lee needing to do very much at all. Yet even this outcome was not just a matter of luck: Lee had earlier judged, correctly, that the leftists had made themselves vulnerable to being targeted for detention by winning a majority on the CEC, and he and his close colleagues had subsequently resigned from the CEC to maximise the left-wingers' exposure to the risk of detention.[29]

Lee himself came close to being detained at Lim's direction early in 1959, but he dodged that fate thanks to the refusal of one of his other political opponents (former chief minister David Marshall) to compromise his liberal principles.[30] That was lucky, but after that break, he made his own luck. In the lead up to the 1959 Legislative Assembly elections, Lee manoeuvred seven out of the eight PAP candidates, who Special Branch suspected of having links with the MCP into standing for unwinnable seats, thus removing them as front-line threats.[31] Upon the PAP winning those elections, he then negotiated for only a very limited number of his left-wing former colleagues to be released from detention and then ensured that they were relegated to subservient junior partners in government, dependent on Lee's goodwill.[32]

In his quest to remove threats and rivals, Lee even took Singapore into Malaysia as a constituent state in 1963, which he reasoned was the only way to fully neuter his domestic opponents. Certainly, he had other, higher reasons for wanting to 'merge' Singapore with Malaya to make Malaysia, but it was the domestic political dimension – the ongoing threat from the left to the PAP's supremacy – that gave the push its urgency.

The push to take Singapore into Malaysia highlights many of the more public aspects of Lee's leadership technique: his tireless, relentless capacity to campaign; his superb tactical mind; and his powerful oratorical skills. It was also a demonstration of his skilful manipulation of state power to tilt the playing field against his opponents: he called a plebiscite in September 1962 to decide on merger and then manipulated the plebiscite questions so that every option was a vote in favour of merger. Even a blank or spoilt vote was counted as 'yes'!

The key element in his associated year-long, state-sponsored public campaign was a series of 12 radio talks of approximately 15–25 minutes' duration each, written and read personally by Lee over September–October 1961, not just in English but also in Malay and Mandarin. The talks, which Lee collectively titled 'The Battle for Merger,' were also broadcast in Tamil, Hokkien, and Cantonese, so that every significant language spoken on the island was covered without his opponents having any right of reply, let alone a comparable opportunity to campaign.[33] The messaging was simple to the point of being simplistic: only the communists stood to gain from keeping Singapore out of Malaysia, so anyone who opposed the merger was a communist or a stooge or a fool. Furthermore, these broadcasts revealed the

32 Michael D. Barr

secret story of Lee's engagement with the MCP over the previous decade, which highlighted both the deadly seriousness of the threat and Lee's credentials as someone who knew from first-hand experience what he was talking about.

The master of messaging

Lee's messaging in his campaign for merger has a significance beyond its impact on the outcome of the plebiscite. It played a pivotal role in the construction of his much grander leadership programme and also it put on display the populist element of his leadership technique. Lee routinely derided populism in politics, but in fact he was a master at constructing populist messages, in which he always offered simplistic binary choices purportedly between good and evil, whether it was communism versus freedom, racial harmony versus race riots, independence versus subjugation, strong government versus anarchy, capitalism versus poverty, or Western decadence versus Confucian/Asian values. The 'good' was always the very precise policy prescription that Lee was proposing, but every other option was a step on the path to ruin.

The dichotomous pattern of his messaging was remarkably consistent throughout his public life, even if the subjects changed over the decades. There was always a kernel of truth in the choices he presented, but the picture was never as black and white as he maintained. Take, for instance, his presentation of communism as the primary evil in his self-styled 'Battle for Merger' in the early 1960s. Yes, the MCP was engaged in clandestine operations in Singapore, and yes, some of its operatives and associates held key leadership roles in trade unions and in the Chinese schools, but its glory days were well and truly behind it.

By the early 1960s, the MCP in peninsular Malaya was on its way to military defeat, having been reduced to a few isolated units scrambling around the jungle, with its leader Chin Peng unable to communicate with personnel in Singapore. As for Singapore itself, according to Internal Security Department (ISD) records, the MCP never recovered from the destruction of the party's Singapore Town Committee (STC) by Special Branch, which conducted a series of highly effective operations against it over 1948–1950.[34] The vacuum created by the demise of the STC left the radical nationalist and leftist movements in the island's trade unions and Chinese schools to grow through the 1950s and 1960s without much contact with or direction from the party. The MCP did what it could to restore its fortunes by successfully building new united front organisations, but the new operations proved to be loose cannons: thoroughly undisciplined, populist, and answerable to no one, least of all to faceless MCP apparatchiks isolated on some of the smaller Indonesian islands in the Straits of Malacca and in the even more remote jungles of Malaya and southern Thailand.[35]

Lim Chin Siong emerged as the effective leader of this mass movement (with a much more direct leadership role than 'the Plen'), but he was no party functionary.

The description of Lim by the British Deputy High Commissioner to Singapore in July 1962 confirms the picture:

[W]hile we accept that Lim Chin Siong is a Communist, there is no evidence that he is receiving his orders from the CPM, Peking or Moscow. Our impression is that Lim is working very much on his own and that his primary objective is not the Communist millennium but to obtain control of the constitutional government of Singapore.[36]

This revisionist account of the 1950s and 1960s is not meant to imply either that the communists were benign in their intent or that the radical movements more generally were harmless or free of MCP influence, but it does suggest that Lee's presentation of the MCP and the leftist movements as a monolithic, disciplined, and existential threat was a self-serving parody of the truth. In any case, in 1963 Lee proved that he was fully capable of dealing with any threat from communism when he destroyed the remnants of the MCP along with the entire radical-leftist wing of Singapore politics by ordering their detentions in a mass security sweep before Merger even took place.[37]

None of these shades of grey, however, were allowed to stand in the way of Lee's 1961 campaign to present merger as the only defence against a communist insurgency. With this campaign technique, he not only won his victory – Singapore became a constituent state of Malaysia in September 1963 – but he established the communist menace as a cornerstone of his political messaging for the next quarter century. (It was still doing faithful service providing a fanciful justification for a round of detentions as late as 1987.)[38]

Lee enshrined the communist threat as a core element of Singapore's foundation myth, where it was eventually joined by a litany of other mythologies: most notably the threat of race riots, Chinese 'chauvinism,' Western decadence, the demographic threat posed by a supposedly dysgenic pattern of population growth, and the challenge of religiously motivated subversion. With this developing record of changing foci, Lee's form of leadership came to resemble a series of identifiable campaigns. He never slipped out of frenetic campaigning mode or gave himself or his constituents a chance to draw breath because there was always a new crisis to grab attention or an old one to be revisited. Such was the centrality of crisis identification in Lee's political technique – which clearly owed a debt to Arnold Toynbee – that his public career can be tracked by identifying the crises upon which he built his messaging, always with gross oversimplification, and often with outright lies.

The lies that built a nation

The most powerful and enduring lie was the story of Singapore's supposed 'expulsion' from Malaysia in August 1965. This narrative sits at the heart of

34 Michael D. Barr

Singapore's founding mythology and is even more central than the story of the communist threat. And yet it is a lie. In fact, Singapore's departure from Malaysia was a negotiated, mutually agreed separation, and it was the Singapore government that initiated the negotiations. The press and every politician except one said that Singapore had been expelled. At 4.30 p.m. on the day of Separation, 9 August 1965, TV Singapura broadcast a recording of Singapore Prime Minister Lee Kuan Yew's press conference from earlier that day at which he famously shed tears for the lost union and bemoaned Singapore's expulsion from Malaysia.[39] By sharp contrast, Malaysian Deputy Prime Minister Tun Abdul Razak denied flat out that Singapore had been 'ejected' from Malaysia and insisted that it had left by mutual agreement.[40] No one in Singapore paid Razak any attention, but he was correct, in both the letter and the spirit of the truth. He should have known, since exactly three weeks earlier, on 20 July, he had met Singapore Finance Minister Goh Keng Swee where they began arranging Singapore's orderly departure from Malaysia after Goh had proposed the course of action a week earlier.[41] After four more meetings held variously in Razak's office and his home, the Separation Agreement was drafted and typed in his office on the evening of 6 August by Singapore Law Minister E.W. Barker and signed at about 1–1.30 a.m. on 7 August.[42] The initiative for these meetings had come from Goh Keng Swee, who told me in interview that he had acted with the full knowledge of Prime Minister Lee.[43] Malaysian Prime Minister Tunku Abdul Rahman agreed to be portrayed in Singapore's historiography as the instigator of Separation, but we now know this was a charade.[44]

Goh Keng Swee revealed the essentials of the true story (along with an extract from his classified file notes of the episode) in a research interview with author Melanie Chew that was published in 1996.[45] At this time the false story had been sustained without anyone suspecting anything for three decades (i.e. from 1965 to 1996), and even then, in supposedly serious history books written for university students, the narrative of the Malaysian Prime Minister 'casting Singapore out' persisted throughout the 2000s.[46] In fact, after the revelation of 1996, we still had to wait another 23 years (till 2019, four years after Lee's death) before any history textbook intended for use in either university or schools overtly acknowledged that Separation was initiated by the Singapore government.[47]

Flaws and foibles living in the shadows of success

Several elements of the story of Singapore's exit from Malaysia deserve attention in this study of Lee Kuan Yew's approach to leadership. First, he used the profound sense of crisis to justify the curtailment of most civic freedoms and the embrace of unfettered investment by international capital as necessary for Singapore's survival. Second, note the seriousness and success with which Lee maintained the lie, long after it was serving any useful purpose except to sustain Lee's personal legacy as Singapore's hero.

Yet perhaps the most interesting observation is not what the story of merger and separation tells us about Lee's strengths as a leader but about his shortcomings. What, after all, went so badly wrong in Malaysia that Singapore needed to leave in such a tearing hurry? The truth is that Singapore's two years in Malaysia reveal a catastrophic series of misjudgements on Lee's part that very nearly saw him detained by the central government.[48] Lee presumed that Singapore was entering Malaysia as an equal partner with the other 13 states, that the PAP and Lee personally would be welcomed as partners in government, and that Singapore's manufacturers would be given unfettered access to the new domestic market on the Malay peninsula. In fact, Singapore was barely tolerated as a Chinese-majority add-on to the existing Federation of Malaya, and there was never going to be any place for Lee or the PAP in the central government.[49] To top it off, after political relations between Kuala Lumpur and Singapore began deteriorating (which happened very quickly), the central government went out of its way to put the Singapore economy at a disadvantage in what Singapore's Finance Minister Goh Keng Swee described as an act of 'utter bad faith.'[50]

The plunge in relations between the Singapore government and the central government began early in 1964, just a few months after the merger, when Lee decided that the PAP would contest the Malaysian Federal elections on the peninsula in direct contravention of the terms of an agreement he had settled with the Malaysian Prime Minister Tunku Abdul Rahman.[51] Lee belatedly recognised this decision as a turning point in his relations with the government in Kuala Lumpur,[52] but according to a friend, Maurice Baker, who later discussed the matter with him, Lee did not even appreciate that his actions would cause offence. He completely misunderstood a conversation with Tunku in which Lee had asked Tunku how he would feel if the PAP contested the election after all, and Tunku replied, 'Well if that's the way you feel, go ahead.'[53] Amazingly, he interpreted this comment as approval. After that breach, an escalating war of words between Lee and the Malay leadership in Kuala Lumpur spiralled out of control, until Lee launched his final, suicidal dive into communal politics in June 1965 with a campaign for what he called a 'Malaysian Malaysia.'[54] This was explicitly a campaign to end Malay political hegemony in Malaysia, and it led directly to Singapore's theatrical 'expulsion' from Malaysia just two months later.[55]

In retrospect, the gulf between the parties' expectations and the outcomes was so vast that it would be churlish to blame Lee alone for the failure of the Malaysia experiment, but it is nevertheless instructive to consider what Lee's conduct in the episode might tell us about the man himself and his leadership skills. The first thing to note is that he retained the same campaigning instincts that served him so well during the merger campaign, but this time the results were disastrous. This raises the question of what might have been different, and the most obvious answer is that this time Lee was not able to develop an insider's access to power.

In Singapore in the 1950s, Lee had built a coalition with the British against his domestic political enemies, but in Malaysia in the 1960s, power sat squarely with

36 Michael D. Barr

the government in Kuala Lumpur, and no one there regarded him or the PAP as a partner. Even those who were most friendly with him in Kuala Lumpur – notably Prime Minister Tunku Abdul Rahman – never really regarded him as an ally or a friend, though Lee seemed to be unaware of this reality. Then, through his campaigning in the 1964 General Elections, Lee managed to turn his tentative colleagues into political rivals, and a year later with the launch of the campaign for a 'Malaysian Malaysia,' he turned his rivals into bitter enemies. Without access to power – and worse still, with power in the hands of his opponents – Lee proved himself a wildcard rather than a leader, something that his allies in Singapore Cabinet freely conceded in research interviews with Melanie Chew decades later.[56]

For all of Lee's strengths as a tactician, such episodes reveal his fallibility, which as I read it, was commonly based on his incapacity to read people, especially those whose world view was different to his own. Both before and after these episodes, his leadership was characterised by instances when he publicly ascribed nefarious motives to other people, giving them no benefit of the doubt. This was generally true whether he was accusing an opposition politician or a newspaper editor of being anti-Christian, a Chinese 'chauvinist,' or an agent of foreign influence; or detaining Catholic and amateur theatre social activists, along with pro bono lawyers, for being Marxist 'conspirators.'[57] When he was launching such attacks from a position of near-absolute power, this was undoubtedly a convenient way to weaponise his personal political agenda, but his dealings with the Malaysian leadership – and Prime Minister Tunku Abdul Rahman in particular – reveal the same flaw when he was in a position of weakness, suggesting that the problem runs deeper.

It is significant that *Men in White* – a fervently sympathetic history of the PAP published in 2009 – opened with an eight-page prologue that was exclusively devoted to the story of one of Lee's more spectacular and consequential misjudgements of a colleague. This episode was set in the early 1960s. The newly appointed Prime Minister Lee had insisted on trusting his own judgement concerning the trustworthiness of Chan Sun Wing – who was both his right-hand man in the prime minister's office and the man responsible for staffing PAP branches and the government's network of community centres. Special Branch and many others had been telling Lee for years that Chan was an MCP operative, but even as Lee acknowledged that Chan was 'a communist sympathiser,' he insisted that he 'had changed.' Except that Special Branch was right, and Lee was left slack-jawed when Chan and all the people he had appointed to the PAP branches and the community centres turned against him and his party in 1961. The authors make a point of describing this episode as 'yet another misjudgement of character' on the part of Lee Kuan Yew.[58]

Tellingly, once he was more comfortably in power and the party had the luxury of offering recruits secure career paths, Lee's colleagues – notably Goh Keng Swee and Lim Kim San and Hon Sui Sen – lifted most of the business of talent spotting from Lee's shoulders,[59] but even then, he could not leave it alone. He continued to immerse himself in both the minutia of talent spotting and the broad-brush work of setting the parameters of recruitment and testing, only to be routinely disappointed with the results.

Note at this point that Lee's approach, and that of the upper levels of government as a whole, was intensely personal. Recruitment and promotion processes in the civil service, the military, and politics were notionally professionalised in the 1980s, but it was still well-nigh impossible to rise to the heights of the elite without having spent time working in Lee Kuan Yew's office, commonly as his personal private secretary.[60] Sometimes, it seemed that the only people he could trust fully were his relatives, followed by those with whom he had formed a close personal bond.

To be fair to the rising stars who disappointed Lee, it is not always clear that the fault lay in the stars themselves but with Lee's judgement in matching people with roles. Two high-profile and closely linked cases come to mind from the mid-1980s: Devan Nair and Lim Chee Onn.

Lee's original recruitment of Devan Nair in the late 1950s cannot be faulted. At that time, Lee needed him in a role to which he was ideally suited and in which he was a great success: head of the trade union movement. At the beginning of the 1980s, however, Lee needed to move him out of the trade union movement because he wanted to give his hand-picked successor, Lim Chee Onn, a free hand. To effect this transfer, Lee took Devan Nair – a hard-drinking, tough-as-nails trade union leader – and made him President of Singapore, which was a highly decorous and isolated role for which he was completely ill-suited. Devan Nair struggled and failed to adapt to the new environment, and Lee came rather quickly to the decision that he had to force him to resign, which he proceeded to do through a public campaign that destroyed his friend's reputation. Lee even went to the extent of accessing and publishing Devan Nair's personal medical records and commissioning a government White Paper devoted exclusively to tearing him down.[61] Furthermore, he engaged in this public campaign without ever acknowledging that the prime responsibility for the sad spectacle was his own lack of judgement in choosing Devan Nair for the role of president in the first place (not to mention the lack of restraint he displayed when he turned so viciously on his friend of nearly 30 years).

Meanwhile, Lim Chee Onn's star was also falling. His tenure as secretary-general of the National Trades Union Congress began at the end of the 1970s, and it was intended by Lee to usher in a golden age of social and institutional leadership by tertiary-educated technocrats (Lim being both a Harvard graduate and a naval architect). Lee should not have been surprised that Lim had difficulty building a relationship with the old-school trade union leaders who had been put under his charge.[62] His problem was very nearly a mirror image of Devan Nair's, but the source of the two men's difficulties was the same.

Lee's chequered record of people management persisted through to the very end of his life: one of his final choices of personal private secretary was Heng Swee Keat, who went on to fail spectacularly as deputy prime minister and heir apparent to Prime Minister Lee Hsien Loong.[63]

38 Michael D. Barr

It was also fundamental to Lee's personality that he never reciprocated loyalty, even to close friends (though family was different). Maurice Baker (mentioned earlier) was Singapore's High Commissioner to Malaysia when Lee set out to destroy the reputation of President Devan Nair in the first half of the 1980s. In 1996, Baker told me in interview:

> I was in KL when this happened to Devan Nair. I saw Musa Hitam, the [Malaysian] DPM, and [PM] Dr Mahathir, and they told me they can never understand how a man can treat a friend like this. . . , a man who has done so much for the country. They were more upset than Singaporeans. Why disagree in public? And Mahathir said, if he could do this to a friend, what would he have done to us [if Singapore had stayed in Malaysia]?[64]

Leadership in power: political management

The limitations of Lee's people management skills have provided a bridge by which this chapter has moved from a consideration of Lee's leadership techniques during the early decades, when he was acquiring power and establishing his dominance, to his later years, when he was secure in power and experienced in running the country. The point at which this transition can be said with confidence to have occurred is necessarily imprecise, but it was certainly sometime during the mid-1970s (probably after he led the PAP to a sweeping victory in the 1976 General Election).

The transition from political insurgent to national office holder is routinely problematic for those who led their countries to independence, both because the two roles require very different skillsets and because too often, insurgent leaders have no serious plans beyond winning. For Lee, however, the shift was seamless, in part because he had always taken the role of governing seriously, and, as we have seen, he was a keen student of power per se. Indeed, the reason I have devoted a disproportionate amount of attention to the early years of Lee's political career in this chapter is that the lines of continuity with his later years are overwhelming.

Beyond his intrinsic personal traits (high intelligence, curiosity, a seemingly limitless capacity for hard work), he basically continued deploying the techniques and habits that he learnt during his rise (perpetual campaigning; simplistic and very effective messaging; ruthless deployment of power in all available forms), but he augmented them with management skills acquired from encounters with the world of professional managers – both public sector managers and those in the capitalist private sector. It was not for nothing that in 1968, Lee launched himself on a residential sabbatical at the Kennedy School of Government at Harvard University, which morphed into a series of visits over the next two years. During these visits his hosts introduced him to America's governing elite. Over the following decades, he sent a caravan of senior political, administrative, and military figures to the Kennedy School to study public administration, beginning with his eldest son, Lee Hsien Loong.[65]

It is tempting to suggest that Lee's excursions to the Kennedy School might have been the source of his focus on governance, but such an assessment ignores evidence from Lee's earlier speeches that show conclusively he had long been focused on – even obsessed with – governance as a supposed science. Government policy, Lee told Singaporeans in 1966, was 'calculated' rather than developed, and policies worked because 'there is a group of men sitting in little rooms, planning, thinking, analysing, watching figures, watching trends.'[66] And as early as 1959, when Lee was still in his first months as prime minister, he described in the Legislative Assembly his government's programme of 're-educating' civil servants (his own choice of words) through a body called the 'Political Study Centre,' which was designed explicitly and openly to bring them into political alignment with his government.[67] After a rocky start in which Lee had trouble getting the messaging right, the programme of re-education succeeded beyond all expectations, turning the civil service into a politicised arm of the government, not just formulating government policy but even staffing many of its grassroots outreach activities.[68] (When I was interviewing the electoral officer and 'grassroots leader' of a senior Cabinet minister in 2003, he went out of his way to explain that although he was himself an unpaid volunteer, the 'young man' who ushered me into the office and served tea was a civil servant doing his day job.)[69]

The civil service also became the main recruiting ground for Cabinet, and to this day nearly all of Cabinet are drawn from the public sector,[70] though since the mid-1980s the civil servants have had to share the table with former university-trained military officers, beginning with Lee Hsien Loong. Lee Kuan Yew came to regard this section of the officer corps as a superior form of civil servant, explicitly trained in leading men and getting things done.[71]

Lee's new relationship with the Kennedy School reflects a second key element in his successful conversion from an insurgent politician to an institutional office holder: notably, his apparently insatiable curiosity about new ideas and opportunities. This curiosity was particularly strong when it came to big-picture ideas that offered grand explanations of history and society – hence the appeal of Arnold Toynbee's *A Study of History* when he was young.

Lee's relative freedom from conventional ideological approaches had the great advantage of opening his mind to new possibilities. On balance, this proclivity served him well in government, except that his curiosity was too easily satiated: once he had found a new idea, he 'knew' that he was right and needed no further advice until this idea had run its course. To make matters worse, he had the power to give most of his whims concrete form as well as the skill to broadcast his message convincingly.

Albert Winsemius, Lee's friend and long-term economic adviser, spoke of this characteristic in the 1980s, identifying it as a recurring source of trouble:

I don't know if you've ever noticed that Singapore and its government often behave like adolescents in a one-sided way, over-stressing a thing and forgetting

40 Michael D. Barr

the rest; then dropping the subject and focusing, once more one sided, on the next thing.[72]

On this particular occasion, Winsemius was arguing that Lee was dead wrong in his public statements about the quality of Singaporean workmanship (suggesting it was substandard), and Winsemius was explaining the difficulties he faced in getting his message through to the prime minister, once he had an idea fixed in his head.

It is good to keep a healthy awareness of Lee's foibles, but let us not dismiss the greater advantages that his curiosity and formidable mind brought to his leadership techniques. Lee had a remarkable ability to assimilate new ideas and information. This knack, combined with his capacity for forensic yet imaginative analysis, earned him the respect of leaders the world over. Such characteristics raised his and Singapore's standing in global affairs, which played well both at home and abroad.

Leadership in power: business management

Beyond connections in government, there was another strand to the set of introductions Lee enjoyed during his American sabbatical: his hosts arranged for him to meet and deliver sales pitches to the most important players in American capitalism. This move not only launched independent Singapore as a successful node in the global capitalist economy, but it was also integral to its new strategic alignment with the United States. And thanks to Lee's capacity for both pragmatic policy shifts and 'big picture' thinking, he identified the embrace of American-anchored capitalism as a prerequisite for Singapore's American-anchored security. In his mind, a partnership with American capitalism and the American defence and diplomatic establishment became two sides of the same coin, with each being the guarantor of the other. It is not mere chance that they were both seeded and nurtured during Lee's sabbatical at the Kennedy School at the end of the 1960s.

I highlight this feature because it headlines a key strand of continuity in his repertoire that came to assume new importance as Lee moved from 'insurgency' to 'governance' mode: his leadership in business management. Not that Lee had ever been a great business manager himself, but in the chaos of the immediate postwar period he was engaged in a successful manufacturing and wholesale business (selling gum), as well as the prime agent in several more dubious back-alley and waterfront enterprises that skirted the law. Between them, they were sufficiently successful for Lee to both support his family and fund himself through his law degree in England.[73] Then after his return from England, he and his wife and brother started a new family law firm, Lee and Lee, which prospered after he became prime minister. As the company website tells us rather coyly, 'Lee and Lee has grown and developed in tandem with Singapore.'[74] His wife and other family members continued to be actively engaged in other business ventures long after Lee Kuan Yew's rise to power, making million-dollar direct investments in enterprises.[75] We also know from a real estate scandal in 1996 that he was not above making direct million-dollar business investments in his own name.[76]

Whether or not these various life experiences affected his attitude to business, it is undoubtedly the case that as he moved further and further into governance mode, Lee came to have increasing respect for business success and was pleased to facilitate it – provided they posed no potential political threats. Hence, for decades he treated local Chinese banks, newspapers, and SMEs (Small- and Medium-Sized Enterprises) with overt hostility because they had a collective record as a rival centre of power. Chinese businesses were eventually rehabilitated but only insofar as they had accepted a subordinate, dependent relationship with the government.[77] By contrast, he was keen to welcome foreign direct investment (FDI), since the multinational companies (MNCs) associated with FDI generally had no interest in local politics, provided profits and stability were assured.

Yet the businesses that Lee really wanted for Singapore were those that were actively integrated into his government's policy agenda; and this is what he set out to build. Within a few years of taking office in government, he and his closest colleagues began corporatising government statutory boards and turning them into the seeds of a new type of business that has since become known as the government-linked company (GLC). The early management of GLCs was placed in the hands of people who happened to be known to Lee or one of the other key members of his Cabinet so that their political reliability was assured.[78] It is vital to note, however, that this did not usually involve the appointment of incompetent relatives or lackeys; they were mostly highly experienced and competent men, so the GLCs flourished despite the obvious pitfalls that could have engulfed them.

Generational change in GLC leadership was decades in coming, but when it did, Lee's holistic and expansive vision of leadership – combined with his attention to detail – began paying dividends. From the very beginning of his premiership, Lee had been paying close attention to human resource planning at the national level. This took two distinct forms. First, there was education for the masses in ordinary 'neighbourhood' schools and local post-secondary education institutes and universities. Second, there was elite education, which was conducted in a clutch of elite schools that acted as de facto feeder schools for competitive government scholarships to elite overseas universities. Mass education trained a workforce for industry and the lower and middle levels of the government and tertiary industry sectors. Elite education trained future generations of leaders, not just for GLCs but also for the civil and military services and eventually for the political service (Cabinet).[79] In fact, GLC personnel came to be so mobile – moving back and forth between GLCs and the various arms of the public sector – that we can legitimately ask whether they were really business managers or just public servants with business experience. Certainly, the end product was everything that Lee ever dreamed of: a highly professional business elite dependent upon and loyal to the political establishment.[80]

42 Michael D. Barr

It took a couple of decades for these programmes to start producing cohorts of business leaders who were ready to take over at the highest levels, but as they did – in the 1980s – Lee became increasingly confident that he could trust both their professional competence and their political loyalty. Lee had already started ceding some degree of autonomy to GLCs in 1974, through the creation of two government-owned holding companies that in turn managed some of the GLCs. At this time his trusted colleagues were still in harness, but in retrospect we can see him preparing the GLCs for generational transfer. Concomitant with loosening direct control of GLCs, the 1980s saw an increase in Lee's indirect control of GLCs. He expanded the footprint of the government's holding companies so that between them their coverage of GLCs was comprehensive; strengthened the family's lines of communication with the holding companies by enacting critical personnel changes at the peak levels; imposed increasingly intricate patterns of cross-ownership of GLCs with other GLCs and other government-linked entities; and ensured the ubiquitous presence on GLC boards of company directors who had close personal and professional links to the ruling elite.[81] With the completion of such indirect inputs into GLCs in the 1980s, direct control was hardly necessary – and would have been cumbersome and counter-productive.

Having ensured that management of GLCs at the highest levels was in the hands of people he trusted, Lee was then willing to allow the GLCs to be run by the professionals with only a very light touch of direct interference from the government itself – in sharp contrast to other arms of society, which were much more oppressively subject to government 'leadership.'

Thus far, the description of Lee's approach to business fits readily with that which we have already seen in Lee's ultra-realist approach to power: economic power is a form of power, so it needs to be tamed and tethered, but there is another aspect. Beyond the straightforward matter of constraining the rise of potential rivals and subordinating business to government, Lee was also convinced that the government (though not necessarily Lee personally) knew best about the economy – as it did about everything else. This conceit began waning only in the mid-1980s, which was when Lee allowed Goh Chok Tong to shift the government towards a more 'business-friendly' stance.[82]

It is true that the lines of patronage in the government-linked business sector were and are evident, and any GLC could find itself required to do the government's bidding at a moment's notice, but on a daily basis and in their long-term planning and hiring, GLCs were expected to display high levels of professionalism in their governance and to turn profits for their stakeholders. We cannot be sure why Lee's leadership of business displayed such an uncharacteristic restraint. Perhaps, it was his own experience in business that made the difference, or perhaps, he accepted good advice from people who he recognised as knowing more than he did. It could simply be that he was convinced that Singapore's international economic success was so dependent on factors he could not control that he decided to scale back his micro-management instincts somewhat. Regardless of the true origins of 'the Singapore approach' to business, there can be no denying that thanks to his self-restraint, Lee managed to find a sweet spot between the extremes of a centrally planned economy and American-style 'wild west' capitalism.

From chilli-hot politicians to bloodless technocrats

Lee and his colleagues had, in fact, invented a world-class form of state capitalism.[83] They also gave birth to a new type of technocratic business/administrative professionals who would work in tandem with the political leadership: highly competent and easily capable of independent action but ultimately quiescent to the will of the political centre. That worked for GLCs and the civil service, but then Lee applied the same template to Cabinet-level appointments. Thus, since the 1980s, Cabinet has been full of highly educated professionals from the public sector (including from the GLC sector since the turn of the century) who have all been invited/appointed into political office without any political experience and only known leadership within contexts characterised by performance reviews and annual bonuses. And judging by their typical acceptance speeches and introductory press conferences, they seem to be proud to treat politics as a profession rather than a passion or a cause; a challenging extension of their civil service, military, and/or GLC careers.[84]

This legacy sits oddly with Lee's own origins as a chilli-hot politician who had to fight his way into power, risking much to win it all. One of the most important lessons in Lee's playbook is surely the distinction between leading and ruling: between leadership and the mere exercise of power. Lee was a master of both, but with his successors being gifted power as part of their career advancement, we are entitled to wonder whether leadership has been overlooked.

Lee Kuan Yew passed away in 2015, leaving in place a Cabinet led by his eldest son, Prime Minister Lee Hsien Loong, who was heading a so-called third-generation (3G) leadership team. In the years that followed Lee Kuan Yew's death, his children, their spouses, and his grandchildren engaged in very public disputes over his will and his legacy. This was mixed with talk of one of Lee's grandsons possibly entering politics.[85]

Perhaps, the third generation of Lees in politics will never happen, but this very recent history highlights the importance of the Lee family brand in Singapore.[86] This is both a tribute to the depth and seriousness of Lee Kuan Yew's lifetime in leadership and perhaps an unconscious indicator of the fundamental problem in Lee's attempted micro-management of elite regeneration: the gap left by the necessary absence of Lee Kuan Yew.

Lee has left behind a national government modelled on a leadership structure he designed for GLCs; but GLCs are themselves dependent parts of a whole that looks, however indirectly, to the political centre for leadership. In the political centre itself, there needs to be someone who can provide the sort of visionary and autonomous leadership that Lee himself did over many decades. This begs the

44 Michael D. Barr

question: how long can a system designed to be run with a Lee Kuan Yew at the centre function without Lee Kuan Yew? The fact that such a question can even be reasonably asked (regardless of the answer) is a tribute to the man's record of achievement.

Notes

1 Lee Kuan Yew, "Interview With Roy Mackie and Quek Peck Lim," *The Business Times*, 16 September 1987, cited in Lee Kuan Yew, *Prime Minister's Speeches, Press Conferences, Interviews, Statements, etc.*, Singapore: Prime Minister's Office, 1959–90.
2 Lee Kuan Yew, "Broadcast Version of a Talk to Civil Servants at the Political Study Centre," 14 June 1962, cited in Lee, *Prime Minister's Speeches, etc.*
3 Michael D. Barr, "Perpetual Revisionism in Singapore: The Limits of Change," *The Pacific Review* 16, no. 1 (2003): 77–97.
4 The full text of the speech is available at Han Fook Kwang, Warren Fernandez, and Sumiko Tan, *Lee Kuan Yew: The Man and His Ideas* (Singapore: Times Editions and The Straits Times Press, 1998), 256–62. A one-page précis is available at Michael D. Barr, *Lee Kuan Yew: The Beliefs Behind the Man* (Richmond, Surrey: Curzon, 2000), 17.
5 Maurice Baker chaired the meeting at which Lee spoke and remembered it as being 'a very good talk.' Goh Keng Swee remembered hearing Lee's presentation, but despite being generally impressed with Lee's intelligence, the speech itself made no impression on him at all. 'It was just one speech among many.' Interviews with Maurice Baker, September 25, 1996 and with Goh Keng Swee, September 1, 1996.
6 Barr, *Lee Kuan Yew*, 98–108, Chapter 2; James Minchin, *No Man Is an Island: A Portrait of Singapore's Lee Kuan Yew*, updated ed. (North Sydney: Allen & Unwin, 1986, 1990), 44.
7 Interview with Wang Gungwu, September 8, 1996; Lee Kuan Yew, Legislative Assembly Debates, Official Report (1946–1965), 12 April 1956.
8 Lee in Han, Fernandez, Tan, *Lee Kuan Yew*, Chapter 8; Barr, *Lee Kuan Yew*, Chapter 6.
9 For examples of Lee's characterisation of people as 'digits,' see Lee Kuan Yew, *New Bearings in Our Education System* (Singapore: Ministry of Culture, 1966–1967), 19; Lee Kuan Yew in "Questions and Answers after Prime Minister's address on 'University autonomy and social responsibility' at the Historical Society Meeting at the University of Singapore," November 24, 1966, in Lee, *Prime Minister's Speeches, etc.*; Lee Kuan Yew, "Change Is the Essence of Life in the World Today," *The Mirror* 3, no. 19 (May 8, 1967): 6; Lee's address to University of Singapore Matriculation Ceremony, 5 September 1969, *University of Singapore Students' Union Journal* [n.d., c. 1970], 87; Lee Kuan Yew's speech at the University of Dar-Es-Salaam, September 6, 1970, in Lee, *Prime Minister's Speeches, etc.*
10 Interview with Goh Keng Swee, September 1, 1996; Barr, *Lee Kuan Yew*, Chapter 3.
11 Barr, *Lee Kuan Yew*, 79, 83–85.
12 Lee Kuan Yew, "Speech to the Royal Society of International Affairs (Chatham House), London," May 1962, in Lee, *Prime Minister's Speeches, etc.*; Lee, *New Bearings in Our Education System*, 10.
13 Lee Kuan Yew, *The Singapore Story: Memoirs of Lee Kuan Yew* (Singapore: Prentice Hall, 1998), 132–40.
14 Special Branch Report on Lee Kuan Yew, June 1954, FCO 141–15306, Foreign and Colonial Office, UK, National Archives of United Kingdom.
15 Lee, *The Singapore Story*, Chapters 9–10.
16 See Sonny Yap, Richard Lim, and Leong Weng Kam, *Men in White: The Untold Story of Singapore's Ruling Party* (Singapore: Singapore Press Holdings, 2009), Part 1.

17 Report by M. Higham to H.E. [His Excellency the Governor], December 3, 1955, 10, FCO 141–15298, Foreign and Colonial Office, UK, National Archives of United Kingdom; Report from Officer Administering the Government to Secretary of State for the Colonies, May 29, 1957, paragraphs 20 and 31, FCO141–15306, Foreign and Colonial Office, UK, National Archives of United Kingdom; Monthly Intelligence Report No. 8, May 29, 1957, paragraphs 30, 31, FCO 141–14773, Foreign and Colonial Office, UK, National Archives of United Kingdom.

18 Lee, *The Singapore Story*, 137.

19 Ibid., 157–58.

20 Special Branch Report on Lee Kuan Yew, June 1954, p. 5, FCO 141–15306, Foreign and Colonial Office, UK, National Archives of United Kingdom.

21 Letter from R.M. Broome, Secretary for Chinese Affairs, Singapore, to Mr Fairbairn, Special Branch – March 18, 1955, SCA.006/55, Report on meeting with Lee Kuan Yew, FCO 141–14582, Foreign and Colonial Office, UK, National Archives of United Kingdom.

22 Note by E. Melville, Colonial Office, London, on meeting with Lee Kuan Yew, December 3, 1957, FCO 141–15306, Foreign and Colonial Office, UK, National Archives of United Kingdom; Note by H. E. the Governor regarding a meeting with Lee Kuan Yew, September 18, 1958, FCO 141–14651, Foreign and Colonial Office, UK, National Archives of United Kingdom; Note by H. E. the Governor regarding a meeting with Lee Kuan Yew, December 1, 1958, FCO 141–14651, Foreign and Colonial Office, UK, National Archives of United Kingdom.

23 Note by H. E. the Governor regarding a meeting with Lee Kuan Yew, March 17, 1959, FCO 141–14651, Foreign and Colonial Office, UK, National Archives of United Kingdom.

24 Note by H.E. the Governor, on meeting with Lee Kuan Yew, April 23, 1959, FCO 141–14651, Foreign and Colonial Office, UK, National Archives of United Kingdom.

25 D.B.S. to C.S. – 10.12.1958 [Verbatim extracts from Goh Keng Swee's report "on the City Council, gangsters, P.A.P. cadres and membership, P.A.P. policy if they form the Government," December 11, 1958, FCO 141–14783, Foreign and Colonial Office, UK, National Archives of United Kingdom.

26 Lee, *The Singapore Story*, 157–60, 290–93.

27 Michael D. Barr, *Singapore: A Modern History* (London and New York: I.B. Tauris and Bloomsbury, 2019), 106–7.

28 Summary of Intelligence – Singapore No. 8/59 for the period April 19–May 2, 1959, p. 2, FCO 141–14631, Foreign and Colonial Office, UK, National Archives of United Kingdom.

29 C. M. Turnbull, *A History of Singapore: 1819–1988*, 2nd ed. (Singapore: Oxford University Press, 1989), 259–60; Lee Kuan Yew, *The Singapore Story: Memoirs of Lee Kuan Yew* (Singapore: Prentice Hall, 1998), 268–71; Yap, Lim, and Leong, *Men in White*, 105–6.

30 John Drysdale, *Singapore: Struggle for Success* (Singapore: Times Books International, 1984), 206–7.

31 Summary of Intelligence – Singapore No. 8/59 for the period April 19–May 2, 1959, p. 2, FCO 141–14631, Foreign and Colonial Office, UK, National Archives of United Kingdom.

32 Note by WAC Goode, Governor, on meeting with Lee Kuan Yew, May 14, 1959, FCO 141–14651, Foreign and Colonial Office, UK, National Archives of United Kingdom.

33 Yap, Lim, and Leong, *Men in White*, 234–37; Lee Kuan Yew, *The Battle for Merger*, 2nd ed. (Singapore: National Archives of Singapore and Straits Times Press, n.d. (original 1962)). See "Message by Mr. Lee Kuan Yew," which appears before the sequence of numbered pages begins. Included with the second edition is a CD of the complete series of broadcasts in English, Mandarin, and Malay.

46 Michael D. Barr

34 Alexander Nicholas Shaw, "The British Intelligence Community in Singapore, 1946–1959: Local Security, Regional Coordination and the Cold War in the Far East" (PhD thesis, University of Leeds, 2019), 136–60.

35 See Poh Soo Kai, Tan Kok Fang, and Hong Lysa, eds., *The 1963 Operation Coldstore in Singapore: Commemorating 50 Years* (Petaling Jaya and Kuala Lumpur: Strategic Information and Research Development Centre and Pusat Sejarah Rakyat, 2013); Poh Soo Kai, *Living in a Time of Deception* (Singapore: Function 8, 2016); C. C. Chin and Karl Hack, eds., *Dialogues with Chin Peng: New Light on the Malayan Communist Party* (Singapore: NUS Press, 2004); Said Zahari, *Dark Clouds at Dawn: A Political Memoir* (Kuala Lumpur: Insan, 2001), 301; C. C. Chin, "The United Front Strategy of the Malayan Communist Party in Singapore, 1950s and 1960s," in *Paths Not Taken: Political Pluralism in Post-War Singapore*, ed. Michael D. Barr and Carl A. Trocki (Singapore: NUS Press, 2008), 58–77; Barr, *Singapore*, 105–9.

36 T. N. Harper, "Lim Chin Siong and the 'Singapore Story'," in *Comet in Our Sky: Lim Chin Siong in History*, K. S. Tan Jing Quee and Jomo (Kuala Lumpur: Insan, 2001), 39. Also see Kevin Y. L. Tan, "Lim Chin Siong and His Legacy of Left-Wing Activism in the Fight for Nationhood," in *A General History of the Chinese in Singapore*, ed. Kwa Chong Guan and Kua Bak Lim (Singapore: Singapore Federation of Chinese Clan Associations and World Scientific, 2019), 1173–98.

37 Geoff Wade, "Operation Coldstore: A Key Event in the Creation of Modern Singapore," in *The 1963 Operation Coldstore in Singapore: Commemorating 50 Years*, ed. Poh Soo Kai, Tan Kok Fang, and Hong Lysa (Petaling Jaya: Strategic Information and Research Development Centre; Kuala Lumpur: Pusat Sejarah Rakyat, 2013), 55, 60–62, 68.

38 In 1987, Lee initiated and managed the detention of 22 people associated variously with the Catholic Church, the Law Society, and independent theatre, claiming they were part of a 'Marxist conspiracy' to overthrow the state. See Michael D. Barr, "Marxists in Singapore? Lee Kuan Yew's Campaign Against Catholic Social Justice Activists in the 1980s," *Critical Asian Studies* 42, no. 3 (2010): 335–62.

39 "Singapore Is Out: Tengku Pledges Support for Admission to Commonwealth and United Nations," *The Straits Times*, August 10, 1965.

40 "Razak Rejects 'Ejection' of S'pre: Bill Passed 126-0," *The Straits Times*, August 10, 1965.

41 Goh Keng Swee in Melanie Chew, ed., *Leaders of Singapore* (Singapore: Resource Press, 1996), 147.

42 Michael Barr's interview with E. W. Barker, Singapore, October 16, 1996; Tan Siok Sun, *Goh Keng Swee: A Portrait* (Singapore: Editions Didier Millet, 2007), 116–23.

43 Interview with Goh Keng Swee, Singapore, October 1, 1996.

44 "Tengku: It Was My Idea," *The Straits Times*, August 10, 1965; National Heritage Board, *Singapore: Journey Into Nationhood* (Singapore: Landmark Books, 1998), 96–97; Alex Josey, *Lee Kuan Yew: The Crucial Years* (Singapore: Times Books International, 1968 [(1980]), 284.

45 Goh in Chew, *Leaders of Singapore*, 147.

46 Edwin Lee, *Singapore: The Unexpected Nation* (Singapore: Institute of Southeast Asian Studies, 2008), 260.

47 Kwa Chong Guan, Derek Heng, Peter Borschberg, and Tan Tai Yong, *Seven Hundred Years: A History of Singapore* (Singapore: National Library Board, 2019), 268.

48 Discussion of the possibility of Lee's detention by the Central Government is reported in *The Straits Times*, 9, 10, 14 July 1965.

49 Albert Lau, *A Moment of Anguish: Singapore in Malaysia and the Politics of Disengagement* (Singapore: Times Academic Press, 1998).

50 Lee, *The Singapore Story*, 601.

51 Michael D. Barr, "Lee Kuan Yew in Malaysia: A Reappraisal of Lee Kuan Yew's Role in the Separation of Singapore from Malaysia," *Asian Studies Review* 21, no. 1 (1997): 1–17.

52 Lee Kuan Yew's secret letter to Sir Robert Menzies, Prime Minister of Australia, April 20, 1965, A1209, 1965/6571, National Archives of Australia.
53 Interview with Maurice Baker, October 25, 1996; Barr, *Lee Kuan Yew*, 30.
54 Lee Kuan Yew, speech at the University of Malaya, Kuala Lumpur, August 28, 1964, in Lee Kuan Yew, *Some Problems in Malaysia: Three Speeches by the Prime Minister of Singapore, Mr. Lee Kuan Yew* (Singapore: Ministry of Culture, c.1965), 1–11; Lee Kuan Yew, *The Battle for a Malaysian Malaysia* (Singapore: Ministry of Culture, 1965); Lee Kuan Yew, *Towards a Malaysian Malaysia* (Singapore: Ministry of Culture, 1965); Lee Kuan Yew, *Are There Enough Malaysians to Save Malaysia?* (Singapore: Ministry of Culture, 1965).
55 Goh, cited in Tan, *Goh Keng Swee*, 117.
56 Lim Kim San and Toh Chin Chye in Chew, *Leaders of Singapore*, 98, 167.
57 James Chin, "Anti-Christian Chinese Chauvinists and HDB Upgrades: The 1997 Singapore General Election," *South East Asia Research* 5, no. 2 (1997): 217–41; Francis T. Seow, *The Media Enthralled: Singapore Revisited* (Boulder and London: Lynne Rienner, 1998); Chng Suan Tze, Low Tit Leng, and Teo Soh Lung, eds., *1987: Singapore's Marxist Conspiracy 30 Years on* (Singapore: Function 8, 2017); Jothie Rajah, *Authoritarian Rule of Law: Legislation, Discourse and Legitimacy in Singapore* (New York: Cambridge University Press, 2012); Michael D. Barr, "Singapore's Catholic Social Activists: Alleged 'Marxist Conspirators'," in *Paths Not Taken: Political Pluralism in Post-War Singapore*, ed. Michael D. Barr and Carl A. Trocki (Singapore: NUS Press, 2008), 228–47.
58 Yap, Lim, and Leong, *Men in White*, 8.
59 Ngiam Tong Dow, *A Mandarin and the Making of Public Policy: Reflections by Ngiam Tong Dow*, ed. Simon S. C. Tay (Singapore: National University of Singapore Press, 2006), 62; Asad-ul Iqbal Latif, *Lim Kim San: A Builder of Singapore* (Singapore: Institute of Southeast Asian Studies, 2009), 48, 50.
60 Michael D. Barr, *The Ruling Elite of Singapore: Networks of Power and Influence* (London and New York: I.B. Tauris, 2014), 24–30, 43–49, 86–96.
61 Devan Nair, "An Open Letter to Lee Kuan Yew for the Editor," *The Straits Times*, Singapore, July 8, 1988, cited in "Singapore Repository: A Collection of Historical Articles/Documents," accessed August 9, 2022, https://sgrepository.wordpress.com/2015/03/16/devan-nair-letter/; Ruth Youngblood, "Government's Disclosure Rocks Medical Profession," *UPI*, July 11, 1988, accessed August 9, 2022, www.upi.com/Archives/1988/07/11/Governments-disclosure-rocks-medical-profession/3877584596800/.
62 Michael D. Barr, "Trade Unions in an Elitist Society: The Singapore Story," *Australian Journal of Politics and History* 46, no. 4 (2000): 481–98; "Great National Honour for SMU Chancellor Mr. Lim Chee Onn," Singapore Management University website, accessed August 8, 2022, https://admissions.smu.edu.sg/our-community/news/great-national-honour-smu-chancellor-mr-lim-chee-onn.
63 Emma Connors, "Singapore Deputy PM Steps Aside as Future Premier," *Australian Financial Review*, April 9, 2021.
64 Interview with Maurice Baker, October 25, 1996.
65 Barr, *Singapore*, 122–23.
66 Lee Kuan Yew, "Discipline for Survival: Speech to Political Study Centre, July 13, 1966," *Mirror: A Weekly Almanac of Current Affairs*, July 25, 1966; Lee Kuan Yew, "Transcript of Speech Made by the Prime Minister, Lee Kuan Yew," Queenstown Community Centre, August 10, 1966, in Lee, *Prime Minister's Speeches, etc.*
67 Lee Kuan Yew, "Debate on Motion of Thanks to His Excellency the Yang Di-Pertuan Negara, Refutation and Exposure of Ong Eng Guan," Legislative Assembly Debates, Official Report (1946–1965), August 10, 1959.
68 Barr, *Constructing Singapore*, 78–80, 238–240.
69 Interview with a de-identified GRO (Grassroots Organisation) leader, April 8, 2003.

48 Michael D. Barr

70 Michael D. Barr, "The Singapore School: Technocracy or Less," in *China's 'Singapore Model' and Authoritarian Learning*, ed. Stephan Ortmann and Mark R. Thompson (London and New York: Routledge, 2020), 54–71. At the time of writing (August 2022), 12 of the 18 members of Cabinet entered politics directly from the public sector (including GLCs), and another three had close connections with the public sector or the inner circle of the ruling elite before entering politics. See accessed August 23, 2022, www.pmo.gov.sg/The-Cabinet.

71 Barr, *The Ruling Elite of Singapore*, 81–86. Also see Samuel Ling Wei Chan, *Aristocracy of Armed Talent: The Military Elite in Singapore* (Singapore: NUS Press, 2019), Chapter 7, "Scholars and Stars by Numbers and Cases" (277–313) and Appendix A (362–411). The attraction of recruiting former military officers to Cabinet peaked early in the 2010s, when six out of 15 members of Cabinet had military backgrounds (40%). As of August 2022, only three of 18 members of Cabinet are retired military officers (18%). See accessed August 23, 2022, www.pmo.gov.sg/The-Cabinet. Also note that two retired generals were publicly canvassed as candidates to succeed Lee Hsien Loong as prime minister, but both were overlooked in favour of two civilians, Heng Swee Keat and Lawrence Wong.

72 "Winsemius: How I Risked the Prime Minister's Wrath," *The Sunday Times*, January 27, 1985.

73 Minchin, *No Man Is an Island*, 35.

74 Lee and Lee website, accessed August 11, 2022, www.leenlee.com.sg/our-people/the-firm/.

75 Photo caption: 'Lee Kim Yew, Lawyer and Younger Brother of Prime Minister Lee Kuan Yew. Lee Kim Yew and Kho Yen Bock were the largest and (sic) private individual shareholders in Tat Lee Bank with $1 million worth of shares each. The Monetary Authority of Singapore (MAS) has given consideration to Tat Lee Bank's application for a banking licence before Lee Kim Yew was named a Director and Subscriber of the bank.' Image PCD0496-0103, November 23, 1978. Caption supplied by Singapore Press Holdings. Available in National Archives of Singapore, accessed August 23, 2022, www.nas.gov.sg/archivesonline/photographs/record-details/a7f0d72f-1162-11e3-83d5-0050568939ad.

76 Barr, *The Ruling Elite of Singapore*, 62–63.

77 Sikko Visscher, *The Business of Politics and Ethnicity: A History of the Singapore Chinese Chamber of Commerce and Industry* (Singapore: NUS Press, 2007).

78 *Ibid.*; Barr, *The Ruling Elite of Singapore*, 32–39.

79 Michael D. Barr and Zlatko Skrbiš, *Constructing Singapore: Elitism, Ethnicity and the Nation-Building Project* (Copenhagen: Nordic Institute of Asian Studies, 2008), Chapters 7–10.

80 Barr, *The Ruling Elite of Singapore*, 109–11.

81 Ross Worthington, *Governance in Singapore* (London and New York: Routledge Curzon, 2003), 15–37; Werner Vennewald, "Technocrats in the State Enterprise System of Singapore," Working Paper, No. 32, Asia Research Centre, Murdoch University, Perth, 1994; Barr, *Singapore*, 122–27, 158–59; Barr, *The Ruling Elite of Singapore*, 125–26.

82 Shashi Jayakumar, *A History of the People's Action Party: 1985–2021* (Singapore: NUS Press, 2021), 171–73.

83 Joshua Kurlantzick, *State Capitalism: How the Return of Statism Is Transforming the World* (New York: Oxford University Press, 2016), 29.

84 " 'I've Never Hankered for Post, Position or Power': Read PAP's 4G leader Lawrence Wong's Speech', *The Straits Times*, April 16, 2022, www.straitstimes.com/singapore/politics/ive-never-hankered-for-post-position-or-power-read-paps-4g-leader-lawrence-wongs-speech; "Eight New Faces Introduced at First Virtual Candidate Introduction Press Conference," People's Action Party website, www.pap.org.sg/

news/ge2020-news/pap-introduces-first-slate-of-new-candidates/. Both accessed August 17, 2022.

85 "Lee Family Feud in Singapore," *Financial Times*, June 15, 2017, accessed August 22, 2022, www.youtube.com/watch?v=phiqbCB3ruM.

86 Michael D. Barr, "The Lees of Singapore: A Quality Brand," *South East Asia Research* 24, no. 3 (2016): 341–54.

3

FIDEL CASTRO

The eternal leader of a revolution or the leader of an eternal revolution?

Vinicius Mariano de Carvalho

> Condemn me, it doesn't matter, history will absolve me.
> (Fidel Castro's statement in his trial for the attack on
> the Moncada barracks, on 16 October 1953)*

Introduction

It may seem a little strange to start a chapter for an academic book talking about oneself. Especially because this is not a chapter about myself or my theories or academic thoughts, rather it is a chapter about a global leader who left a huge impact on generations both during and after the Cold War. My chapter is about Fidel Castro (1926–2016), but to introduce the character, I may need a small autobiographic digression.

For a young boy, born during a right-wing military dictatorship (1964–1985) in Brazil, one among several that were in place in many Latin American countries, growing up in poverty in a socially unequal society, under political repression, disappearances, tortures, and death, merely developing political consciousness was already an act of rebellion. Grassroots movements, like workers' unions, students' unions, and social movements, had a strong role in this process of political education. Even the Catholic Church became a powerful space for political resistance, thanks to the Theology of Liberation being practised in the region since the early 1960s. As every teenager around the world, we were also searching for our idols, our exemplary figures. Besides the traditional rock stars or famous actors, for many of my generation, we also had our political idols. And in Latin America, undoubtedly, those would be Che Guevara and Fidel Castro. At that time, Che Guevara was already dead, killed in the jungles of Bolivia in 1967, fighting another Quixotesque guerrilla war. The one alive and sound was Fidel

DOI: 10.4324/9781003426165-3

Castro. My political engagement during my youth was strongly impacted by this controversial leader that on one side was seen as the only one in Latin America who managed to not only win a revolution but also establish a regime against American imperialism; who survived several botched assassination bids by the CIA; that from a small and poor island, continuously challenged the predatory capitalist model implanted in the Latin American region. Of course, I was aware of the other side of this history, such as the executions of political opponents – described as traitors of the revolution –, the repression to the GLBTQ+ on the island, the restriction of the press, and other repressive actions of Fidel Castro. However, the simple fact that he managed to break the path of US imperialism in the region was enough for propelling him into an iconic position. So, on the walls of my bedroom, instead of posters of singers and actors or actresses, I had on one side Che Guevarra and on the other Fidel Castro. Overlaid on both posters were quotations of some of their speeches.

As many other leaders around the world, biographies of Fidel Castro proliferate in several languages. They range from very critical biographies, highlighting the dictatorial and totalitarian behaviour of the leader, to almost hagiographic ones, praising and glorifying this mythological man.[1] In this chapter, I don't intend to write another one. What I will highlight, however, is how Castro's leadership model was formed and evolved during his long 47 years as the political leader of Cuba and the symbol for the left-wing movements that emerged around the world. I have divided the evolving nature of his leadership into four periods and will show how Castro used historical events to build and consolidate his leadership model. I will avoid biographical references to Castro directly and focus much more on the political events that forged his leadership style.

The creation of a leader

Son of a wealthy farmer, Castro started his involvement in politics while studying law at the University of Havana. After participating in rebellions against the right-wing governments in the Dominican Republic and Colombia (he was in Bogotá on the day that Jorge Eliécer Gaitán Ayala was assassinated, starting the period called 'La Violencia' in Colombian history. In this event, Castro took up arms on the side of the Liberals, against the *Conservadores*).[2] Back in Cuba, thereafter, he planned to overthrow the Cuban dictator Fulgencio Batista, launching an unsuccessful attack on the Moncada Barracks in 1953.

This first revolutionary movement already showed many characteristics of this 'Leader to be.' There, one can see the construction of what has been historically called the 'Fidel-Centrism,' a term describing the conceptual fog created over the decades which depicts the overwhelming tendency of so much of the writing on the revolution to focus exclusively on the person and personality of Fidel Castro.[3] This 'Fidel-Centrism' poses a fundamental problem that confronts anyone seeking to understand the complex processes and trajectory of the post-1959 revolution.

52 Vinicius Mariano de Carvalho

Rooted in familiar traditions of the 'great men,' the 'caudillos,' this strong central figure reproduces patriarchal colonial models of Latin American countries, and Castro managed to operate very well with this image, combining the characteristics of both a martyr and a hero.

In this first essay of revolution, 'The Vanguard,' the period between 1953 and 1958 was fundamental for the consolidation of what would be the inner circle of the revolution of 1959.[4] Since the violent actions of 26 July 1953 in the cities of Santiago de Cuba and Bayamo, aiming at dethroning the group led by Fulgencio Batista that had seized power on 10 March 1952, the group led by Fidel Castro did everything possible to keep exclusivity in the decision-making process and in presenting themselves as the leaders of the revolutionary movement. Fidel Castro also emulated the nineteenth-century mythological leadership figure, Jose Martí, and went on an excursion to the United States, following the footsteps of Martí and in the hope of gaining the support of the Cuban émigrés wherever he went.[5]

Castro managed to present himself as not aligned with any other opposition groups or parties that contested Batista's coup. The fragmentation of the opposition allowed guerrilla tactics to fill the void between them. There were two main opposition forces that existed on the island: the Authentic Cuban Revolutionary Party (*los Autenticos*), who presented themselves as nationalists, anti-corruption, and revolutionaries but proved to be as hypocritically corrupt as any other government, and the Cuban People's Party (*Ortodoxos*), who were the real opposition to Batista, the party that Fidel was a member of and which struggled internally in finding a singular leadership. There was also a Popular Socialist Party, a Marxist-Leninist group that had in their past forged an alliance with Batista (in 1939).[6]

The novelty was the creation of the National Revolutionary Movement in 1952, led by Rafael García Bárcenas. This was a small and previously unknown group, with an ambitious plan to attack the main military base in Cuba. The plan was pre-empted by security forces, and most of the plotters were arrested. This opened the space for Fidel to exploit and construct his own movement, called *Generation of the Centenary*, again making reference to the anniversary of José Martí's birth. With this group, Fidel launched the twin attacks in Santiago on 26 July 1953, targeting two garrisons, a small outpost near Bayamo and the Moncada Army Barracks (*Quartel de Moncada*). Both attacks failed spectacularly as the attacking force was outnumbered and outgunned and didn't manage to bring off the surprise that they had hoped to effect. Many were killed after their arrest.[7] Fidel was duly arrested but survived to stand trial for orchestrating the attack. Although a grisly failure, the attack brought Fidel Castro into the public light, and during his trial he used his speeches as the first real manifesto of his political views. It was in a speech at his trial that he said the words used as an epigraph to this text: 'Condemn me, it doesn't matter, history will absolve me.'[8] At this point, one can see already Castro's ability with rhetoric. Prone to grandiloquence, he developed his own way of producing and delivering speeches that would become from henceforth a mark of his communication model with the Cuban people.

The Moncada adventure also shone an early light on the 'inner circle' approach that Castro would follow later after the success of the revolution in 1959. Very few people participated in the planning of the attacks in Santiago. This same group would be around Fidel Castro in the future successful revolution, but none of them really managed to gain prominence over the central figure of Fidel Castro.

The prisoners of the Moncada misadventure were sent to Presidio Modelo, a prison located on the Isle of Pines. From there, the movement was given a name and direction: *Movimiento Revolucionário 26 de Julio – M-26–7* (26 July Movement).[9] This movement was actually founded in 1955 and began to take shape under the leadership of Frank Pais and those who hadn't been imprisoned, drawn mostly from Havana and Santiago.[10]

Fidel Castro's leadership of this group started in mid-December 1957, when he signed a letter addressed to the other opponents of Batista, claiming power over the group. While Castro's group was shown to be solid in its political competition with the other groups on the political scene, the real leadership of the M26J was concentrated in the military group, in the guerrilla elite that fought in the Sierra Maestra. In other words, in approximately one year, the urban guerrilla group founded by Frank País had been absorbed by the rural guerrilla group led by Fidel Castro.

In these events, other characteristics of Fidel Castro's leadership model can be noticed. He managed to, step by step, neutralise any other possible leadership to the movement, absorbing pragmatically groups that disagreed with some of his ideas or methods and making himself the only person fit for this role of leader of a revolution against Batista. It is in this period that Raul Castro, Fidel's young brother, joined the group as well. Raul would become a complimentary figure to the Cuban revolution, asserting Fidel's leadership, never putting himself in competition with his brother, and acting like a real 'lieutenant' of Fidel. And he would be the one selected by Fidel to succeed him when his health removed him from the public arena.

Fidel Castro, with other prisoners, was fortuitously released from prison on 15 May 1955 and went into a strategic exile in Mexico. From there, the movement acquired another function: to prepare for a rebellion that would coincide with the landing of an armed force on the island, that took place on 2 December of 1956, when 82 rebels aboard a small yacht called *Granma* landed on the island.[11]

The landing was a notable failure. Due to bad weather, navigational incompetence, and a lack of fuel, the ship arrived late (failing to coincide with the soon suppressed rebellion of 30 November in Santiago), and to cap it all the yacht ran aground far from the planned beach (where disembarkation would have been easy and transport/supplies awaited). Impenetrable swamp separated the rebels from dry land and safety, and it took several hours to cross this swamp. Their only advantage was that they were not attacked as they landed; however, within three days, their progress inland was interrupted at Alegría de Pío by an air force bombardment and an encounter with the army, resulting in many deaths and the dispersal of the rebel

54 Vinicius Mariano de Carvalho

force, after which only a handful made it into the nearby Sierra Maestra as planned, to regroup and form the basis of the guerrilla force.

The exact numbers became shrouded in myth and imprecision, and this became another important aspect of the Cuban guerrilla movement. The important thing, however, is to identify those who remained central or influential thereafter, either supporting or opposing Fidel's leadership. In the heroic group of *Granma* were Fidel, Raúl, and Che Guevara (who had joined the group in Mexico and from this moment on began to play a fundamental role in consolidating Fidel's leadership, either reinforcing or questioning it); Faustino Pérez (who ran the Mexico 'training farm' and became the movement's National Coordinator), Juan Almeida; Camilo Cienfugos Gorriarán; Universo Sánchez; Efigenio Ameijeiras; Ciro Redondo; Montané and Ramiro Valdés Menéndez (Moncada veterans).

The mythical aspect refers to the notion of *the twelve*, who supposedly survived the Alegría counterattack. The reality was more mundane: in Alegría, 24 were killed during or after the fighting, 21 were arrested, and 19 escaped from encirclement, leaving 21 in total, divided into four small groups who regrouped in the following days. Eight of these were with Fidel by 18 December, and other straggler groups arrived in the following days, gradually totalling 15 (at one point there were 12, but they were then joined by the remaining three). The numbers of combatants were fluid and difficult to calculate, and once Cienfuegos and Guevara started their march westward, members flooded into the ranks, swelling from an original of 300 or so in early 1958 to approximately 3,000 by the end of the year.

Rebellion developed and opposition to Batista grew significantly after 1955; the Movement created several adjacent organisations to give the Movement a broader image, consisting of several other groups, and all became known broadly as the **Llano**. Nonetheless, the armed guerrillas in the **Sierra** were the core and vanguard of the Movement and those with the greatest popular respect and legitimacy. Sierra's prestige was a source of tension within the Llano.[12] Due to the prestige of the Sierra group, the groups of Llano signed an unconditional commitment, drawn up entirely in the Sierra Maestra, dissolving the political groups that supported dialogue with Batista, the reorganisation of the armed forces, the confiscation of assets, and reinforcing the leadership of the movement around the 'Holy Trinity' formed by Fidel, Che, and Raúl and the inner circle, formed by men and women who would play a very significant role in the future success of the revolution and the consolidation of Fidel's power and leadership. Most of those from the inner circle took important political positions after the success of the 1959 revolution, and the most dramatic case would be the relationship between Fidel and Che Guevara, whose personality and leadership competed with Fidel in both popularity and power.

Patria o Muerte

This almost romantic group of guerrillas managed to gain popular support after the *Granma*'s arrival on the island, and despite all the repression by Batista finally on 8

January 1959, Fidel Castro victoriously entered Havana, deposing the government and establishing a new regime.

Eleven of the 19 ministers of the transitional government headed by lawyer Manuel Urrutia were prominent members of the *Movimiento Revolucionário 26 de Julio*. On 13 February, Fidel Castro was appointed prime minister, after the resignation in his favour of José Miró Cardona, also a lawyer, who had previously led the Civic Revolutionary Front. The senior staff of the government, formed of 26 members of the council of ministers, were mostly from his inner circle. Fidel's first address to the public already announced a change in his revolutionary approach, distancing from his previous manifestos publicised during the period of guerrilla activity. The leader became pragmatic and more authoritarian from one day to another. Revealing what would be one of the strongest aspects of his leadership as head of state, Castro presented himself as the voice and will of the people. Instead of addressing the 'People of Cuba,' as in previous manifestos, he took a messianic tone, announcing that 'we are one with the people.' So he literally removed any symbolic need for approval by the people, as he and the people were considered to be the same thing! In his address, he defended the death penalty for any citizen who opposed the revolution and the censorship of public demonstrations while the provisional government lasted. The rationale for these restrictions was as convoluted as it was paradoxical. In essence, he basically said that the revolutionary government was restricting the public's freedom to prevent the enemies of the revolution from behaving in a manner that would force the government to restrict the freedom of the people![13]

The authoritarian turn was completed by expanding a new legal system, created to punish the followers of the Fulgencio Batista dictatorship and to deal with all those who disagreed with the new power. In November of that same first year of the revolution, the council of ministers approved a law that ensured all crimes classified as counter-revolutionary would be tried summarily. Even the slogan of the revolution changed from 'Freedom or Death' to 'Homeland or Death.'[14]

Castro continued to consolidate his leadership and remove anyone who contested his primacy over the revolutionary process. Still, in 1959, Huber Matos, a veteran of the revolution and army commander resigned and accused Fidel of 'burying the revolution.' Matos was accused of disloyalty and was arrested by Camilo Cienfuegos under the orders of Fidel. Together with Matos, 15 other army officers were also imprisoned. Soon after, Cienfuegos would die in a mysterious plane accident.[15]

In the external context, and in the early moments of the new regime, Castro also demonstrated very clearly which direction he was seeking for his 'new Cuba,' and this pointed to the Soviet Union. A series of events defined the pattern of the island in the frame of the Cold War. On 8 May 1960, Cuba established diplomatic relations with the Soviet Union, and in July of the same year, Fidel Castro declared that he would turn 'The Andes Mountains into the Sierra Maestra of the American continent,' supporting any guerrilla movement that was fighting against tyrannic

56 Vinicius Mariano de Carvalho

rulers (meaning: against the United States).[16] Soon after, all big US companies on the island were expropriated and nationalised. At this point, President Eisenhower had already approved and allowed the CIA to form a plan to overthrow Castro. The escalation of tensions with the United States led to the rupture of relations between the two countries in January 1961. And in April 1961, during the events of the Bay of Pigs invasion, Fidel Castro declared the socialist character of the Cuban revolution.[17]

The Bay of Pigs invasion was the perfect opportunity for Castro to impose and definitely consolidate his leadership inside the country and externally, as a Marxist-Leninist Latin American reference point. First, it became clear that the Americans would try everything they could to overthrow Castro, which therefore justified Castro in cementing his Soviet alliance with Khrushchev. Second, the support and engagement of the Cuban émigrés in the Bay of Pigs invasion, many of whom had been expelled from Cuba and now lived in Florida especially, helped Castro to frame them as traitors to the revolution and to the people of Cuba. Third, he went himself to the theatre of operations, leading the reaction and resistance directly. This theatrical bravery played well in the eyes of soldiers and the population generally and reinforced the messianic image of the leader.[18]

On 2 December in the same year, Fidel Castro declared his Marxist-Leninist affiliation. This led to the expulsion of Cuba from the Organization of American States and precipitated the rupture of diplomatic relations with all the member countries (except Mexico) in early 1962. Fidel, then, issued the 'Second Declaration of Havana,' calling again on the memory of José Martí and declaring that 'the duty of every revolutionary is to make the revolution.' At this point, a new aspect of Fidel Castro's leadership in the context of the Cold War begins. He presents himself as the reference point for and supporter of all revolutionary movements in Latin America and Cuba as the space for the articulation and promotion of the ideals of Marxism-Leninism on the subcontinent. In February 1962, Kennedy's government in Washington declared an embargo on the island. At this point, Cuba was already in the arms of the Soviet Union, and the episode of the Cuban Missile Crisis would make this more evident than ever.[19]

Narratives about the installation of atomic missiles by the Soviet Union in Cuba oscillate between Castro's approval and disapproval of it. Some reports claim that he was not in favour, because this would make Cuba look more like a puppet state of the Soviet Union. Alternatively, others suggest that he was in favour of Khrushchev's Operation *Anadyr* from the outset. What is certain, however, is that Fidel perceived the outcome of the crisis as a gross betrayal by the Soviets, as the decision to resolve the crisis was made exclusively between Khrushchev and Kennedy. In these negotiations, Cuban interests, such as resolving the status of the American hold on the Guantanamo Naval Base on the island, were not even discussed with him. Furious with Khrushchev, Castro evidently felt that an opportunity had been lost to put some pressure on the United States. Unquestionably, thereafter relations between Havana and Moscow were never the same again.[20]

Among the Cuban leadership, however, the one who was more critical about the Soviets' behaviour was Che Guevara. Guevara became increasingly critical of the Soviet Union, arguing that it was too focused on building up its own power and neglecting the needs of the global socialist movement. In 1965, Guevara resigned from his government positions and left Cuba, citing his desire to continue the fight for revolution elsewhere.[21] This decision of Che Guevara was actually timely for Fidel Castro, as the Argentinian hero was, if not a competitive figure to Castro, at least a leader with a similar aura and power among the generation of the revolution. The departure of Che served Fidel in two ways, removing a possible competitor while promoting revolutionary ideas in Africa and Latin America. Castro and Guevara remained in contact after Guevara's departure, and Castro reportedly provided him with support for his revolutionary activities in Africa and Bolivia. In 1967, Guevara was captured and executed by the Bolivian army. Che Guevara became the martyr that Fidel needed for his revolutionary cause and for the narrative of Cuba being the reference point of a successful revolutionary movement in Latin America. For Fidel Castro, it was easier to deal with a myth than with the real person of Che Guevara as a potential competitor.[22]

In the internal context of Cuba, Castro implemented a socialist economic system, nationalising most of the industries and promoting the collectivisation of the agricultural sector, the main strength of the island. In a few years, Cuba achieved high levels of literacy and universal access to healthcare, both free to all citizens. By the end of the first decade of the revolution, illiteracy had been eradicated from the island, and the country had the lowest infant mortality rates in Latin America – both of which were very notable achievements.

Under Castro's leadership, a major land reform programme was carried out that redistributed land from large landowners to peasants, providing land to thousands of people who had previously been landless. This helped to reduce inequality and promote social justice in rural areas. In addition, the revolutionary government established social programmes to provide basic needs, such as food, housing, and utilities to the entire population. This helped to reduce poverty dramatically, and living conditions for many Cubans changed substantially for the better.[23]

On the other hand, Fidel Castro dealt with his leadership rivals in a variety of ways, ranging from imprisonment to exile and even execution. Castro's government imprisoned thousands of people who were considered political dissidents, opponents of the government, or threats to the revolution. Many of these people were subjected to harsh treatment and torture in prisons such as La Cabana and the Isle of Pines. Thousands of executions, many of them by firing squad, were carried out as well, often without a fair trial and were used to eliminate political opposition and deter others from challenging the government. The government forced many people into exile, including political opponents, intellectuals, and members of the middle and upper classes. These people were often stripped of their property and assets and were not allowed to return to Cuba. Propaganda and surveillance were used systematically to monitor the population and suppress dissent. The

58 Vinicius Mariano de Carvalho

state-controlled media was used to promote the government's ideology and to portray dissenters as enemies of the revolution. Personality cults flourished with Fidel Castro (and Che Guevara) faces everywhere (as they still are). His speeches held in public squares for thousands of people were repeated by the official state TV and Radio, the only media outlets allowed on the island. Harassment and intimidation were also instruments to silence critics of the government. This included raids on opposition offices and homes, confiscation of property and assets, and physical violence against opposition leaders.[24]

Fidel Castro was definitely a pragmatic leader – or if one prefers, a leader full of contradictions. In the 1970s, he managed to integrate Cuba into the Council of Mutual Economic Assistance of the Soviet bloc; he organised the First Congress of the Communist Party of Cuba (1975); and the Socialist Constitution was approved in a referendum (1976). From one perspective, Fidel completely integrated Cuba into the Communist bloc of countries, under the influence of the Soviet Union. But it was also in this decade that the Organization of American States revoked the sanctions against the country (1975), and Havana and Washington opened diplomatic offices with one another (1977). Commercial flights between the United States and Cuba were resumed in 1979, and in the same year Cuba released more than 3,000 political prisoners. It was clear to Fidel Castro that at least negotiations with the Americans should take place, considering the impact that the economic embargo of 1962 had upon Cuba. In return, American demands were mostly focused upon getting Cuba to stop supporting the Latin American guerrilla groups, seeking the withdrawal of Soviet military advisors from the island, and respect for human rights.

It was in this period that many left-wing movements in Latin America, especially in countries living under military dictatorships sponsored by the United States and with an anti-communist ideology, like Brazil, looked to Fidel Castro as a model of leader who had learnt how to create socialism with a Latino face and one that was adapted to the reality of the subcontinent. These contradictions, as exposed in the previous paragraphs, were seen as a necessity, considering the socio-historical-cultural aspects of Latin America. It was this Fidel Castro who became the idol of my generation, in terms of possible socialism in Latin America.

Reinventing socialism

The 1980s, however, arrived with events that called for a rethink of this *socialismo moreno*. Exactly in April 1980, several Cubans started to seek asylum in embassies of Latin American countries based in Cuba. Fidel Castro then declared that those who wanted to leave the country were free to do so, if other countries granted them entry. The result was that from April to September of that year, about 125,000 Cubans arrived in the United States, escaping in boats leaving the Mariel Harbor in Cuba.

And it was not only in Cuba, but in the Soviet Union itself, that socialism was passing through a radical transformation. A series of events required a change in the model of leadership represented by Fidel Castro. In 1988, Cuban troops finally left Angola; in November 1989, the Berlin Wall fell; in 1990, the Sandinistas suffered a defeat in Nicaragua (they had been supported by Cuba); in 1991, Soviet troops withdrew from Cuba; and on 25 December in the same year, the Soviet Union disintegrated. Fidel Castro needed to reinvent socialism in Cuba or suffer the same fate as had befallen the communist leaders of the entire Soviet bloc.

Fidel Castro declared the so-called *Período Especial en Tiempo de Paz* (Special Period in Time of Peace). This was a sort of revolution within the revolution. A national defence council was established, responsible for the declaration of a state of emergency and regulated the right to use violence to defend the power constituted more than 40 years before. The Socialist Constitution, promulgated by the Fourth Congress of the Communist Party and approved by the National Assembly (July 1992), eliminated the reference to the hegemony of the former Soviet Union and to the Marxist-Leninist doctrine. Atheism was also removed from the constitution.[25]

The 'war of narratives' also intensified. A mausoleum to Ernesto Che Guevarra was erected in Santa Clara, and the remains of the leader were returned to Cuba 30 years after his death. A diplomatic battle between the Cuban community in the United States and the Cuban government was also picked up by the world's media, surrounding the custody of a young boy Elián González, who was being kept in the United States with his Cuban relatives, although his father in Cuba was demanding his return. With the return of the boy to his country, Fidel Castro took personal interest in the case and used it for his fight against American interests. A new law 'for the Protection of the National Independence and the Economy of Cuba' was approved in 1999. This toughened the penalties against those who disseminated information criticising the regime.

By the 1990s, Fidel was facing a terrible dilemma. Without the economic support of the Soviet Union, he was forced to authorise the possession of dollars, the opening of bank accounts in this currency, and money remittances from abroad. In addition, foreign tourism was encouraged, and private professions were authorised once again on the island. These measures just accentuated what was already notorious: the equalitarian model preached by Castro at the beginning of the revolution was not anymore a clear goal. Social inequalities became evident, with an extremely impoverished population, surveilled and repressed, dependent on a government that was economically fragile and with an elite which had privileges and resources to travel and live in a capitalist lifestyle.

Fidel Castro always blamed this crisis on the US embargo on Cuba. At this time, in another Latin America country, a new leader emerged, inspired by Fidel Castro and the Cuban revolution, and, like Fidel Castro, someone who would be controversial, ambiguous, and, most-importantly, a staunch opponent of the United States – Hugo Chaves, in Venezuela. Thanks to the revenues of oil exploration, Chaves didn't have to face the dilemmas that Fidel confronted in Cuba, and, by

60 Vinicius Mariano de Carvalho

simply ignoring the American embargo, he supported the Cuban regime economically, assuring a survival to Fidel Castro's regime.[26]

The last years

In July 2006, Fidel Castro underwent intestinal surgery for an undisclosed illness, temporarily transferring power to Raul Castro, who was then the vice-president. Fidel remained out of the public eye for several months, leading to speculation about his health and the future of the Cuban regime. In February 2008, in an article to the official newspaper *Granma*, he announced that he would not seek re-election as President of the Council of State and Commander in Chief. The time of the *Comandante* who had outlasted ten American presidents was officially over. Raúl Castro was elected as the new President of Cuba. Fidel continued serving as the First Secretary of the Communist Party of Cuba until April 2011 and wrote prolifically for *Granma* in his years of retirement. He died on 25 November 2016.[27]

To summarise, one could say that Fidel Castro's leadership led to the assumption that he alone created, engineered, determined, and perhaps distorted/destroyed the Cuban revolution. He was undoubtedly a very skilled revolutionary leader and maybe not so much a leader of a democratic regime. Maybe, this is the reason why he always insisted that Cuba was in a constant state of revolution, that the revolution which had started in the Sierra Maestra, was not concluded yet.

Still in his lifetime, Fidel Castro was testimony to the so-called Pink Tide in Latin American countries, with the ascension of many leaders and governments left-wing oriented, with presidents who have also fought revolutions in their countries. Some of these governments ended quite dramatically, with impeachments or coups; others managed to stay longer but also fragilising the democratic institutions and becoming quasi-dictatorial, as happened in both Bolivia and Venezuela. For many of those leaders, Fidel Castro was a reference point of leadership. His legacy is still strongly alive not only in Cuba, that still lives under the shadows of his revolution, but also in many countries of the region. Maybe, the perception of his leadership is more critically understood today, than when I was a young teenager starting to learn about politics.

Writing the final lines of this chapter in Brazil, I asked a teenager wearing a school uniform in Rio de Janeiro if he knew who Fidel Castro was. The answer was revealing: 'Of course I know. The Cuban dictator who was a mix of Jesus Christ and Karl Marx.' After this answer, I am not sure if history has absolved or condemned Fidel Castro.

Notes

* Fidel Castro, *La historia me absolvera* (La Havana: Ediciones Politicas, 1985).

1 Tad Szulc, *Fidel: A Critical Portrait* (New York: William Morrow and Company, 1986); Ignacio Ramonet and Fidel Castro, *Fidel Castro: My Life: A Spoken Autobiography* (New York: Scribner, 2008); Juan Reinaldo Sanchez and Axel Gyldén, *The Double*

Fidel Castro **61**

Life of Fidel Castro: My 17 Years as Personal Bodyguard to El Lider Maximo (New York: St Martin's Press, 2015); Jean-Pierre Clerc, *Fidel de Cuba* (Paris: Ramsay, 1988); Sebastian Balfour, *Castro* (Harlow: Pearson, 2008).

2 René de la Predaja, *War of Latin America, 1948–1982: The Rise of the Guerrillas* (Jefferson, NC: McFarland & Co, 2013), 7.

3 Antoni Kapcia, *Leadership in the Cuban Revolution* (London: Bloomsbury, 2014).

4 Ramón Bonachea and Marta San Martín, *The Cuban Insurrection, 1952–1957* (New York: Routledge, 1970).

5 Kapcia, *Leadership in the Cuban Revolution*, 82.

6 Samuel Farber, *The Origins of the Cuban Revolution Reconsidered* (Chapel Hill: University of North Carolina Press, 2006).

7 Steve Cushion, *A Hidden History of the Cuban Revolution* (New York: Monthly Review Press, 2016); Julia Sweig, *Inside the Cuban Revolution* (Cambridge: Harvard University Press, 2002).

8 Rolando E. Bonachea and Nelson P. Valdés, eds., *Revolutionary Struggle: The Selected Works of Fidel Castro 1947–1958* (Cambridge: MIT Press, 1974).

9 Robert Taber, *M-26 – The Biography of a Revolution* (New York: Lyle Stuart, 1961).

10 Bonachea and San Martín, *The Cuban Insurrection, 1952–1957*, 153.

11 Kapcia, *Leadership in the Cuban Revolution*, 138.

12 Sweig, *Inside the Cuban Revolution*, 173.

13 Marta Harnecker, *Fidel Castro's Political Strategy: From Moncada to Victory* (New York: Pathfinder Press, 1987).

14 Joan de Alcazar and Sergio Lopez Rivero, "Fidel Castro: Cuatro fases de un liderazgo inacabado," in *Araucaria. Revista Iberoamericana de Filosofía, Política y Humanidades, año 15, n° 30. Segundo semestre de 2013* (Sevilla: Editoral Universidad de Sevilla, 2013), 3–24.

15 Sweig, *Inside the Cuban Revolution*, 182.

16 Leo Huberman and Paul Sweezy, *Socialism in Cuba* (New York: Monthly Review Press, 1969).

17 Louis A. Pérez, *Cuba and the United States: Ties of Singular Intimacy* (Athens, GA: University of Georgia Press, 1990).

18 René de la Predaja, *War of Latin America, 1948–1982: The Rise of the Guerrillas* (Jefferson, NC: McFarland & Co, 2013), 86.

19 Alcazar and Rivero, "Fidel Castro," 10.

20 Andrés Suárez, *Cuba: Castroism and Communism: 1959–1966* (Cambridge, MA: MIT Press, 1967)

21 Jon Lee Anderson, *Che Guevara: A Revolutionary Life* (London: Bantam, 1997).

22 Mike Gonzalez, *Che Guevara and the Cuban Revolution* (London: Bookmarks, 2004).

23 Edward Boorstein, *The Economic Transformation of Cuba: A First-Hand Account* (New York: Monthly Review Press, 1968).

24 Kapcia, *Leadership in the Cuban Revolution*.

25 Alcazar and Rivero, "Fidel Castro," 12.

26 José Alvarez, *Principio y fin del mito fidelista* (Bloomington: Trafford, 2008).

27 Alcazar and Rivero, "Fidel Castro," 21–22.

4

THE UNLIKELY PRIME MINISTER

Rethinking Sirimavo Bandaranaike's
leadership in a bipolar nation and world

Darinee Alagirisamy

It is both ironic and remarkable that an individual once dismissed as one who 'had not the foggiest idea of how to run a government' should have had the double distinction of rising to power as the first elected female prime minister in the country of their birth and globally as well. The individual was Sirimavo Bandaranaike, the year was 1960, and *Time* magazine had issued the verdict on the occasion of the leader's swearing-in ceremony.[1] Mrs Bandaranaike would in fact attend several such ceremonies in her lifetime, logging a total of 18 years in the highest political office over three terms between 1960 and 1965, 1970 and 1977, and 1994 and 2000. Although she inherited her surname from her husband, it is she and not he who is credited with launching the Bandaranaike name into political immortality. In fact, a relative went so far as to pronounce 'Aunt Sirima' the most 'formidable and charismatic leader' in Sri Lanka's history.[2] Her magnetism was almost unbearable for some observers who read in her leadership certain worrying megalomaniacal tendencies.

Up until the 1990s, most scholarship was focused on male leadership in Western societies. The feminist turn in leadership studies resulted in a slew of works from the early 1990s that undertook two important related tasks. First, they examined women's role and impact in politics at the national and international levels. Second, scholars prioritised shifting the focus of their enquiry to women as leaders in the Global South.[3] As case studies, the careers of Indira Gandhi, Aung San Suu Kyi, Megawati Sukarnoputri, Benazir Bhutto, Corazon Aquino, and Khaleda Zia have thrown light on various aspects of leadership struggles especially relevant to female politicians in conservative Asian societies. The fact of women acquiring leadership positions in these societies cannot be taken for granted. The particular sociocultural dynamics that enabled them to acquire power as well as the levers on which their power subsequently turned

DOI: 10.4324/9781003426165-4

would suggest that the phenomenon of women as political leaders needs to be carefully accounted for.

The factors that paved the way for male leadership frequently fall short in explaining the rise and consolidation of female political leadership in these contexts. Whereas the rise and consolidation of male leadership has conventionally been discussed with reference to personal charisma, political competition, or signature policies attributed to the leader in question, scholars have looked to such factors as culture and women's proximity to politically connected, powerful male relatives to account for their rise to positions of power. One of the most notable analytical frameworks to emerge from this focus on factors specific to women as political leaders is 'the widow's walk to power,' wherein scholars have emphasised the sudden, often dramatic, demise of a close male relative as the springboard enabling entry into politics for women in traditional Asian societies.[4] There is some credence to this argument, as, besides Sirimavo Bandaranaike, Indira Gandhi, Khaleda Zia, and Corazon Aquino's respective paths to power were also paved with tragedy and tears.

The 'weeping widow' argument, however, meets its limits in accounting for how women as leaders were able to forge long political careers in spite of the overwhelming odds they faced. Once in power, all the leaders referenced here faced situations wherein their leadership was challenged by great instability in the societies they inherited and conniving political rivals who sought to exploit their relative inexperience. Linda Richter, in an essay that has since the time of its writing remained seminal in reclaiming women's place in leadership studies in the Global South, argues that certain circumstances have historically proven more amenable in enabling women's rise to, and consolidation of, power in traditionally patriarchal societies. These include proximity to power, the social class of the women in question, and the structure of the electoral systems they inherited.[5] With the important exception of Indira Gandhi, whose career inspired numerous studies that have prioritised personality as a key factor accounting for leadership style and decisions, Asian strongwomen in politics have largely been subjected to the same broad brushstroke of their being female first and foremost. Richter, for one, claims that 'politics is more personal and familial in most of south and southeast Asia.'[6] It would appear then that women's accession to the highest political office through democratic processes in Asian societies has been explained largely with reference to the interplay of the circumstances and political culture that paved the way for them to emerge and consolidate power as leaders.

Whilst surfacing insights on the broad structural similarities that influenced the nature of female political leadership in South and Southeast Asia, the extant scholarship has also proven to be something of a double bind. Its value lies more in establishing patriarchy as a simultaneously limiting and enabling factor for women's political advancement than in offering a meaningful explanation of how their unlikely rise to power was conditioned by the individual qualities and responses of the leaders in question. Moreover, there appears to be something remarkable

64 Darinee Alagirisamy

about the global context that facilitated women's disproportionate representation in Asian politics between 1960s and 1980s. Considering that the trend of women's laying claim to power played out across several South and Southeast Asian societies over roughly the same period, the broader international milieu appears to be a factor that influenced women's preponderance as prime ministers and presidents. This line of reasoning leads one to the question: would examining the domestic and international contexts in post-colonial Asia in tandem with leaders' responses to those contexts enable a more complete understanding of the nature and limitations of their power?

Such an approach would be especially relevant here considering the hats that Sirimavo Bandaranaike consciously chose to wear – that of populist, nationalist, and internationalist. The road to her rise to power was certainly paved by the personal and familial while the maintenance of this power was sometimes aided and at other times bedevilled by nepotism. Equally relevant in explaining her equation with power, however, would be the factors embedded in Sri Lankan politics and society, in combination with the opportunities presented by the global climate in the 1960s and 1980s. It is this particular interaction, between the individual and the structural, and between the personal and the political, that I examine in tracing the rise and eventual fall of the world's first democratically elected female prime minister. Specifically, I propose an analytical framework in which opportunity, response, and personality form the three axes that frequently intersected against a backdrop of domestic and international bipolarity to shape Asian female political leadership between the 1960s and 1980s. The utility of this framework becomes amply evident when we consider the nature, limitations, and legacies of Sirimavo's long, if chequered, career as prime minister.

Turbulent times: decolonisation, the Cold War, and internal strife

When Mrs Bandaranaike first became prime minister, Ceylon was still Ceylon, preoccupied with exorcising the ghosts of colonialism; it was a nation struggling to come into its own. By the time she well and truly left the prime minister's office, it had become Sri Lanka, a change that the leader had personally pushed for at the height of her career in 1972. The move had everything to do with her aim of distancing herself and her nation from the memory of colonialism. It was, in other words, yet another symbolic feather in her populist cap. But this was arguably the least significant of the legacies that she would leave behind; by that point in time, the nation was still struggling to come into its own, torn apart as it was by a civil war that showed few signs of abating.

Tempting as it is to jump the gun and launch straight into legacies, it is important to begin with inheritances. The year 1960 marked an especially turbulent point in post-independence Sri Lankan history. Independence from British rule had been achieved a short 12 years previously in 1948, the decision to withdraw from Ceylon having followed on the heels of the British withdrawal from India. Decolonisation had been a hushed affair negotiated between elites – British and Sinhalese – thus reducing opportunities for the emergence of the nascent national identity that anti-colonial mass movements had breathed life into elsewhere in the former British Empire. Alongside the uncertainties visited by decolonisation, which, among others, had left the economy in shambles and a soaring unemployment situation, Sri Lanka found itself facing the perilous prospect of establishing a foothold as a sovereign nation in a global order dominated by superpower rivalry. Cold War calculations meant that the United States and the Soviet Union were likely to perceive decolonisation as a potential threat to their respective blocs and equally likely to intervene in the affairs of small states to prevent such an eventuality. Although the period between 1960 and 1979 marked detente, formally the easing of tensions between the United States and the Soviet Union, the superpower-backed war ravaging Vietnam at the time did little to ease the threat to national sovereignty that loomed large for newly decolonised Asian countries. The problem was compounded by the fact that Sri Lanka had to figure out its foreign policy strategy entirely from scratch. Until as late as 1944, external affairs and defence had been left to the colonial state to manage. It was only after independence that the External Affairs Department was set up. The prime minister had near-free reign of external affairs under Article 46(4) of the Soulbury Constitution, adopted for the administration of independent Sri Lanka, so much so, in fact, that she or he did not need the legislature's consent for any matter other than the allocation of finances.

Nevertheless, Ceylon (Sri Lanka) had the best prospects for democratic governance in all of Asia.[7] Since the constitutional experiment of 1931, Sri Lankan society had uninterrupted tutelage in exercising the right to vote. This 30-year experience of universal franchise – in terms of the processes and precedents that had been established as a result – marked a promising start, although a democratic culture had yet to take root amongst the populace. Moreover, although women's suffrage had become a reality for close to two decades before decolonisation, Sri Lankan society remained deeply patriarchal and categorically dismissive of women's involvement in public life. The extent of this bias becomes evident when we consider that in 1960, the House of Parliament had only seven elected female representatives, all of whom belonged to elite families and boasted political connections through powerful male relatives. At any rate, by 1948, the foundations of a welfare state were in place, and the basis of the model of governance that Bandaranaike's party would champion – democratic socialism – had been laid. There was free schooling and free healthcare, and public food provisions were heavily subsidised. The rice ration, for instance, became a non-negotiable commitment for successive governments, which quickly realised that it came with costly consequences for the country's balance of payments.

Socially, strains were beginning to deepen between the Sinhalese Buddhist majority and Tamil minority, with the withdrawal of the divide and rule system of patronage between the ethnic communities that the colonial state had carefully nurtured for its survival. In the immediate aftermath of independence, a tinderbox

66 Darinee Alagirisamy

situation emerged with the government's move to disenfranchise the Estate Tamils on the grounds that they were Indian nationals.[8] This event was directly responsible for triggering the formation of the Federal Party among the Tamils. The party clamoured for a federal solution for the Tamils and subsequently posed innumerable difficulties for Mrs Bandaranaike's administration. In 1958, a rumour that a Tamil had killed a Sinhalese triggered the first major episode of nationwide communal violence in which more than a hundred people – mostly Tamil – lost their lives. Coming in an already restive context, the riots had the effect of further poisoning relations between the Sinhalese majority and Tamil minority. Her husband's government responded by declaring a state of emergency and forcibly relocated more than 25,000 Tamil refugees from Sinhalese areas to Tamil areas in the north. In the absence of a cohesive national identity, such tensions had the effect of shaping political trajectories along distinctly communal lines. At the same time, the discourse of Sinhala Only – Sinhala as Sri Lanka's sole official language – was rapidly gaining ground. Solomon Bandaranaike was in the vanguard of the movement fanning the flames of Sinhalese nationalism. His emphatic electoral speeches, to the tune that the 'fear of the inexorable shrinking of the Sinhalese language . . . cannot be brushed aside,' had paved the way to his short-lived premiership. Solomon wasted no time making good on his electoral promise. As soon as he became prime minister following his party's electoral victory in 1956, he saw to it that Sinhala replaced English as Sri Lanka's sole official language.

As Solomon Bandaranaike would find out soon enough, however, talk was not going to be enough, especially when that talk itself seemed half-hearted and insincere. In fact, he would pay with his life in what would become the nation's first assassination, owing to a perceived lack of commitment on his part to the Sinhalese cause. Whilst committing his party to the promotion of the Sinhalese people's interests and Sinhala's enshrinement as the sole official language, the prime minister had also stated that this course would not engender 'the suppression of such a minority language as Tamil whose reasonable use would receive due recognition.'[9] He proceeded to sign the ill-fated Bandaranaike–Chelvanayakam Pact in 1957. The agreement, concluded with the leader of the main Tamil political party of that time, sought to assuage Tamil anxieties.[10] In practice, it failed to appease Tamils whilst simultaneously presenting Sinhalese hardliners with the proof they needed to accuse the government of reneging on its promise to put the majority community's interests first. The damage had already been done by the time the pact was unilaterally abrogated by the Bandaranaike government in 1958. Amidst rising grievances brought about by the government's vacillation between a Sinhala-only course and accommodating Tamil interests, the prime minister's assassination at the hands of a Buddhist monk brought the situation to a tipping point.

From Sirima to Sirimavo: the individual behind the leader

Born Sirima Ratwatte on 17 April 1916 in Ratnapura, near Kandy, the suffix 'vo' in Sirimavo's name was a later addition signifying respect and authority. Whereas

Solomon Bandaranaike's stature as a politician had been built up over decades of campaigning, Sirimavo apparently 'donned hers like a cloak that had been lying in her wardrobe for years, unworn, but which had been pressed and kept ready for wearing at any given moment.'[11] She had a compelling personality that lay dormant until the opportunity both necessitated and facilitated its explosion into public life. The undeniable presence that Sirimavo brought to politics is perhaps best understood with some reference to her aristocratic bearings. Hers was a thoroughly Anglicised family, having consolidated its fortunes and influence through generations of loyal service to the British colonial machinery in Ceylon. Consequently, the family's comfort with English culture extended even to their naming traditions. Sirimavo's father, for instance, was named Barnes Rattwatte, after a British governor-general. The family, however, drew the line at religious conversion. Like her parents, siblings, and almost everyone else in her social circle, Sirimavo was educated in Catholic convents in the capital, Colombo, for all 11 years of her formal schooling. This early exposure to Christianity notwithstanding, she remained a practising Buddhist throughout her life.

As a child born into one of Sri Lanka's most influential families, the oldest of six children had a privileged upbringing and, by all accounts, a happy childhood. Her mother was a doctor, and her father was involved in politics as a district leader and member of the Senate. During her childhood and adolescence, Sirimavo often accompanied her father in his official visits into Sri Lanka's rural interior. These experiences provided valuable opportunities to acquaint herself with various women's welfare programmes in two areas that would hold enduring interest for her throughout her life: healthcare and education. She remained committed to social work following her marriage as well. Owing to this early and sustained engagement with public life, Sirimavo was fluent in her command of Sinhala and its cadences, particularly as it was spoken in the Sri Lankan countryside. Standing her in good stead to appeal to her rural constituencies, this skill enabled her to consolidate and extend the vote banks that her husband, Solomon West Ridgeway Dias Bandaranaike, strived to build during his lifetime. Forged at the nexus of opportunity, response, and personality, these circumstances were to mould Sirimavo's signature leadership style.

In 1940, Sirimavo married the Oxford-educated lawyer turned politician, Solomon, in what was dubbed 'the wedding of the century.'[12] As with her parents before her, the alliance had been carefully arranged to ensure the continuity of two powerful elite lineages. Solomon was the heir of a feudal family that had thrived under British patronage. Fondly referred to as 'the bell of Asia' by his supporters, he was an affable and charismatic leftist who had shed the most conspicuous aspects of his Anglicised, upper-class background to transform into a populist in Sri Lankan politics. Having converted from Catholicism to Buddhism, Solomon literally shed his lounge suit to don the 'cloth and banian' of the masses when he ventured into the countryside to canvas support.[13] He was a rising star in politics, a well-heeled match for Sirimavo. She would have three children with Solomon, two daughters, Sunethra and Chandrika, and a son, Anura. Of her three offspring, two would end

68 Darinee Alagirisamy

up in politics, but in opposing camps. If Sirimavo made history as the country's first woman prime minister, Chandrika holds the distinction of being the republic's first female president between 1994 and 2005.

At any rate, life, which was humming along pleasantly for the couple, took an unexpectedly bloody turn when Solomon was shot to death on 26 August 1959. The fact that the murder took place in the privacy of the Bandaranaike residence, by a Buddhist monk no less, sent shock waves throughout Sri Lanka. It triggered all sorts of anxieties about the tenuous state of ethnic relations in the country, the majority's dissatisfaction with the perceived fecklessness of political parties, particularly where the Tamil issue was concerned, and finally, the future of the nation. More crucially for our purposes, it thrust Sirimavo, who had up until then apparently 'presided over nothing fiercer than the kitchen fire,' into the raging inferno of Sri Lankan politics.[14]

The year 1960 witnessed two parliamentary elections in Sri Lanka. The first took place in March in a context wherein the incumbent Mahajana Eksath Peramuna (MEP) coalition – with its reliance on the popularity of Solomon Bandaranaike and his Sri Lanka Freedom Party (SLFP) – was rapidly coming apart at the seams. The parties that had thrown their weight behind the coalition were internally divided over the question of paddy lands. The biggest point of contention arose between the SLFP and other minor parties, which were all loosely united under a Marxist banner. Adding to the upheaval was the acrimonious power struggle that the SLFP found itself embroiled in following Solomon's sudden demise. Out of this morass, the United National Party (UNP) and the SLFP emerged as the parties to watch in the elections of March 1960, although it was hardly an equal fight. The UNP was projected to win the elections with its relatively strong organisational base, the support it enjoyed amongst the majority of Sinhalese and considerable numbers of Tamils, as well as able leadership by the charismatic Dudley Senanayake.

The SLFP, however, had an ace up its sleeve. The party decided to parade Sirimavo about the country as a 'weeping widow' whose tears would do her talking for her. Sirimavo's vulnerability, party stalwarts calculated, would be their answer to Dudley's undeniable strength. They saw in the situation an opportunity to use Solomon's widow as a pawn to be moved and manipulated to their will. She was, on the one hand, the perfect representation of all that the assassinated prime minister had stood for, whilst, on the other, serving as the ultimate reminder of the enormous debt that the nation owed to the bereaved family. The party saw in the situation potentially great dividends to be reaped from 'moral capital,' a political store of virtue enabling followers to confer respect, authority, support, and patronage to a leader who utilises – or who, conversely, can be manipulated into utilising – it as a political resource to further their goals.[15] Party cadres stood to gain if they could groom Sirimavo into a pliant figurehead, which they were convinced would be the inevitable outcome. Both the UNP and the SLFP championed a pointedly anti-Tamil stance and promised a Sinhala Only future for the nation in these elections. Equally importantly, the failure of both parties to secure a clear majority paved

The unlikely prime minister **69**

the way for a tiebreaker, which came in the form of the elections of July 1960. In a replaying of the proverbial fight between David and Goliath, Sirimavo's SLFP pulled off the seemingly impossible to come out on top.

Enter the populist: the Sirimavo formula

Sirimavo's entry into politics required her to canvas and consolidate support for her party at a time when the party's future was mired in uncertainty. Solomon's assassination had raised pertinent questions about the nature of the leadership that the fledgling nation – and fractured party – needed going forward. These circumstances encouraged her young nephew, the ambitious Felix Dias Bandaranaike, to push for her candidacy.

In the elections of July 1960, Sirimavo seized the opportunity by taking it upon herself to visit every constituency where the SLFP fielded a candidate and relied heavily on the goodwill that her dead husband had amassed during his lifetime to ingratiate herself to the masses. At the risk of confirming her party cadre's plans to groom her into a willing puppet, she eschewed the chance to speak at these rallies, relying instead on replaying audio tapes containing Solomon's speeches. She thus exploited 'inherited charisma,' realising that there was real power to be mined by remaining in the sidelines for the time-being, shrouded in the cloak of mourning and inexperience that confirmed her virtue in the eyes of Sri Lankan society.[16] The grieving widow, propped up from the afterlife by the martyred former prime minister, had an electric effect on the electorate, who voted the party into power with a majority of 75 of 151 elected seats in Parliament. Notably, the majority of the votes that secured Sirimavo's premiership came from rural areas. From this point onwards, through to the 1970s and 1980s, Sirimavo's SLFP would dominate politics; the UNP, along with the Federal Party representing Tamil interests, led the opposition.

Time magazine made the disparaging comment of Sirimavo's inability to lead government owing to the tearful damsel in distress figure that she cut, made perhaps even more apparent by her stated reluctance to take over the premiership.[17] The most painful barbs came, perhaps predictably, from those closest to Mrs Bandaranaike. 'What does she know of politics?' mused a relative with all the scorn and none of the sympathy that might be expected given the circumstances. The scepticism was echoed by political observers whose biggest concern was that she would go on to ruin her personal reputation and family name. Her stated commitment to achieving the nebulous programme that her husband had outlined and admission that she was going to be 'lean(ing) heavily' on her nephew, Felix, must have convinced her colleagues in the party and world at large that they were right in their assessment: she seemed poised to be the perfect puppet. Sirimavo, however, clearly thought otherwise.[18] To her detractors, her response was simultaneously stoic and steely: 'A woman's place is everywhere and anywhere; that duty requires her to be *also* in her kitchen!'[19]

70 Darinee Alagirisamy

Having clinched the reins of power, Sirimavo's next challenge was to consolidate support as prime minister. Here she understood, almost instinctively, that she would be walking a delicate tightrope; she had the dual challenge of convincing her people that she was an able and effective leader whilst at the same time avoiding giving her male colleagues and critics, many of whom were in her own party, the impression that she would thwart their political ambitions. Sirimavo's first line of defence was to install close family members in key positions. She named Felix Reginald Bandaranaike as her finance minister and appointed her brothers as her private secretary, a Supreme Court judge, the leader of the state-owned plantation company, and the director of exports, respectively.

Like others after her who would inadvertently echo aspects of her political style, most famously Jayalalitha from the neighbouring Indian state of Tamil Nadu, Sirimavo transformed herself into the 'Mother of the People.'[20] Deliberate populist measures, including her advocacy for children's protection from the dangers of nuclear activity and crediting all her victories to her people, alongside the rapid strides that Sri Lanka recorded in the areas of maternal health and women's education under her premiership, buttressed this political image. Besides these measures that exalted her in the view of the public as a champion of women and children's welfare, Sirimavo cemented her position as mother of the nation, albeit one that was defined along communal lines, through her deliberate overtures to the Sinhala-Buddhist cause. Sinhala was enshrined as Sri Lanka's sole official language in January 1961, and the link between Sinhala and Buddhist strains of nationalism was cemented with the Schools Takeover Act of 1961. With the latter, Sirimavo's government bowed to the pressure that Buddhist leaders had long mounted on the government to open more Buddhist schools and break the near-monopoly that Christians, and Catholics in particular, held over Sri Lanka's network of schools.[21] While the Church responded with predictable chagrin, with Archbishop T.B. Cooray promising to 'fight to the end even by shedding blood,' Sirimavo remained singularly unmoved.[22] If anything, she would speak with pride about the Schools Takeover Act until her death.

Sirimavo thus consolidated the moral capital that she had inherited with Solomon's passing. Opportunity intersected with response and personality to enable her to stake her place as generalissimo in an intensely male-dominated battlefield. Her personality, inflected by the successes she had recorded in social work before assuming political office, came together with her colleagues' underestimation of her abilities, the space afforded by patriarchal society for women's participation, and her newly won position to aid her in carving out a prime minister's profile that was as powerful as it was non-threatening.

Entrenching the nationalist: Sinhala Only in practice

Having risen to power on the coat-tails of her husband's memory, Mrs Bandaranaike encountered several challenges to her leadership during her long political career. Within a year of her first electoral victory, she found herself having to declare a state of national emergency. The pro Sinhala-Buddhist stance that Solomon had flirted with and that Sirimavo consolidated with her language and education policies, alienated the Westernised Sri Lankan elite. The latter interpreted these measures as deliberate attempts to undermine and reverse the old colonial order that they were familiar with. One of the greatest sources of opposition came from the nation's Christians, who were especially aggrieved by the new government's encroachment on the autonomy enjoyed by their schools. In January 1962, Christian police and military officers led a coup to topple the government. Sirimavo's government put a decisive and swift end to the uprising with her right-hand man, Felix Bandaranaike, taking the lead. The incident ended up proving, in the eyes of most Sinhalese Sri Lankans, the pressing need for a pro-Buddhist, pro-Sinhala brand of governance.

Sirimavo's inability to address pressing economic problems paved the way for her electoral defeat of 1965. Although she tried to exploit the image of the grieving widow once again, the combined pressure from rising costs of living, shortages of essential goods, strikes, and high rates of unemployment proved insurmountable for the SLFP, which managed to secure only 39 seats out of a total of 157. However, this defeat did not mark the end of Sirimavo's career. On the contrary, she bounced back five years later with a big majority in the 1970 elections, which she campaigned on a stridently anti-Tamil platform. Having swept the polls with a two-thirds majority in Parliament, her party won without the support of minority groups. This was the beginning of the prime minister's attempt to shore up her popularity by playing to the majority: an ultimately destructive strategy that looked to the escalating ethnic conflict as an opportunity to be milked.

Sirimavo quickly positioned herself as a leader by laying down deep roots of patronage and support among the Sinhalese people. The brand of partisan politics that she threw her weight behind promoted the rights and interests of the majority over that of other communities. It was Sirimavo's silver bullet; the open secret to her electoral success. From the outset, the prime minister worked on entrenching a national discourse of the Sinhalese people having been systematically weakened by the growing ascendancy of the minority Tamil 'other.' 'The Tamil people,' she asserted, 'must accept the fact that the Sinhala majority will no longer permit themselves to be cheated of their rights.'[23] This polemic appears to have been motivated as much by the aim of forging an electoral platform that would remind her Sinhalese voters of her late husband's promises, whilst simultaneously superseding them with more tangible results. As part of this nationalist project, the contours of which became more sharply delineated over the course of the 1960s and early 1970s, she moved to ban the country's Dravida Munnetra Kazhagam (Dravida Progress Party, DMK), which championed Tamil interests and was modelled on the neighbouring Indian state of Tamil Nadu's ruling DMK party. Although the DMK had a relatively small political presence in Sri Lanka, Sirimavo's symbolic move cut where it hurt the most. It signalled the government's intention to undermine the

72 Darinee Alagirisamy

Tamil position wherever it could, beginning, significantly, with existing avenues for political representation.

Sirimavo adopted a stance that cast the Tamil minority in a state of perpetual alienation and opposition to the national community; her policy measures enabled the resultant unequal status quo to be written into the very workings of the state. She subsequently moved to rewrite the university admissions policy to benefit the Sinhalese in a programme that was spuriously called 'standardisation.' Sri Lanka boasted near-universal literacy by the 1960s owing to the government's provision of free education. Moreover, university education had been made available in the Sinhala and Tamil languages beginning in 1959. By 1970, despite their minority status, Tamils were over-represented in Sri Lankan universities' most prestigious courses; Tamil dominance in the fields of engineering and medicine especially stoked majority anxieties of losing out. Between 1970 and 1973, the policies put in place tried, in vain, to increase Sinhalese university enrolment relative to Tamil enrolment. Sirimavo presided over the introduction of predetermined minimum qualifying marks that were higher for the Tamil medium than for the Sinhalese medium. In 1973, the district quota system that replaced them sought to reverse the monopoly over education that the English-educated held, regardless of whether they were Sinhalese, Tamil, or of other ethnicities, and confer these advantages to Sinhala-speaking youth instead. Regardless of specific points of difference, taken together, the slew of policies that targeted education had the effect of alienating Tamil youth and breeding a grave sense of betrayal of their interests by the government.

Reappointment as prime minister also enabled Mrs Bandaranaike to push through a new republican constitution through which it became possible to affirm all the bills that had been introduced under the Sinhala Only Act. With this constitution, the state formally committed itself to the promotion of not only the language of the majority but also the religion of the majority, Buddhism. Aggrieved by this latest development, which effectively translated into the systematic exclusion of minority communities from the constitution, the Tamils responded by forming the Tamil United Front on 14 May 1972. Alongside this political response, however, a much more militant Tamil response was also taking shape.

The formation of the Liberation Tigers of Tamil Eelam on 5 May 1976, under the leadership of Vellupillai Prabhakaran, confronted not just Mrs Bandaranaike but every subsequent government with the ultimate consequence that may be expected when the flames of ethnic nationalism are fanned. Playing the nationalist card not only brought division and sowed the seeds of distrust amongst Sri Lankan Tamils, the vast majority of whom felt personally and deliberately sidelined, they also earned her bitter criticism that would last the test of time. One such critic was the Sri Lankan-born journalist and writer, Varindra Tarzie Vittachi, who was outspoken in deriding what he saw as Mrs Bandaranaike's neocolonial excesses. Moreover, the 30-year civil war that tore Sri Lanka apart from the inside had its origins in the LTTE's guerrilla struggle against the state, which it commenced shortly after its

The unlikely prime minister **73**

formation. While playing to the majority may have brought Sirimavo impressive political dividends in the short run, the long-term effects were explosive. Chandrika Kumaratunga, Sirimavo's daughter, who served as Sri Lanka's president between 1994 and 2005 felt, all too powerfully, the heat of the Sinhala Only firestorm that her mother had nurtured.

Playing the internationalist: non-alignment and selective engagement

Foreign policy in Sirimavo's Sri Lanka rested on two main tenets: the first was establishing a harmonious relationship with its neighbouring regional power, India, and the second was charting a neutral course in a world that was rapidly being carved up into distinct capitalist and communist spheres of influence. Central to both were concerns relating to the maintenance of national sovereignty. As a small state, Sri Lanka had everything to lose in dealing with larger countries that wielded far greater influence in the regional and international theatres.

The dynamic of Cold War rivalry provided Sirimavo with an opportunity to cement her leadership beyond the national arena. Specifically, she saw in it an opportunity to marry her role as prime minister with her aspirations as a rising star in the Non-Aligned Movement. At the first NAM Summit in Belgrade, Yugoslavia, Sirimavo became a founding member, standing shoulder to shoulder with other luminaries such as Nehru, Tito, and Sukarno. At the summit, Sirimavo made connections that made evident her unique position in the movement. She said, 'I am happy to attend this great conference not only as a representative of my country but also as a woman and a mother who can understand the thoughts and feelings of those millions of women.'[24] Soon afterwards, Mrs Bandaranaike extended her unequivocal support to Nelson Mandela in his fight to end apartheid in South Africa. The leader thus demonstrated a keen awareness of the urgency of staking a claim for her nation as an equal among equals. Equally importantly, she understood the importance of staking a claim as a leader of international standing on a global platform that was as male-dominated as the national stage. Sirimavo knew that the two were inextricably linked in shoring up power: the image of the nation and the reputation of the leader had to be cultivated in tandem if small nations were to have any hope of self-preservation in the great game of superpower rivalry.

Sirimavo's efforts in the direction of building a globally prominent role paid off soon after her second term in office as prime minister commenced. When the next major hurdle came in the form of the leftist Janatha Vimukti Peramuna (People's Liberation Front, JVP) uprising of 1971, the country's non-aligned friends helped to prop up the government when the nation's weak military could not. In an unexpected but fortuitous turn of events, India and Pakistan, which had been locked in their own tense stand-off since 1947, sent troops to Colombo, enabling Sirimavo to defeat the insurgents and reassert control. The uprising, which left an estimated 20,000 people dead, was met with Sirimavo's steely response, earning

74 Darinee Alagirisamy

her a reputation amongst her officials that 'she was the only man in her cabinet.'[25] Sri Lanka's regional and international standing thus came to the aid of Sirimavo's national standing as prime minister. Having thus thrown in her lot with left-leaning countries under the NAM banner, she rose to a leadership position as their chairman in 1976. Hosted by Colombo that year at the newly constructed Bandaranaike Memorial International Conference Hall, a gift from the Chinese government no less, the international NAM summit provided yet another opportunity to the prime minister to cement her role as a leader of international importance. In her speech, Sirimavo noted:

> Detente among the great Powers and between their alliance systems does not, however, meet the needs of the smaller and weaker nations as long as it perpetuates rivalry for spheres of influence, or condones manifestations of imperialism, colonialism and outside intervention in the internal affairs of States. It is even less attractive to us if it permits attempts at domination of some countries by others and lends credence to concepts of balance of power or of unequal relations between States.[26]

When Sirimavo highlighted the problem of unequal interstate relations, she was not only referencing superpower dynamics but also alluding to Sri Lanka's position vis-à-vis the regional hegemon to the country's north, India. India had to be managed carefully for several reasons. For one, the close geographical proximity between Sri Lanka and India necessitated the maintenance of amicable ties. Second, Sri Lanka's handling of its Tamil minority evolved as a matter of political interest in the southern Indian state of Tamil Nadu owing to the rise of Dravidian political parties there that drew a parallel between centre–state relations in India and the majority Sinhalese and minority Tamil communities in Sri Lanka. Following the 1962 Sino-Indian border conflict, Sirimavo undertook a diplomatic visit to Beijing and New Delhi to try and salvage relations between the two feuding countries. She did this after holding a meeting with the heads of various non-aligned nations, Myanmar, Cambodia, Ghana, Indonesia, and the United Arab Republic, to discuss the issue, thus buttressing her influence as a leading light of the NAM.

Sirimavo's foreign policy thrust relating to India included reckoning with the status of Indian-origin individuals in Sri Lanka. In this regard, the signing of two agreements was imbued with as much symbolic as strategic significance. The Indo-Ceylon Pact of 1964, more popularly known as the Sirima–Shastri Pact was signed between Indian Prime Minister Lal Bahadur Shastri and Mrs Bandaranaike. It set out to settle the future and status of persons of Indian origin who had been recruited by the British in India to work as indentured labourers on Sri Lankan plantations.[27] Of the approximately 975,000 Estate Tamils, the agreement guaranteed citizenship for 300,000 individuals while India accepted repatriation of 525,000 persons. The remaining 150,000 people's fate was to be determined by a second, separate agreement between the Indian and Sri Lankan governments. This agreement was

The unlikely prime minister **75**

concluded in 1974 between her and India's Indira Gandhi. The Sirima–Gandhi Pact, concluded between two women leaders who were also good friends in a personal capacity, divided the remaining people of Indian origin equally between India and Sri Lanka.[28] In sum, a lopsided 600,000 Tamils were to be repatriated to India while 375,000 were to remain in Sri Lanka. Although the process of repatriation, which began in 1968, came to an abrupt halt in 1983 with the outbreak of the Sri Lankan civil war, the two agreements helped to shore up Sirimavo's reputation as a decisive and capable leader in the eyes of the public: she had brokered a settlement on the long-standing issue of Tamil statelessness in Sri Lanka. Perhaps, more importantly, she had pulled this off without compromising the Sinhalese position.

Downfall: nationalisation, corruption, conspiracy

By the end of the 1970s and beginning of the 1980s, however, Sirimavo's star was in decline. While membership in the NAM club conferred several undeniable benefits, it did not come without its share of problems. Alongside the nationalisation of schools, Sirimavo moved to nationalise several foreign enterprises, the press, banking and insurance sectors, the petroleum industry, and the import and distribution of essential commodities, which were now placed under the Cooperative Wholesale Establishment. In fact, Sirimavo's heavy-handed nationalisation programme during her second term in office extended much farther than Solomon Bandaranaike's efforts had, motivated primarily by a myopic assessment of the political gains that it would score against her party's right-wing rival, the UNP. Coupled with other controversial decisions, such as ordering the US Peace Corps programme out of the country in 1970 and the abrupt closure of the Israeli embassy in the country, these actions invited the ire of the Americans and the British.[29] When the allies imposed an aid embargo on Sri Lanka, Sirimavo's response was to align her country even more closely with China and the Soviet Union, albeit under the banner of non-alignment. The cost of alienating the United States became obvious during the oil crisis of 1973, which further devastated the Sri Lankan economy. Cut off from access to Western aid and reeling under the effects of ill-advised socialist policies that had brought soaring rates of unemployment and a massive drain on existing reserves, the economy careened out of control.

The clouds of economic collapse were hanging over Sri Lanka even as Sirimavo once again faced the spectre of political instability. Accused by her political opponents of autocratic rule and corruption, she found herself beleaguered and with few allies outside her immediate family circle that she could count on. Mrs Bandaranaike's arch nemesis, Junius Jayawardene, made rapid political gains when he succeeded Senanayake as leader of the Opposition to Sirimavo's government and clinched political power as prime minister in 1977, before stepping down to become president in 1978. Jayawardene would in fact initiate a witch hunt against her that would trigger an official enquiry. To make matters worse, Russia had withdrawn its support for the SLFP government by the late 1970s following

76 Darinee Alagirisamy

the latter's ouster of the more radical leftist Lanka Sama Samaja Party (LSSP) and the Communist Party from the coalition government. Sirimavo's government had prorogued Parliament to stall the discussion on a no-confidence motion. This had embarrassingly triggered the resignation in protest of five party members, including the industries minister. Meanwhile, the national media relentlessly heaped praise on the SLFP's supposedly democratic brand of governance, in full glaring view of policies that were anything but democratic, thus further reinforcing the feeling of disconnect and distrust with which many Sri Lankans regarded their government.

Developments in neighbouring India did not help, either. By 1977, observers were drawing unfavourable parallels between Mrs Bandaranaike and Indira Gandhi. Sirimavo seemed to be headed on the same ill-fated electoral path that Gandhi's Emergency laws had led her down.[30] In the midst of – and in response to – the dire lack of public confidence in the government's ability to fix the problems that needed urgent fixing and point the way to a better future, finance minister Felix Bandaranaike announced the revaluation of the Sri Lankan rupee relative to the US dollar and the pound sterling. Aimed at salvaging its plummeting popularity ahead of the 1977 elections and contrary to the advice of the Monetary Board advisors who issued ominous warnings about the likely economic fallout of such an action, the government pressed ahead with currency revaluation. The general election of 1977 showed what the electorate thought of revaluation along with the government's balance sheet for the seven years it had been in power. The SLFP, as part of the United Left Front coalition, was crushingly defeated in the 1977 general elections. To add insult to injury, both Sirimavo and Felix were stripped of their civic rights and expelled from Parliament for seven years on 16 October 1980. They had been found guilty of corruption and grievous abuse of power.

Along with her grievous mishandling of the ethnic conflict, Sirimavo's legacy today remains marred by criticism of nepotism. By the late 1970s, things were not looking good for her on the family front either. Her children, Chandrika and Anura, crossed swords over the party leadership after the former returned from self-imposed exile in London following her husband's assassination. Tragically, Solomon's assassination would not be the last that Sirimavo would witness. Her son-in-law, Vijay Kumaratunga, also met his end owing to his political career. The widowed Chandrika eventually won out after Sirimavo's resignation in 1994, prompting her brother, Anura, to cross over to the United National Party. While Chandrika, who briefly broke ranks with her parents' party, remained firmly within the Sri Lanka Freedom Party camp, Anura etched out a career as leader of the opposition, a dynamic that often led to the siblings being at loggerheads professionally. Amidst these developments, Mrs Bandaranaike's final act was to vote in a parliamentary election that she hoped would return the family's party to power leading a coalition known as the People's Alliance. She died at the ripe old age of 84 from a heart attack on Election Day in the year 2000. Even death seemed poetically timed for the woman who, against all odds, had made politics her family business and whose political career had spanned a long four decades.

Conclusion

This chapter set out to examine Sirimavo Bandaranaike's equation with power, positing that its tenets may be located in the particular ways in which opportunity, response, and personality intersected against a backdrop of domestic and global bipolarity. Specifically, these three axes conditioned both the nature of the power that she wielded and its limitations.

Opportunity knocked on Sirimavo's door at several points over the course of her life, both in and out of politics, although her personality and responses shaped the final outcome. Her birth and upbringing in an influential aristocratic family stood her in good stead for a future life in politics, a connection that was further reinforced with her arranged marriage to the then-rising star in national politics, Solomon Bandaranaike. Tragic as it was, Solomon's assassination proved to be a golden opportunity that catapulted the grieving Sirimavo into the heart of Sri Lankan politics as a prime ministerial candidate. Her inexperience, along with the deeply entrenched sexist attitudes that prevailed in Sri Lankan society, translated into her peers underestimating her potential, convinced that they could use her as a pawn to further their own interests.

Once in power, Sirimavo proved adept at manipulating circumstances to her advantage, although the repercussions were neither immediately apparent nor always favourable. Her consolidation of power was aided by several factors that worked together in her favour, at least initially. Domestically, the Sinhala Only discourse that her late husband had strived to launch played into her hand, although her response to the tenuous state of ethnic relations in the country complicated the situation even further in the long run. Whilst her pro-Sinhalese Buddhist policies entrenched her popularity amongst the majority community, the prime minister was to find out that short-term electoral gains would come at the cost of long-term instability. Although the seeds of ethnic conflict had been sown long before Sirimavo assumed power in 1960, the soil was conditioned in large part by her initiatives and responses to a rapidly escalating situation that she had completely lost control of by 1976. Playing the nationalist card put numerous challenges in her way as she consolidated her electoral gains. It also plagued successive administrations that would inherit a devastating civil war situation.

Internationally, Cold War politics and simmering tensions between its neighbours in the Asian theatre provided opportunities for Mrs Bandaranaike to etch out a role of global prominence. She exploited the Non-Aligned Movement as a platform to stake her place – and that of her country's – as an equal among equals. These overtures proved to be a double-edged sword. Some of her responses to foreign policy opportunities proved to be advantageous, as during the time when India and Pakistan sent aid that helped her put an end to the coup of 1971. Other responses, however, proved to be far less favourable. Her efforts to align Sri Lanka closer to China and the Soviet Union served to antagonise the Western allies, with devastating consequences for the country's economy.

78 Darinee Alagirisamy

Where double-edged swords are concerned, Sirimavo's decision to rely on familial networks proved both advantageous and damaging at various points in her career. Family fostered her entry into politics and made the subsequent storms easier to endure. This was a winning formula as long as Sirimavo's star was on the rise. However, when that star started to wane, owing to a combination of crises which rendered the prime minister more a liability than an asset in the public eye, crippling charges of nepotism played into the hands of her political rivals. The blurred lines between the personal and the political became one of the final nails in the coffin of Sirimavo's career. Making national politics family business also meant that political divisions could spill over into and poison blood ties, as evident in the wedge that they eventually drove between her own children who emerged as bitter political rivals.

Sirimavo's early experience with social work in the Sri Lankan countryside stood her in good stead for the future role that she would play in public life. She drew on this rich reserve of experience as well as her ability to switch effortlessly between her command of the English language and familiarity with the local register of Sinhala that ingratiated her to the masses. Indeed, she mastered the art of continual reinvention. Sirimavo's dexterity in transforming herself from a diminutive damsel riding on the coat-tails of her husband's memory to a formidable and charismatic leader in her own right showed a degree of political cunning that completely blindsided her rivals. She had an uncanny ability to hold back when circumstances demanded it, just as her steely resolve shone through when the situation necessitated decisiveness. From being dismissed as a clueless housewife who had fumbled her way into politics, to being termed the only man in her cabinet, Mrs Bandaranaike's political career as prime minister remains a compelling study: not just of female political leadership in the Asia-Pacific region but of leadership in general in a bipolar world.

Notes

1 This chapter foregrounds Sirimavo as the political personality who set in motion policies that were to have lasting consequences for Sri Lankan politics and society. In recognition of the leader's agency and to distinguish her premiership from that of Solomon Bandaranaike, it often refers to the leader by her first name, 'Sirimavo,' instead of using the more conventional Bandaranaike or Mrs Bandaranaike.

2 Yasmine Gooneratne, *Relative Merits: A Personal Memoir of the Bandaranaike Family of Sri Lanka* (London: Hurst, 1986), 160.

3 See, for instance, Rounaq Jahan, "Women in South Asian Politics," *Third World Quarterly* 9, no. 3 (July 1987), 848–70; Linda K. Richter, "Exploring Theories of Female Leadership in South and Southeast Asia," *Pacific Affairs* 63, no. 4 (Winter 1990–1991), 524–40; Francine D'Amico and Peter R. Beckman, eds., *Women in World Politics: An Introduction* (London: Bergin & Garvey, 1995); Gail Omvedt, "Women in Governance in South Asia," *Economic and Political Weekly* 40, no. 44–45 (October 29–November 4, 2005), 4746–52; Claudia Derichs and Mark R. Thompson, eds., *Dynasties and Female Political Leaders in Asia: Gender, Power and Pedigree* (Berlin: LIT Verlag, 2013).

The unlikely prime minister **79**

4 Francine D'Amico and Peter R. Beckman, "Introduction," in D'Amico and Beckman, *Women in World Politics*, 1–15, especially 18.

5 Richter, "Female Leadership in South and Southeast Asia," 524–40, especially 524–27.

6 See, for instance, Mary C. Carras, *Indira Gandhi: In the Crucible of Leadership: A Political Biography* (New Delhi: Beacon Press, 1979); Pupul Jayakar, *Indira Gandhi: A Biography* (New Delhi: Penguin, 1992); Blema S. Steinberg, *Women in Power: The Personalities and Leadership Styles of Indira Gandhi, Golda Meir, and Margaret Thatcher* (Montreal: McGill-Queen's Press, 2008); Nayantara Sahgal, *Indira Gandhi: Tryst With Power* (New Delhi: Penguin, 2017).

7 For the purpose of continuity, this chapter will refer to the country in question as Sri Lanka from this point onwards. The name change from Ceylon to Sri Lanka took place in 1972.

8 The Estate Tamils lived almost exclusively in the Kandian hills for generations and formed almost half the total Ceylonese Tamil population at that time.

9 Joint Programme of the Mahajana Eksath Peramuna (People's United Front) Colombo, 1956.

10 The Bandaranaike–Chelvanayakam Pact sought to assure Tamils that Tamil would be used as the language of administration in the country's Northern and Eastern provinces.

11 Sirimavo Bandaranaike, *Tribune*, May 7, 1967, cited in Nira Wickramasinghe, *Sri Lanka in the Modern Age: A History of Contested Identities* (Honolulu: University of Hawaii Press, 2006), 161.

12 Maureen Seneviratne, *Sirimavo Bandaranaike, the World's First Woman Prime Minister: A Biography* (Colombo: Hansa Publishers, 1975), cited in p. 75.

13 Nira Wickramasinghe, *Dressing the Colonised Body: Politics, Clothing, and Identity in Sri Lanka* (London: Orient Blackswan, 2003), 21.

14 Paul Pieris Deriyanagala quoted in Gooneratne, *Relative Merits*, 160. Deriyanagala was best man at the Bandaranaikes' wedding.

15 John Kane, *The Politics of Moral Capital* (Cambridge: Cambridge University Press, 2001).

16 Derichs and Thompson, *Dynasties and Female Political Leaders in Asia*, 15–17.

17 Sirimavo Bandaranaike quoted in *Tribune*, May 7, 1967, cited in Wickramasinghe, *Sri Lanka in the Modern Age*, 161.

18 Seneviratne, *Sirimavo Bandaranaike*, 76.

19 Ibid. Cited in p. 204. Emphasis in original.

20 Bradman Weerakoon, *Rendering Unto Caesar: A Fascinating Story of One Man's Tenure Under Nine Prime Ministers and Presidents of Sri Lanka* (Colombo: New Dawn Press, 2004), 123.

21 A. Jeyaratnam Wilson, *S.J.V. Chelvanayakam and the Crisis of Sri Lankan Tamil Nationalism, 1947–1977: A Political Biography* (London: C. Hurst, 1994), 100–2.

22 *Dinamina*, June 30, 1959.

23 Sirimavo Bandaranaike, *Tribune*, May 7, 1961, cited in Wickramasinghe, *Sri Lanka in the Modern Age*, 161.

24 Sirimavo Bandaranaike, Speech at Non-Aligned Conference, Belgrade, 1961.

25 Warnakulasuriya Thomas Aquinas Leslie Fernando, *Reflections on a Changing Society* (Colombo: Samayawardhana, 1997), 67. This quote is attributed to Sir John Kothelawala.

26 Sirimavo Bandaranaike, "The Non-Aligned Movement and the United Nations," *The Black Scholar* 8, no. 3 (December 1976): 27–31, 34–38.

27 A. Jeyaratnam Wilson, *Politics in Sri Lanka, the Republic of Ceylon: A Study in the Making of a New Nation* (New York: Palgrave Macmillan, 2016), 345.

28 India abrogated both treaties in 1982. At this point 90,000 Indian Tamils who had been granted Indian citizenship were still in Sri Lanka while 86,000 were still in the process of applying for Indian citizenship. See, for instance, Anoma Pieris, *Sovereignty, Space*

and Civil War in Sri Lanka: Porous Nation (Oxon and New York: Routledge, 2019), 128–30.

29 Saman Kelegama, *Development Under Stress: Sri Lankan Economy in Transition* (New Delhi: Sage, 2006), 49–51.

30 Arthur S. Banks, *Political Handbook of the World Governments, Regional Issues, and Intergovernmental Organizations as of January 1, 1978* (London: McGraw-Hill, 1978), 30. Echoing the sentiment that prevailed at that time among political analysts, Banks argued that Sirimavo's leadership was becoming increasingly heavy-handed, in much the same way as Gandhi's handling of Indian politics had paved the way to Emergency. This analysis was subsequently extended in other publications of that time. See, for instance, *Political Science Review*, vol. 18–19 (Rajasthan: University of Rajasthan, 1979), 128.

5

JULIUS NYERERE

African leadership as a moral project

Sara Lorenzini

> Leaders must set a good example to the rest of the people in their lives and in all their activities.
>
> Julius Nyerere, *Arusha Declaration*, 1967

Julius Nyerere was one of the most acclaimed and longest-lasting leaders in the history of contemporary Africa. He entered politics right after completing his studies at the University of Edinburgh, becoming the president of the Tanganyika African Association (TAA), soon renamed Tanganyika African National Union (TANU) in 1953. He became the first Prime Minister of Tanganyika in December 1961, then its president after the proclamation of the Republic in 1962, and lastly, the President of the United Republic of Tanzania (Tanganyika and Zanzibar) in 1964. He resigned from office in 1985, belonging to that small pantheon of African founding fathers who passed down a lasting legacy of institutional legitimacy to the republican institutions they had contributed to creating.[1] Although his economic development strategy failed in bringing prosperity to Tanzania, Nyerere was regarded with reverence, at home and abroad, and was remembered as *Mwalimu* (teacher) also by people too young to have experienced his leadership. During office and even after abdicating power, he used his prestige to urge ethical political choices at home and abroad.

What are the traits of his charismatic personality and his guidance? I argue in this chapter that his capacity to adapt his goals to the times was crucial in establishing an enduring legacy and that the moral inspiration of his political action was essential to his leadership style.

In the half-century after independence, Tanzania enjoyed a degree of stability, peace, and cohesion that few African states could claim. Nyerere deserves a great

DOI: 10.4324/9781003426165-5

82 Sara Lorenzini

deal of credit for this. 'His life and leadership encompassed the contradictions of his age,' writes Paul Bjerk in the latest (short) biography that appeared in 2017.[2] With this, he means that, like in the case of many heroes of national independence, Nyerere's time in office was not a story of blinding success. Instead, it was a story punctuated by questionable economic choices and with a dubious democratic record. In international politics, however, the picture is overall positive, with Nyerere consistently acting on his ideals of freedom and according to undisputed moral principles. Two priorities guided him: preserving national independence and practising international solidarity and justice in the Cold War setting both at home and abroad.

Nyerere's trajectory as a leader can be divided into three phases: the first with him as the 'father of the nation,' when he articulated his national project in pan-African terms. This was followed and dominated by African Socialism, with the promotion of *Ujamaa* as an ideology and the plan to build a socialist state based on self-reliance. Finally, there was a period of Third-Worldism, with Nyerere becoming an inspiring voice of the Global South around projects designed to transform the international economic order.

The father of the nation: Nyerere as the leader of independence, 1953–1965

In 1959, Eleanor Roosevelt conducted an intriguing 'Prospects of Mankind' round-table interview on Africa.[3] The main guest was Julius Nyerere, in his position as the president of TANU. Other guests were Ralph Bunche, the UN under-secretary-general for special political affairs and a Nobel Peace Prize laureate, Barbara Ward, the British economist who was a resident of Ghana and lecturer at Harvard University, and Saville R. Davies of *The Christian Science Monitor*. The opening question was 'Is independence coming too quickly?' While the other respondents, in one way or another, confirmed that yes, the pace of national liberation in Africa came as a surprise to many, and yes, it was somehow too rapid, Nyerere was offended by the query and by the underlying idea that Africans 'were not ready' for independence. After all, he argued, colonialists had taken what was not theirs. Now they were finally returning power to the legitimate owners who had succeeded in 'making the colonial powers go out.' The round table touched upon a few more topics, revealing a clear distance between Nyerere and the other participants. For example, Nyerere rebuffed the description of Tanganyika as an extraordinary case of a multiracial society. The expression, he claimed, was devised by the colonial powers to describe East Africa, and it was used instrumentally to discredit the prospects for democratic government in Africa. In his opinion, the main goal to be pursued once the nation was built was economic development. Nyerere argued that technical assistance was needed ideally within a new regime to be initiated by the United Nations and under a common umbrella, without distinctions between East and West. Like Kenya's Tom Mboya around the same time, Nyerere was always mindful of 'wrapping the quest

Julius Nyerere **83**

for foreign aid into the language of African sovereignty,' and he was resolute in asserting the right to accept aid from every quarter.[4] In would-soon-be-independent Tanganyika, he was willing to cooperate with foreign private capital to promote economic development. His country was poor and needed a flow of technical and financial aid from any source available, provided there were no political strings attached. The donors, he insisted, 'must not exploit our need in order to force us into one or the other of the blocs.' Finally, on pan-Africanism, Nyerere spoke of 'a sentiment of oneness in Africa that you can't find anywhere else.' The borders of the states now fighting for independence were arbitrarily cut out by the colonial powers, and the tendency was now to regroup in bigger units as a way to overcome artificial divisions. But he concluded that whether plans for federation or regional unity would become a reality were not clear.

This interview is especially illuminating. It touches upon several essential points that define Nyerere's policymaking in the early stage of independence: revolution, democracy, multiracial representation, economic development, and Cold War dynamics. More importantly, it describes Nyerere's personality as a political leader. In 1953, Julius Nyerere was elected president of the Tanganyika African Association, a 20-year-old organisation representing the interests of a tiny African middle class of educated civil servants and businessmen. He transformed it into a different party, an umbrella organisation to coordinate the efforts of various African political groups. With brilliant eloquence, he toured the country, obsessively repeating that the key to success in the struggle for independence was unity against the divide-and-rule policy of the colonial powers. He succeeded with the help of fellow activists Bibi Titi Mohamed and Oscar Kambona, who built up TANU's membership from 2,000 members at the beginning of 1955 to over 40,000 by the time of general elections in 1958–1959.[5]

Nyerere was often described as a pleasing personality, inspired by gradualism and negotiation. Anyone listening to the 1959 interview, however, may form the impression that Nyerere, while no doubt polite, was far from accommodating. Instead, he sounds pretty confrontational. Throughout the conversation, he countered with determination all elements touched upon by the other speakers and made his point, exposing the patronising tones of his interlocutors. Especially trenchant was his point on financing development because here he bluntly exposed the inconsistency of colonial narratives about aid, arguing against the myth of colonial aid, which was never substantial. His replies to the many questions raised in the interview were very well articulated. The exception being the question about democracy. Mrs Roosevelt posed the question: how could a one-party system like the one established in Tanganyika by TANU be democratic? Nyerere answered vaguely and shifted the attention to the fight for independence. To exist, he contended, democracy did not need a multiparty system. The true expression of democracy in Africa was the existence of a nationalist movement with freedom as its primary goal. In successive interviews, he would formulate a much more articulated answer to this kind of question. We are democratic, he would argue, because the

84 Sara Lorenzini

essence of democracy is that individuals do not feel harassed, that they are free to choose. He was convinced that there was not just one way to understand democracy. Democracy as a method, he claimed, meant freedom of choice, but the choice need not be between two or more parties. It could be at the level of the individual representative. The system in Tanzania was about this: choosing the individuals, not the party.[6]

Nyerere assiduously cultivated an inclusive political establishment. He held the view that post-colonial countries must eliminate the structures of social inequalities that intersect with racial and ethnic divisions.[7] Therefore, he made a deliberate effort to ensure that his government and his closest associates reflected a cross section of Tanzania's diverse society: Muslim, Christian, Hindu, and animist; African, Indian, Arab, and European – the countless religious and ethnic groups and identities of Tanganyika and then Tanzania's broad territory needed to be properly represented.[8] Throughout his political career, Nyerere made a great effort to avoid corruption and keep his bureaucracy accountable to the people, to prevent the waste of resources, and to balance the interests of different parts of the country and various segments of society. The inclusive attitude flaunted by Nyerere throughout the 1950s allowed TANU to gain support throughout the country, bringing together a myriad of local groups with different priorities.

Another principle that ruled action on the eve of independence in the years 1958–1961 was the adoption of moderate policies and a consistent cooperation with the British authorities towards independence.[9] Despite having Africanisation as a goal, Nyerere did not seem the guy who would push in the direction of dramatically cutting off relations with the former mandatory power. On the eve of independence, he addressed a personal letter to the British civil servants asking them not to leave their jobs to provide a smooth transition and support the training of young African civil servants.[10] Andrew Cohen, the UK representative in the UN Trusteeship Council, described him as capable, smart, and 'essentially moderate in politics.' Other British administrators stressed that he was 'no fanatic' and able to advance his demands for self-government without 'bitterness or rancor toward the British Authorities.' UK Governor Edward Twining, instead, held the opposite view. He accused Nyerere of 'black racialism' and, in private correspondence, he described him as a pathetic figure, lonely and unimpressive.[11] After all, unlike the prominent educated chiefs working with Twining, Nyerere rejected the ethnic boundaries within which the British administration had contained local politics. Moreover, increasingly inspired by Kwame Nkrumah's example, Nyerere, who had begun as a territorial nationalist, quickly advanced into pan-African nationalism. Convinced that Africans were to surpass the boundaries imposed by the colonisers and think in a larger collaborative setting, he worked towards the idea of an East African Federation with Kenya and Uganda. On this, he had significant support from the United States, interested in a federation with solid ties to the West. President Kennedy saw Nyerere as one of the most promising politicians on the African continent and invited him on an official visit in July 1961, before

Tanganyika achieved formal independence. The project of the East Africa Federation, however, never materialised.[12]

Negotiation as a method did not imply renouncing the constant emphasis on independence and on maintaining an independent foreign policy. Furthermore, on this point, Nyerere was adamant with any interlocutor in the West and the East alike. In the Communist countries, and especially in the Soviet Union, Nyerere did not get a good press. Until the early 1960s, Tanganyika did not seem to take a path to distance itself from the West. Therefore, his project was judged with scepticism, if not hostility, by the communist parties, in the Soviet Union and China. Nyerere's attempt to frame his policies into the language of African Socialism was perceived and commented upon as an ideological deprivation. *Ujamaa*, the unique form of African Socialism adopted as the political ideology of TANU, was socialism without Marxism. It was explicitly against class conflict and the very concept of the working class. Consequently, it did not deserve to be taken seriously by orthodox socialists.

Nyerere started articulating his ideas on Tanzanian Socialism in 1962, when he wrote a famous pamphlet titled '*Ujamaa*: The Basis of African Socialism.'[13] He introduced the concept of *Ujamaa*, or familyhood, which he defined as 'the foundation, and the objective, of African socialism.' *Ujamaa*'s goal was building a happy society based on the belonging of individuals to a community. It was opposed to capitalism, which seeks to build that kind of society based on what he saw as the exploitation of man by man, and to doctrinaire socialism, which he considered sought to build its happy society on a philosophy of inevitable conflict. *Ujamaa* connected ideas of socialism to authentic local traditions: building on the past and forged in or as part of an autonomous design.[14] According to Nyerere, capitalism and socialism were two sides of the same coin. European socialists, he argued, could not think of socialism without its father – capitalism. In this way, they ended up glorifying the existence of capitalism. This was intolerable, lamented Nyerere, who argued that the idea of class and conflict was the product of an alien culture, introduced with colonialism, and that did not exist in African societies before. 'Socialism, like democracy, is an attitude of mind,' he wrote. It could be regained by returning to tradition and applying it to today's societies. According to Nyerere, fundamental to the construction of a socialist society were elements such as the centrality of man, the dignity of individuals (men and women alike), the adoption of democracy as a system, secularism, and the centrality of work without exploitation. As for specific models to follow, Nyerere was caustic: 'There is no model for us to copy.' Instead, learning from others meant studying past experiences and adapting success stories to the local setting.[15] Nyerere's socialist discourse was similar to other African socialist discourses and policies observable in pan-Africanist networks. Many pan-African leaders emphasised economic equality and an aversion to the social alienation they attributed to capitalism. They gave prominence to race over class. Many shared the ambition of claiming the heritage of some pre-modern socialism. Some of them, such as Kwame Nkrumah in

86 Sara Lorenzini

Ghana or Sékou Touré in Guinea, identified explicitly with socialism. Others, such as Jomo Kenyatta in Kenya or Léopold Senghor in Senegal, were less interested in the socialist character. All of them idealised extended family as the fundamental structure embedded at the core of their model of 'tribal socialism.'[16]

Ujamaa was not taken as a serious political project by the Soviet Union. There-fore, the socialist countries did not react with exceptional enthusiasm to Nyerere's attempt to turn to them for aid. The exception was the German Democratic Repub-lic (DDR), which relentlessly tried to find avenues to get international recogni-tion and overcome the principle of the 'sole representation of Germany' claimed by the West Germans. Early contact with Tanganyika started as soon as 1962. A DDR representative was invited to Tanganyika's proclamation of independence in December 1962. Negotiations to establish a trade delegation and sign trade and aid agreements were held between July and September 1962. The (high-ranking) DDR diplomat Gottfried Lessing, who was in charge of the operation, considered establishing trade relations 'a pressing and important political task.'[17] Nonethe-less, the process did not advance much. The first meeting meant to take place in Dar es Salaam in March 1963 was delayed, and negotiations started only in August 1963.[18] Student exchange was activated immediately, but other agree-ments, such as the project to build a printing works, were cancelled or postponed because of constant, specific interference from West Germany.[19] Negotiations were kept top-secret, and Oscar Kambona, Tanganyika's foreign minister who had taken the issue to heart, was often overstepped or kept in the dark because of West German pressures. In September 1963, trade and aid agreements were signed by Tanganyika with Czechoslovakia, Hungary, Poland, and Bulgaria. The Soviet Union signed one, too, but it did not imply any significant commitment.[20] After all, the Tanganyika government had structured its development plan follow-ing the March 1961 World Bank recommendations to transform the rural sector. The World Bank report suggested ways to move towards cash crop production, introducing sisal as the new cash crop. It launched rural experiments based on the village as an organisational unit.[21]

Throughout the 1950s and early 1960s, Nyerere was mostly perceived as a gentle-mannered leader open to dialogue with the former colonial powers and eager to attract direct investments from capitalist countries. The picture of a mild, accommodating, and weak character changed in the mid-1960s, when he became the ultimate symbol of obstinate resistance to what he felt was the arrogance of Western power. What events turned the timid sheep into a fierce wolf? The game changer was the January 1964 coup in Zanzibar and the dynamics ensuing at the domestic and international levels. The revolution in Zanzibar, with the communist takeover headed by Abeid Karume, came as a surprise. It fuelled great expectations in some members of the Eastern bloc, especially in East Germany, still hoping to find in communist-ruled Zanzibar the first newly independent country willing to officially recognise the DDR, notwithstanding the West German threat of with-holding aid in accordance with the Hallstein Doctrine.[22] On 26 January 1964, the

DDR offered immediate official recognition to Zanzibar (26 January 1964) and sent a high-ranking negotiator, Ambassador Fritsch, with what they considered significant aid offers. The action was entirely independent of Soviet policy. The Soviet Union did not react immediately, even though it promised assistance to defend the new country.[23]

To Nyerere, the Zanzibari coup became an opportunity to put into practice the idea of an African Federation in East Africa, albeit on a project of limited dimension. Several members of the new Zanzibari government visited Dar es Salaam in January to talk with foreign minister Oscar Kambona about a union between their islands and mainland Tanganyika. The prospect of a leftist turn in the area awakened worries and hopes in different quarters. A brand-new Cold War mood entered the scene and impinged on Nyerere's golden rule: no interference by any external power. The interference of the British authorities became embarrassing in January 1964, when the British forces intervened to put down the mutiny of the Tanganyika Rifles, the military of the newly independent state, who protested about the slow Africanisation of the officer corps.[24] To show off independent behaviour, Nyerere responded by inviting military instructors from other countries, including seven Chinese advisors. He was offended by the Americans' reaction and by the US ambassador's request to reject the Chinese experts and did not fail to show this on public occasions and press conferences.[25]

Nyerere and Karume agreed to a hastily prepared union treaty, which they signed in April 1964, announcing to the world and baffled hegemonic powers in the region that they had created the United Republic of Tanganyika and Zanzibar, Tanzania. Tanzania's birth is considered one of Nyerere's most significant accomplishments. Seen from the perspective of the Zanzibaris, it looked like an annexation. Nevertheless, it served the purpose of keeping Cold War dynamics under control. After all, Nyerere did not appear to be a radical, and to both sides, he was a guarantee that no major shift was likely to happen. African leaders reacted with enthusiasm. Sekou Touré immediately warned about the dangers of relying exclusively on communist aid. East European countries responded straightaway, offering their assistance, to Zanzibar first and to the whole of Tanzania afterwards. The DDR was especially active. It was so insistent that in April 1964, Nyerere was directly involved. He explained to the DDR emissaries that formalising official relations encountered tremendous obstacles and threatened to repeat the Guinea precedent of 1957, with all the Western powers cutting off relations overnight. He tried to convince the DDR government to exchange the embassy in Zanzibar for a trade mission in Dar es Salaam, asking the Soviet Union representative in London to intercede.[26] He met initially with a scornful reaction. The Soviet Union accused him of playing on the side of the imperialists, but they recalibrated their approach in August 1964, offering to help build up the army and sending weapons and training – provided Tanzania renounced aid from the West, especially from West Germany.[27] In the end, nothing came out of it, because Nyerere did not accept the political constraints attached to the offer.

88 Sara Lorenzini

The year 1965 marked a turning point nonetheless. In May of that year, Nyerere rejected West German pressures to give up trade relations with the DDR. Consequently, West German military personnel left the country without informing him, and aid and official relations were suspended. Nyerere's fundamental ideas did not change. He had no desire to get mixed up in the German question. After all, how could an official recognition of East Germany by Tanzania or Malawi make any difference?[28] The blackmailing attitude of the West, however, was unacceptable. Western countries sided with West Germany and abandoned projects halfway in retaliation. The United Kingdom was one of the first to suspend aid. The socialist countries, however, did not expect any political reversal. DDR's diplomat Lessing, who negotiated agreements to send experts to help with *Ujamaa* and with Tanzania's five-year plan, was pessimistic: non-capitalist development had no chance in Tanzania. Nyerere was a realist, and he was not inclined to revolutionary experiments. Investing in the more radical leadership in Mali and Guinea was a much better option for the DDR.[29]

Tensions between Tanzania and the West were innumerable. They worsened after Southern Rhodesia's Unilateral Declaration of Independence of 11 November 1965. In the Organization of African Unity and elsewhere, Nyerere raised his voice against the West. 'The mutual suspicion which already exists between free African states and nations of the West is in danger of getting very much worse,' he wrote in a damning article in *Foreign Affairs*.[30] It was a responsibility of the United Kingdom to grant gradual constitutional advance towards democracy or majority rule in Southern Rhodesia, condemning regimes where Africans were treated 'as a sub-species of mankind.' Allowing racialism to continue unchallenged on the African continent was the ultimate horror to which no free African country would surrender. A failure to keep to the principles of human equality and freedom, using the Cold War as a pretext, was intolerable to any African leader.

The socialist leader: Nyerere and self-reliance as a political project, between *Ujamaa* and forced villagisation (1967–1976)

Tanzania resulted from the union of two multi-ethnic states that were struggling economically. As in many newly independent countries, development was vital to offer a new perspective. Tanzania's economy was dramatically dependent on external aid. Nyerere was well aware that without economic independence, political independence was a fragile thing. Therefore, he moved towards translating the ideology of *Ujamaa* into an economic development plan. *Ujamaa*, a socialist experiment based on the traditional economy in the countryside, started in 1961, according to the World Bank's suggestions. The organisational social unit around which it was organised was the village, previously at the core of colonial policy as an economic and security structure. *Ujamaa* villages adopted colonial ideas of modernisation, including scientific agriculture, mechanisation, bureaucratic centralism, and modern education. In Nyerere's representation, the village had territorial rootedness and adherence to customary family norms based on familyhood. The principal objectives of *Ujamaa* were self-sufficiency and self-governance. Community members focused on improving agriculture, with common farming at least three days a week and profits shared among the community.[31] They shared equipment, resources, training, and decision-making. Village industries included milling, knitting, and weaving.[32] One of the early *Ujamaa* experiments was incredibly successful: the Ruvuma Development Association (RDA) that united 15 villages in the Songea district in the south-west of the country with local control and non-authoritarian organisation. It was created and managed by Ntimbanjayo Millinga, the secretary of the local branch of the Tanzanian African National Union Youth League. Nyerere was very impressed by how the RDA mirrored the ideas of *Ujamaa* and insisted that it should be replicated at a national level. However, RDA was loathed by many party leaders, envious of its success and independence from governmental authority. It was attacked by TANU's Central Committee and eventually disbanded in 1969.[33]

Ujamaa was born as a political ideology that combined African nationalism with Nyerere's peculiar unorthodox theory of harmonious socialism. His programme was to build socialism without class struggle, starting with agriculture instead of industrialisation and on self-reliance instead of foreign aid. After visiting China, Nyerere was impressed by the austere attitude of the bureaucracy there and began to envision a socialist state modelled on the one built by Chairman Mao. Tanzania, like China, would build socialism in the countryside. In late 1966, he began to work on a policy statement committing Tanzania to a more radical socialist path, to strengthen the state and accelerate the establishment of a single-party government.[34] The result was the Arusha declaration, adopted by TANU's National Executive Committee in January 1967 and published on 5 February. The document began by listing the principles of socialism as laid down in the TANU constitution, beginning with a bill of rights (equality, dignity, freedom of expression, movement, religion, and association), the right to work and receive a just return for labour, and the right to social protection and to participate in politics at all levels. It then moved to the responsibility of the state to intervene actively in economic life and the party's duties to ensure that the state's independence and freedom of its people were respected. The document's language sounded more orthodox than before: 'the state must have effective control over the principal means of production' and 'it is essential that the ruling party should be a party of peasants and workers.' The declaration specifically mentioned cooperation for the liberation of Africa, the promotion of African unity as duties of the state, and the commitment to participating in economic development to eliminate poverty, ignorance, and disease. It then described African Socialism and the features of the policy of self-reliance, stressing the limits of aid. 'It is stupid . . . for us to imagine that we shall rid ourselves of our poverty through financial assistance rather than our own financial resources,' repeated the declaration. 'Independence cannot be real if a nation depends upon gifts and loans from another for its development.'[35] Agriculture was the basis and hard work a

90 Sara Lorenzini

condition for development to thrive. *Ujamaa* villages were socialist organisations created by the people and governed by those who lived and worked in them.

Good leadership was essential: 'Leaders must set a good example to the rest of the people in their lives and in all their activities,' recited the declaration. It was a principle that guided Nyerere's personal life, too. A Leadership Code was introduced as a set of concrete prescriptions to control the activities of political leaders. The Arusha declaration was a coherent and consistent document relevant to Tanzania's social and economic problems. Nyerere had an 'undoubted capacity – if only by African standards – for creative and original thinking,' remarked an Australian diplomat with a smidge of racism.[36] Nyerere hoped that rural cooperatives operating on a voluntary basis could prevent what was called the *kulakization* of Tanzanian agriculture – that is the birth of a class of rich peasants who hired other peasants as labourers.[37] Leaders must not turn masters, he worried, fearing the growth of a class society.[38]

Not all TANU leaders approved the radical turn introduced with the Arusha declaration. The cohesion that characterised the early years disappeared after independence, and the lines between friendship, ideological allegiance, and political loyalty blurred. Oscar Kambona's case was the most dramatic. Kambona was TANU's general secretary, the most prominent party leader after Nyerere, and his close friend. In 1967, Nyerere regarded his opposition as a personal betrayal and forced him into exile, breaking up his previous unitarian ideals. Increasingly, after that time, Nyerere used aggressive tactics against his opponents. Behind the apparent goal of eliminating corruption from the party and government, he established authoritarian practices and crushed any debate about the dangers of socialist policies.[39]

Ujamaa attracted extraordinary attention as a political experiment. Several leftist intellectuals went to study the Tanzania experiment at the University of Dar es Salaam, turning the city into a hub for radical politics.[40] In 1967, Kenyan intellectual Ali Mazrui gave a name to 'the romantic spell that Tanzania casts on so many': Tanzaphilia. It often turned into proper 'Nyererephilia,' he added. Foreign intellectuals praised Nyerere because they recognised him as a fellow intellectual with political power. Original *Ujamaa* plans were widely endorsed by the Catholic Church, too. Special consideration was devoted to education, which had a fundamental role in building Tanzania's national project. Notably, there was an explicit appreciation of the fact that Nyerere – a devout Catholic – did not intend to dismantle the country's missionary-based educational structures.[41] The early enthusiasm of the Church soon turned into scepticism and, later, open criticism. 'Violence, forcing, injustice, and failure' were the words the Episcopal Conference used in 1972 to describe life in *Ujamaa* villages.[42] Capturing the peasants was no easy operation, and *Ujamaa* seemed to have failed at it. Villages lacked funds for both investment and qualified cadres, and the peasants concentrated their efforts on private plots due to the lack of incentives to work on communal farms.[43] Many disillusioned commentators attacked villagisation because it rarely improved production.

Instead, it created economically unproductive communities that refused to cooperate with the state. Mainly, it served as a means for local officials to gain power
over small farmers. To maintain strong leadership and control over the operation,
Nyerere brought labour unions, youth movements, and religious groups into a close
alliance with party policy. However, the concentration of power in local authorities
resulted in widespread corruption, oppressive client networks, and the authorities'
violent response to local resistance against the system.[44] It was exactly a fate that
Nyerere had always wanted to avoid.

In November 1973, disappointed by the results, Nyerere changed the line. 'It is
not easy to change the ideas of peasants,' he commented bitterly. He dismissed his
idea that living in *Ujamaa* villages had to be a free choice.[45] Villagisation became
compulsory. The resettlement campaign (Operation Planned Villages) lasted until
1976. It reminded too many of the forced population movements and the repressive
policies of colonial times. Farming with modern techniques was equally associated with colonialism.[46] Eventually, some 13 million people, the vast majority of
the rural population, were registered in 7,000 villages. According to a government
survey in 1978, none of them achieved the official targets of the *Ujamaa* policy.
In 1979, Nyerere sadly commented that although 60 per cent of the people were
now living in socialist villages, they did not live as socialists.[47] Overall, the plan
was economically counterproductive and disrupted the ecological balance of the
traditional rural economy.

Ujamaa was popularised from the beginning as a unique model of self-reliance
close to the Chinese experience. It shared with China an ideological emphasis on
agricultural labour and the communal village. In 1965, Nyerere visited China for
the first time. He would go 13 times in total. He admired the discipline and frugal-
ity in the Chinese countryside. He decided to work with the Chinese because they
emphasised non-interference, contrary to the Soviet Union, which insisted on orthodoxy and turning TANU into a vanguard party.[48] Even the Chinese, though, wanted
to use their aid to Tanzania for propaganda purposes. At the end of Nyerere's first
visit, they tried to have him sign a joint communique condemning US aggression
worldwide and asked him to side with China against the Soviet Union officially.
Nyerere did not accept this invitation. 'We will not allow our friends to choose our
enemies,' he declared.[49] Throughout the 1960s, Tanzania's relationship with China
was the most significant of its links to socialist states or foreign entities. Recipro-
cally, the connection to Tanzania was the deepest of China's relationships with
African countries at the time. In 1964 alone, China donated $45.5 million worth of
aid to Tanzania – nearly half of its annual aid to the African continent. This assistance included a whole range of projects, products, and services: a labour-intensive
textile mill, a joint shipping line, state farms, books, broadcasting equipment, and
medical care.[50] In March 1969, China became the main supplier of weapons and
training to Tanzania and Tanzania-based freedom fighters.[51]

From his first visit to China, Nyerere brought home an agreement for the Tanzania–
Zambia railroad, the Tazara Railway, also known as Africa's Freedom Railway.

92 Sara Lorenzini

Chinese teams moved in within a year and began planning a thousand-mile route through the rugged terrain of southern Tanzania. Construction began in 1970 and was completed ahead of schedule in 1975 for $400 million, offered as an interest-free loan. The railway would allow Zambia to export its copper without depending on the railways and ports, still under white minority rule in Rhodesia, Angola, and South Africa. Despite being an old colonial enterprise, it was now reinterpreted as a project for national identity.[52] The fact that other donors, both the superpowers and traditional European donors, had rejected the project because they thought it economically unviable made it the ideal showcase for Chinese aid, the symbol of China's ability to offer an alternative. Moreover, by completing the railway before the original deadline, the entire project was seen as a substantial testimonial to Chinese and African labour efficiency.[53]

The cooperation between Zambia and Tanzania – two former colonies uniting against white imperial rule – added ideological, pan-African meaning to the enterprise. This element was essential to Nyerere. Since the workers came from Zambia and Tanzania and represented several ethnic groups, the project was presented as a way of building solidarity. The workers learnt technical skills through example on-site, a necessity that was soon translated into pedagogical and ideological principles. Tazara Railway stations were incorporated into *Ujamaa* villages, thus uniting the two big projects and symbols of Chinese aid. The first resettlements along the railway track started in 1973 and were to be completed by 1977. Workers who had built the railway were to serve as settlers, an avant-garde of modernisers who would catalyse settlement.[54] This did not happen. On the contrary, locals saw the deeply unpopular population transfers as being brought about by nothing other than violent measures.

The 1970s brought Nyerere to the peak of his power both domestically and internationally, but it was also a decade of enormous frustration. Nyerere's socialist policies, enthusiastically adopted by his compatriots and often supported by sympathetic western European nations in the early 1960s, failed to spur economic development in Tanzania. Villagisation violated Nyerere's repeated statements in support of popular participation in decisions. It disrupted rural farm production, and many villages depended on famine relief for years. Food imports skyrocketed, depleting the foreign exchange reserves. One-third of the national budget was supplied by foreign aid.[55] Negative nicknames started to be associated with Nyerere in popular discussions. He was described as cunning, tricky, and cruel and criticised for the concentration of power in his hands and for his refusal to get advice on economic and political reforms.[56] With Tanzania plunging into an economic crisis that worsened with the 1978–1979 war against Uganda, Nyerere's authority was not uncontested anymore. The merger of TANU with the Afro-Shirazi Party in Zanzibar in 1975 had brought him nearly total control of the country through the party structure. He was now overseeing a police state administered by officials whose habits he could not fully dominate. Regional commissioners used preventive detention against political opponents. The Special Branch of the police force and the

Julius Nyerere **93**

paramilitary Field Force contained strikes, protests, and grassroots resistance. Notwithstanding the best intentions, the one-party state had turned into authoritarian rule. Eventually, in 1983, a group of military officers attempted a coup that did not come off.[57]

The Third World leader: Nyerere's pan-Africanism from anti-apartheid activism to the new international economic order

As a major force behind the modern pan-African movement and one of the founders in 1963 of the Organization of African Unity, Nyerere became an icon of Third-Worldism in the 1970s. Promoting *Ujamaa* as an innovative model of African Socialism based on self-reliance made Nyerere an example of creative leadership worldwide. As the president of a poor nation trying to build socialism on its own while involved in the liberation of the whole of southern Africa, Nyerere positioned himself as a vital spokesman of the Third World. He travelled to Cuba, Sweden, and Yugoslavia and participated in the meetings of the Non-Aligned Movement, the Organization of African Unity, and the United Nations. His engagement on the broader international scene had two components. The first was the political commitment to fighting apartheid and supporting rebellions in southern Africa. The second was a new dedication to radical change in the international economic system, championing the New International Economic Order and promoting South–South agreements.

Nyerere's long-standing view was that freedom in one African country was guaranteed only when the entire continent was free from white minority rule. This led to Tanzania's commitment to aiding African rebel movements in the white-dominated states of southern Africa. Tanzania's leadership in support of the liberation movements bolstered Nyerere's militant credentials and helped him outflank those who criticised his good relations with Western countries. He was a strong advocate of economic and political measures against the apartheid policies of South Africa. Within the Organization of African Unity, Nyerere chaired a group of five African presidents who advocated the overthrow of white supremacy in Rhodesia, South Africa, and South West Africa/Namibia, accusing the white supremacist regimes of violating human rights. At the end of the 1960s, Dar es Salaam became a centre for national liberation fighters in southern Africa. It was a cosmopolitan city hosting multiple strands of political activists: academic 'fellow travelers' and journalists, emissaries of socialist countries, African American activists seeking engagement with the continent (many flocked to the city around the 1974 6th Pan African Congress), and especially members of southern African liberation movements in exile. As a consequence, it became a target of multiple terrorist attacks. The most dramatic case being the assassination of Frelimo's leader Eduardo Mondlane.[58]

Nyerere was on the front line in fighting white minority rule using the language of human rights. He was less vocal in accusing African autocrats because he feared that this would harm the prospect of African unity and could be used

94 Sara Lorenzini

by the countries of the Global North for their divide-and-rule strategy. After all, Tanzania did not have an immaculate record in terms of human rights, especially after the compulsory Operation Planned Villages of 1973–1976. 'For international purposes, we should act together. . . . We may criticize tyrannical, brutal, or unjust governments and regimes in the Third World, but we must not do this in the context of the North-South debate.'[59] This was Nyerere's fundamental concern. An exception was Idi Amin, who represented what Nyerere had most feared for independent Africa, xenophobic rule by populist dictators who instigated violence. He even went to war against him in 1979.

Ujamaa's economic failure was one factor that radicalised Nyerere's commitment to the international political economy. As time went on and agricultural production failed to increase, Nyerere blamed the situation on the iniquitous structure of international trade and became one of the most vocal sub-Saharan African proponents of the New International Economic Order (NIEO). By the mid-1970s, Tanzania received more foreign aid than any of its African neighbours. Paradoxically, much of it came from the very Western or northern countries whose exploitative practices Nyerere critiqued. His model of self-reliance with a tinge of socialism was not performing. A 1974 World Bank report on Tanzania was especially damning: the country had focused on social instead of economic investments and was now paying for its wrong choices with economic losses. Nyerere, however, was determined to resist the World Bank's and the IMF's attempts to impose checks on the Tanzanian economy. He certainly loathed the idea of his country becoming the guinea pig for what would soon go under the name of structural adjustment programmes. Therefore, he started getting involved with the NIEO project, seeking Third World support for a concerted action aiming at a radical reform of the international economic system. Soon, he became the most authoritative spokesperson of the Third World.

By the late 1970s, Nyerere was urging the Third World to come together as 'a trade union for the poor.'[60] In the international arena, he used the language of class struggle that he had rejected for his domestic policy a decade earlier. It was not the only change. Even the recipe of delinking from the world economy to achieve self-reliance was abandoned. In the 1970s, he began calling on the South to intensify its material demands on the rich countries of the Global North. In 1979, at a G-77 ministerial conference in Arusha, a disillusioned Nyerere called for Third World unity as the absolute priority. The world's developing nations discovered 'that hard work and prosperity were not cause and effect' and that 'individual efforts to develop our own national economy kept running into a solid wall of power – the power of the rich nations and the rich transnational corporations.'[61] Therefore, it was vital to negotiate a radical change in those rules that were made 'by the industrialized states to serve their purposes' in a world where

> seventy percent of the world's population – the Third World – commands together no more than 12 percent of the Gross World Product, whereas 80% of

the world's trade and investment, 93% of its industry, and almost 100 percent of its research is controlled by the industrial rich.[62]

The Third World nations, continued Nyerere, did not shape the world's institutions of production and exchange and had virtually no say in them. Nevertheless, they were dominated by them, by forces out of their control. This situation was regrettable and needed change. The only way to effectively change the world economic arrangements, insisted Nyerere, passed through unity. The way to achieve unity was South–South cooperation, a concept Nyerere introduced in 1979 that would soon become a new buzzword. The recipe was building up South–South trade; establishing Third World-owned multinational corporations and Third World international insurance; fostering research on Third World needs and resources, and constituting Third World-dedicated financial clearing institutions.

Nyerere had moved leftward at the international level, still thinking of a particular Third World path to socialism. But, at the dawn of structural adjustment, it was ultimately an impossible task. Unwillingly, pressured by the IMF, Nyerere presided over a domestic structural reform agenda at home. He stepped down from the presidency in 1985, just before his successor Ali Hassan Mwinyi signed an agreement with the IMF to undergo full structural adjustment. The following year, Nyerere was asked to head the South–South Commission, a new institutional home established by the leaders of the Non-Aligned Movement to define a vision and a road map for Third World countries to cooperate on issues of development. The South Commission hoped to give an economic identity to the South.

Devaki Jain, who was a commission member herself and worked in close cooperation with Nyerere, explains how his personality was fundamental to the task.[63] 'Wherever we went, she recalls, Nyerere was revered as a gentle but clear-headed leader of the ex-colonies.' Proud of his culture, he often narrated inspirational parables and anecdotes in Swahili. He was considered the Gandhi of the African continent 'because of his humility and generosity of spirit.' He insisted on building up Third World strength through South–South cooperation. His trust in the power of Third World solidarity and in the report written by the South Commission, titled *The Challenge to the South* and published in 1990, was touching. In November 1989, prior to the publication, he instructed Jain to tell the Chinese Prime Minister Li Peng 'that if India and China combine, they can defeat the North.' In 1990, he met with the prime ministers of Kenya (Daniel Arap Moi), Tanzania (Ali H. Mwinyi), and Uganda (Yoweri K. Museveni) and tapping his fingers on the book cover he said: 'Brothers, this is the book, this is your Bible . . . Take your country on this journey. It will be our second liberation.' Notwithstanding Nyerere's enthusiasm, the reality was that the commission's report was a thick but anaemic document, sanitised by the bureaucratic caution of too many conservative commissioners that were either bankers or senior international civil servants largely above 60 years of age, without any clue about the aspirations of people. The words of the Commission's secretary general Manmohan Singh are telling in this respect. When asked to

96 Sara Lorenzini

consult and give voice to people's movements in the South, he replied that he did not understand the concept of people's movements. Another thing he was probably not familiar with was how to deal with the media: the publication of *The Challenge to the South* went completely unnoticed in the press.[64] Nyerere, though, was unrelenting. He believed in the unity of the Global South as his mission, and whenever possible, he went on to stress the importance of this unity. Appointed as the Chairman of the South Centre, which in his dream should function as the OECD of the Global South, he emphasised the importance of collective action of the developing countries in international fora. He called on the G-77 member governments to fully exercise the potential of their collective influence on the global scene by working more closely together.

After Nyerere's death, a posthumous overall positive and nostalgic historical memory was built around his personality.[65] Romanticising Nyerere meant extolling qualities such as humility, integrity, and incorruptibility. Throughout his life, Nyerere held to high moral principles and did not fail to apply them to himself and to his concept of African leadership. His dream of promoting a moral economy based upon justice and equality for all in a society free of class conflict is a unique feature of Nyerere's leadership style and explains his charisma. Inclusiveness as a key to his political project, at both the national and international levels, is another fundamental element. Nyerere was special also because of his ability to adapt to changing times without giving up his fundamental principles. Some of the principles imbuing his leadership were not exclusive to him. At the turn of the 1960s, other African national independence leaders had similar priorities: the national project, the obsession with independence, and the imputation of all the evils to colonialism. Peculiar to Nyerere, though, was the abhorrence of conflict as a concept, even at a theoretical level, and during the fight for liberation. His special African Socialism without Marxism, rooted in a mythically idealised African precolonial society also shared elements with the inspirational projects of fellow African leaders of the 1960s. It proves how much pan-Africanism was a project with shared ideals, even if it centred on nation-building first. Again, in the 1970s, Nyerere shared a lot with his colleagues. This time it was about the frustration with the results of independence and the betrayal of the revolution of expectations. Such frustration resulted in radicalisation. In the case of Nyerere, radicalisation meant the commitment to transform the international economic order, joining forces to change a system ruled by an oppressive Global North.

Notes

1 Douglas Yates, "Bjerk Paul – *Julius Nyerere*," *Cahiers d'études africaines* 239 (2020), http://journals.openedition.org/etudesafricaines/31896; https://doi.org/10.4000/etudesa fricaines.31896.
2 Paul Bjerk, *Julius Nyerere* (Athens: Ohio University Press, 2017), 11.
3 Prospects of Mankind; Africa: Julius Nyerere Interview, 1959, www.youtube.com/watch?v=MSmYoNmN40s.

Julius Nyerere **97**

4   Daniel Speich, "The Kenyan Style of 'African Socialism': Developmental Knowledge Claims and the Explanatory Limits of the Cold War," *Diplomatic History* 33, no. 3 (June 2009): 449–66, here 451.

5   See also Issa G. Shivji, Saida Yahya-Othman, and Ng'wanza Kamata, *Development as Rebellion: Julius Nyerere – A Biography* (Dar es Salaam: Mkuki na Nyota, 2020), and the review by Suell, David Thomas, "Development as Rebellion: A Biography of Julius Nyerere: Issa G. Shivji, Saida Yahya-Othman, and Ng'wanza Kamata, Mkuki Na Nyota, Dar es Salaam, 2020, Xxiii+1208, ISBN: 9789987084111." *Contemporary Political Theory* 21, Suppl 1 (2022): 38–44.

6   Julius Nyerere on the East African Federation, www.youtube.com/watch?v=76x7K8tF0 9o&list=PLjj3W4i3WnZ7rqnZYJ2LWzba27KdTALJW&index=6.

7   Samuel Zalanga, "Julius Nyerere: Leadership Insights for Contemporary Challenges," in *Governance and the Crisis of Rule in Contemporary Africa: Leadership in Transformation*, eds. Ebenezer Obadare and Wale Adebanwi (New York, NY: Palgrave Macmillan, 2016).

8   Bjerk, *Julius Nyerere*, 14.

9   John Iliffe, *A Modern History of Tanganyika* (Cambridge: Cambridge University Press, 1979).

10 Andreas Eckert, *Herrschen und Verwalten: Afrikanische Bürokraten, Staatliche Ordnung un Politik in Tanzania, 1920–1970* (München: Oldenbourg Verlag, 2007), 232.

11 Ibid., 199–200. Twining was well known in the Colonial Office for his talent in inventing traditions – a talent that was clearly not appreciated by modern leadership in Tanganyika and that ended up being counterproductive; see Terence Ranger, "The Invention of Tradition," in *The Invention of Tradition*, ed. Eric Hobsbawm and Terence Ranger (Cambridge: Cambridge University Press, 2012), 233–36.

12 N. Kamata, "Julius Nyerere: From a Territorial Nationalist to a Pan African Nationalist," *The African Review* 46, no. 2 (2020): 309–32, https://doi-org.gate3.library.lse.ac.uk /10.1163/1821889X-12340003.

13 https://ethics.utoronto.ca/wp-content/uploads/2017/11/Nyerere-UjamaaThe-Basis-of-African-Socialism-1962.pdf.

14 Julius K. Nyerere, *Freedom and Socialism/Uhuru na Ujamaa: A Selection from Writings and Speeches, 1965–1967* (London: Oxford University Press, 1968), Introduction, 28.

15 Ibid., 44.

16 Priya Lal, "A Postcolonial Project in the Cold War World," in *African Socialism in Postcolonial Tanzania: Between the Village and the World* (Cambridge: Cambridge University Press, 2015), 22–77. doi:10.1017/CBO9781316221679.003

17 Politisches Archiv des Früheren Ministeriums für Auswärtige Angelegenheiten (MfAA), A15067.

18 MfAA, A 15068.

19 The West Germans were influential because they were important donors, and they threatened to interrupt all aid flows in case Tanganyika signed an official agreement with the DDR. In July 1964, West German aid allocated for projects in Tanzania totalled DM 78 million Deutsche Mark (about $20 million). In addition, in October 1963, West Germany had sent military aid – planes and Bunderswehr instructors, see Sara Lorenzini, *Due Germanie in Africa: La cooperazione alla sviluppo e la competizione per i mercati di materie prime e tecnologie* (Firenze: Polistampa, 2003), 190–91.

20 https://ethics.utoronto.ca/wp-content/uploads/2017/11/Nyerere-UjamaaThe-Basis-of-African-Socialism-1962.pdf – on the contacts with socialist countries for aid supplies; see Jeremy Friedman, *Ripe for Revolution. Building Socialism in the Third World* (Cambridge, MA: Harvard University Press, 2022), 133.

21 International Bank for Reconstruction and Development, Economic Survey Mission to Tanganyika, *The Economic Development of Tanganyika: Report of a Mission Organized by the International Bank for Reconstruction and Development . . . at the Request*

98 Sara Lorenzini

of the Governments of Tanganyika and the United Kingdom (Baltimore: Johns Hopkins University Press, 1961).

22 William Glenn Gray, *Germany's Cold War: The Global Campaign to Isolate East Germany, 1949–1969* (Chapel Hill and London: University of North Carolina Press, 2003), 160–62, 78–79; Lorenzini, *Due Germanie in Africa*, 189–205.

23 MfAA, A 15113, 14.

24 Charles G. Thomas, "'Disgraceful Disturbances': TANU, the Tanganyikan Rifles, and the 1964 Mutiny," in *Dissent, Protest and Dispute in Africa*, ed. Toyin Falola and Emmanuel Mbah (London: Routledge, 2017).

25 The press conference is quoted in Bjerk, *Julius Nyerere*, 84.

26 MfAA, A 15069 and A 17980. See also for a discussion on this controversy George Roberts, *Revolutionary State-Making in Dar es Salaam: African Liberation and the Global Cold War, 1961–1974 (African Studies)* (Cambridge: Cambridge University Press, 2022), 106–9, doi:10.1017/9781009281621.

27 Bundesarchiv Berlin (BArchB), Nachlass Ulbricht, NY 4182, 1330.

28 MfAA C 779/75.

29 Meeting Babu-Lessing, MfAA A 15080; MfAA C 1467/72, 7.

30 Julius K. Nyerere, "Rhodesia in the Context of Southern Africa," *Foreign Affairs*, April 1, 1966, www.foreignaffairs.com/articles/zimbabwe/1966-04-01/rhodesia-context-southern-africa.

31 A. Grande, "Un maestro in paradiso," *Nigrizia* 94, no. 23 (December 1976): 14–15. See also Sara Lorenzini, *Global Development: A Cold War History* (Princeton: Princeton University Press, 2019), 113–19.

32 Dave Darby, "Ujamaa Undermined," *The Land* 19 (2016): 51–53, www.thelandmagazine.org.uk/articles/ujamaa-undermined.

33 On the Ruvuma Development Association: Andrew Coulson, *Tanzania: A Political Economy* (Oxford: Clarendon Press, 1982), 310–18.

34 Bjerk, *Julius Nyerere*, 98.

35 Julius K. Nyerere, *Ujamaa: Essays on Socialism* (Oxford: Oxford University Press, 1968), 13–37; quotes at 22–23, 35.

36 Australian High Commissioner, "The Arusha Declaration: A Novel Approach to African Problems," quoted by Friedman, *Ripe for Revolution*, 126.

37 Julius Nyerere, "Socialism and Rural Development, 1967," in Nyerere, *Freedom and Socialism*, 337–66.

38 Julius Nyerere, "Leaders Must Not Be Masters," in Nyerere, *Freedom and Socialism*, 136–42.

39 Bjerk, *Julius Nyerere*, 98–99. On the impact of the Leadership Code on Tanzania's politics on leadership, see Roberts, *Revolutionary State-Making in Dar es Salaam*, 85–93.

40 Ali Mazrui, "Tanzaphilia," *Transition* 31 (1967): 24–25 quoted in Eckert, *Herrschen und Verwalten*, 218.

41 P. R. Ballan, "Tanzania: La battaglia più dura," *Nigrizia* 86, no. 12 (December 1968): 16; also see "Speranze per il socialismo africano," *Nigrizia* 97, no. 20 (December 1979): 13.

42 A. De Carolis, "Dove va la Tanzania?," *Nigrizia* 90, no. 13–15 (July–August): 11–12.

43 Goran Hyden, *Beyond Ujamaa in Tanzania: Underdevelopment and an Uncaptured Peasantry* (Berkeley: University of California Press, 1980).

44 "Tanzania: Pace e comprensione reciproca," *Nigrizia* 90, no. 21 (November 1972): 40–43.

45 Bjerk, *Julius Nyerere*, 106.

46 On the downsides of Ujamaa, see Michael Jennings, *Surrogates of the State: NGOs, Development, and Ujamaa in Tanzania* (Bloomfield, CT: Kumarian Press, 2008), 37–74, 139–57.

47 P. Walbert Bühlmann, "Chiesa e socialismo in Africa: Speranze messianiche?" *Nigrizia* 97, no. 20 (1 December 1979): 32.

Julius Nyerere **99**

48 Friedman, *Ripe for Revolution*, 164, quoting the Soviet ambassador in 1974.
49 The Soviet report is quoted by Friedman, *Ripe for Revolution*, 136.
50 Lal, "A Postcolonial Project in the Cold War World," 62.
51 BArchB, NY 4182, 1330.
52 Jamie Monson, *Africa's Freedom Railway* (Bloomington: Indiana University Press, 2009), 15–20.
53 Jamie Monson, "Working Ahead of Time: Labor and Modernization During the Construction of the Tazara Railway, 1968–86," in *Making a World After Empire: The Bandung Moment and Its Political Afterlives*, ed. Christopher Lee (Athens: Ohio University Press, 2010), 239.
54 James C. Scott, *Seeing Like a State: How Certain Schemes to Improve the Human Condition Have Failed* (New Haven: Yale University Press, 1999), 227–29.
55 Coulson, *Tanzania*, 185–201, 235–62.
56 Marie-Aude Fouéré, "Julius Nyerere, Ujamaa and Political Morality in Contemporary Tanzania," in *Remembering Nyerere in Tanzania: History, Memory, Legacy* (Nairobi: Africae, 2015 (generated October 24, 2022), http://books.openedition.org/africae/713, ISBN: 9782957305803.
57 Bjerk, *Julius Nyerere*, 116–17, 141–42.
58 Andrew Ivaska, "Liberation in Transit. Eduardo Mondlane and Che Guevara in Dar es Salaam," in *The Routledge Handbook of the Global Sixties: Between Protest and Nation-Building*, C. Jian, M. Klimke, M. Kirasirova, M. Nolan, M. Young, and J. Waley-Cohen, 1st ed. (London: Routledge, 2018), 27–38, https://doi.org/10.4324/9781315150918. On the role of Dar es Salaam as a hub of radical politics around 1968 see Roberts, *Revolutionary State-Making in Dar es Salaam*, 173–83.
59 Nyerere's words are quoted in Samuel Moyn, *Not Enough: Human Rights in an Unequal World* (Cambridge, MA: The Belknap Press of Harvard University Press, 2018), 117.
60 Priya Lal, "African Socialism and the Limits of Global Familyhood: Tanzania and the New International Economic Order in Sub-Saharan Africa," *Humanity: An International Journal of Human Rights, Humanitarianism, and Development* 6, no. 1 (2015): 17–31, https://doi.org/10.1353/hum.2015.0011.
61 Julius K. Nyerere, "Unity for a New Order," *The Black Scholar, AFRICA: The New Societies* 11, no. 5 (May–June 1980), 55–63.
62 Nyerere was quoting Barbara Ward's data from J. D. Runnalls, Lenore D'Anjou, and Barbara E. Ward, *The Widening Gap: Development in the 1970s: A Report on the Columbia Conference on International Economic Development, Williamsburg, Virginia, and New York, February 15–21, 1970* (New York: Columbia University Press, 1971).
63 Devaki Jain, "Looking Back at the South Commission," *Economic and Political Weekly* 51, no. 9 (February 27, 2016): 62–66.
64 South Commission, *The Challenge to the South: Report of the South Commission* (Oxford: Oxford University Press, 1990).
65 Fouéré, "Julius Nyerere, Ujamaa and Political Morality in Contemporary Tanzania."

6

LEONID BREZHNEV

Rule through trust and care

Susanne Schattenberg

In Brezhnev's time, Soviet people joked that the country's history was divided into three eras: the pre-Petrine period, the Petrine period, and the Dnepro-Petrine period – that is the rule of Brezhnev, who filled many posts with his followers from Dnepropetrovsk.[1] This 'anecdote' is an important indication that the 18 years from 1964 to 1982 under Brezhnev were already understood by the population at that time as epoch-making: after the Middle Ages (pre-Petrine period) and the pre-modern era under Peter I came Soviet modernity: economic reforms, prosperity for all, and the status of the feared world power. Contrary to the mocking writings of the dissident and historian Roy Medvedev, Brezhnev was not a party secretary who left hardly any traces behind[2] but one who decisively shaped the Soviet Union. Admittedly, the points of reference for evaluating Brezhnev were and are usually less the Moscow and Petersburg empires than Stalin and Khrushchev. In fact, Brezhnev must be read as the antithesis or answer to both: After Stalin's terror and Khrushchev's reformist furore, he wanted to bring safe and satiated times to both the Central Committee (CC) and the people. As he himself is said to have put it:

> Under Stalin, the people feared repression; under Khrushchev, reorganisation and transfers. The people did not know what tomorrow would bring. That is why the Soviet people should live in peace in the future, in order to be able to work fruitfully.[3]

The argument to be put forward here is that Brezhnev was the most important and successful leader of the Soviet Union, who made it what it is remembered and glorified as today: a modern country with enormous economic potential, even if the second industrialisation did not succeed, a welfare state, albeit at a low level, a superpower that the West feared without reservation. He, and not Stalin

DOI: 10.4324/9781003426165-6

or Khrushchev, was thus the 'real' representative of the Soviet Union because he succeeded in stabilising the country and ensuring a 'normality' that made both Soviet citizens and people in the West believe that the Soviet Union would last forever.[4] In the best Foucaultian sense, Brezhnev made the Soviet Union a truth that – except for a few dissidents – no one questioned any more. But because extremes were expected of Soviet party leaders, especially in the West, Brezhnev was denied leadership qualities for a long time.[5] Stalin and Khrushchev fascinated: the first as a perpetrator of violence, the second as an intrepid enlightener. Brezhnev, on the other hand, appeared faceless, boring, grey. This impression was reinforced by his infirmity from the mid-1970s, when he appeared increasingly apathetic, bloated, and unable to act. For a long time, historians not only found him boring and vacuous; research on him was difficult because, unlike for the Stalin era, the archives were largely closed: his personal archive has become available only in 2014 but still only in parts, the Politburo minutes are accessible since 2018 but poorly indexed. Brezhnev's 'memoirs' were written by ghostwriters,[6] and his work diaries are to a large extent only 'to-do lists.'[7] It is therefore not surprising that until recently there were hardly any – especially serious – biographies of Brezhnev.[8]

It will be argued here (1) that Brezhnev was originally a completely apolitical person who would have liked to become an actor. He was a typical representative of Stalin's generation, born around 1905 and virtually forced into a career in vacant posts and in the reconstruction of the country not only by the terror but also by the devastation of the Second World War; (2) that after Stalin and Khrushchev he was not a 'stopgap' or interim candidate but brought with him the qualities for which the CC members yearned: He was friendly, even-tempered, obliging, and listened to his comrades; (3) that precisely in response to the miserable times of war and terror, he declared 'prosperity for all' to be the party's general line. He wanted to see the petit-bourgeois dream of a home of one's own – a dacha – and a car realised for all Soviet people, while in foreign policy he invested all his energies in a new rapprochement with the West.

From apolitical extra to party secretary

Childhood in Ukraine

Contrary to what is repeatedly assumed, Brezhnev was not of bourgeois but actually proletarian origin. Both his father and his mother's parents had come to Ukraine from Kursk and Belgorod respectively at the turn of the century to Kamenskoye (1936–2016 Dneprodzerzhinsk, today Kamianske) to find work in the ironworks there. Brezhnev's father Ilya had been working as an assistant at the iron rolling mill since 1900, where he met the young Natalya Mazolova, who brought lunch to her father.[9] In 1904, they married; in 1906, Leonid was born, and in 1910 and 1912 the siblings Vera and Jakob. The family lived four to a room as subtenants in the cottage of a blast furnace foreman.[10] Father Brezhnev, who started out as

102 Susanne Schattenberg

an unskilled assistant, did not rise to shift foreman until 1917.[11] Despite the confinement and modest means, Brezhnev seems to have had a carefree childhood. His biographers later had him say: 'Childhood is childhood. Here by the Dnieper everything was a joy to us: We would run down the steep slope, bathe, and swim over to the island.'[12] Football was probably one of his main pleasures.[13] There was nothing revolutionary about the family. On the contrary, Brezhnev's mother hung icons and had the children baptised.[14] What's more, the Brezhnevs belonged to the 'labour aristocracy,' which strove to achieve social advancement through education: both parents could read and write, owned a Sunday best in which they had themselves photographed in the photo studio, and they spared no expense to send their Leonid to the local grammar school from 1915, which was actually reserved for the sons of engineers and white-collar workers.[15] Brezhnev's mother apparently nursed the wish for her son to become an engineer, Leonid fancied the notary's car, and his father's most political act was to hide Jewish neighbours from pogroms.[16] The Brezhnevs were so far away from revolutionary activities that not even the ghostwriters of Brezhnev's memoirs dared to ascribe such things to them. Brezhnev's biographers also described his enthusiasm for Soviet power in 1917 only very discreetly, and even that was probably fictitious.[17] The revolution and the subsequent civil war destroyed the Brezhnevs' meagre prosperity. They experienced the killing, looting, and raping by the 'Reds' and 'Whites' from 1918 to 1920, between which the city alternated more than 20 times.[18] Leonid barely survived a typhus epidemic, and with famine looming, the Brezhnevs decided to flee Kamenskoye for their father's home in Kursk in the summer of 1921. The fact that Brezhnev became a worker in the metalworks that summer at the age of 15 was freely invented by his biographers – the factory had been idle since 1919.[19]

Jobbing and studying in Kursk

What followed for Brezhnev were four years of unskilled work as a packer in a cooking oil factory in Kursk, a job that served only to survive and was so 'unproletarian' that his biographers later avoided mentioning it.[20] Brezhnev toiled for two years solely to contribute to the family's upkeep before taking up studies at the Technical College for Land Survey in 1923. Whether he didn't know what to do during this time, whether he didn't get a place at university, or simply didn't have time besides the hard work – we don't know. His fondness for theatre began with his studies at the latest. He played in an amateur acting troupe and is said to have earned his studies as an extra at the local theatre.[21] In the 1960s and 1970s, he still entertained his staff with his acting talent when he recited the poem 'Anna Snegina' by his favourite poet Sergei Yesenin or Dmitri Merezhkovsky's ballad 'Zakya Muni' by heart while standing on a chair at the hunting lodge Zavidovo.[22] A few days before Khrushchev's fall, he told the opera singer Galina Vishnevskaya: 'No, why drink to me, we drink to the artists. What are politicians anyway, today we're here and tomorrow we're gone. But art is eternal. Let's drink to the artists!'[23] While he joined the communist youth organisation, the Komsomol, much too late at the age of 17, perhaps only to get a place at college, and was otherwise not involved with the communists,[24] Leonid amused himself with theatre, poetry, and dance, where he also met his wife Viktoriya in 1925.[25] When Brezhnev was transferred to the Urals in 1928, a year after graduating, they registered their marriage; their children Galina and Yuri were born in 1929 and 1933. Viktoriya, who was a qualified midwife, henceforth devoted herself to the children and the household.[26]

Flight from collectivisation

The fact that Brezhnev worked as a land surveyor from 1927 to 1930, first in the Kursk Oblast and then in the Sverdlovsk Oblast, later gave him the great advantage of also being considered an agricultural expert.[27] But at that time he was caught in the middle of the onset of collectivisation and *dekulakisation*, from whose excesses he finally fled to Moscow: his task was to survey the expropriated land and mark it out with stakes, to allocate the best land to the *kolkhozes,* the worst to the tolerated individual farmers, and to record this in the land register.[28] Brezhnev not only gave up the post of head of the Sverdlovsk land registry; he also joined the party very late. In 1929, he had applied and, being the employee he now was, had to hold out as a candidate for two years before becoming a full member in 1931.[29] This happened in Kamenskoye because the Brezhnev couple had only lasted three months in Moscow before fleeing from there as well: the city was overcrowded with peasants who had fled, so they could not find housing and returned home, where Leonid first hired himself out as a factory worker in the neighbouring town.[30] Later, the official biographies also kept this quiet: they simply postponed Brezhnev's change from agriculture to industry to 1931 and did not mention the months in Moscow and the double flight at all.[31]

From 1931 Brezhnev worked in the Kamenskoye metalworks during the day and studied at the Arsenichev Institute of Metallurgy in the evening.[32] In 1932, he became party secretary of the institute and had to go into battle against the 'kulaks' again.[33] In 1933, two years before graduating, he became head of the workers' and peasants' faculty in Kamenskoye. When he graduated as a thermal power engineer in 1935 and became a shift supervisor at the metal plant,[34] only to be drafted for one year's military service at the end of 1935,[35] the local newspaper raved,

> I can't imagine where this person gets so much energy and ability to work. . . . If he goes into production now, it is to be expected that the young engineer Leonid Brezhnev will give a lot. And he will give it . . . For he is forged of hard metal.[36]

Rise during the great terror

Until 1937, Brezhnev had distinguished himself through his acting and organisational skills; instead of Lenin or Stalin, he had fancied the avant-garde poet

104 Susanne Schattenberg

Vladimir Mayakovsky, he had only joined the Komsomol and the party when he could no longer avoid it, and he had fled hunger, violence, and housing shortages three times. Nothing pointed to a significant party career until the Great Terror of 1937/1938 created so many vacancies that Brezhnev was literally catapulted up the ranks. After his return from military service in the Far East at the end of 1936, he was in charge of the Dneprodzerzhinsk Technical College for a few months[37] and was targeted by the NKVD because he had added an extension to the teaching building without the party's permission.[38] Nevertheless, in May 1937, he was elected to the city party committee and in August, as the arrests increased, he became deputy chairman of the city council, a kind of mayor, with responsibility for building and public utilities.[39] From now on there was no meeting that did not deal with 'enemies of the people.' Brezhnev was also forced to take a stand on the expulsion from the party of his comrades, colleagues, and friends. We do not know what was going on inside him when his former supporters from the Institute and the party were shot. At the party meetings, however, he was one of those who did not yell 'shoot to kill' but tried to steer the discussion back to the substantive issues at hand.[40] It is significant that he asked – in vain – that his candidacy for the party office be cancelled.[41] At that time, hardly anyone made a career because he or she liked it but because the party demanded it. So the promotions followed every year: in 1938, he moved there as head of the trade department of the party area committee of Dnepropetrovsk. Here he became secretary for propaganda in 1939, third secretary in 1940, and secretary for armaments in March 1941.[42]

Stalinist methods, Khrushchev's protection

Even in these years Brezhnev profited from the indirect protection of Khrushchev, who in 1938 as the new party secretary of Ukraine built up his own clientele, which soon included Brezhnev through a few intermediaries.[43] Since these years, the patron–client relationships developed that were later to become infamous as the 'Dnepropetrovsk Mafia.' It can only be assumed that it was the experience of the terror of 1937/1938, the inhuman pressure to succeed, which could tip over into accusations of sabotage at any time, and the omnipresent enemy hysteria that welded the Dnepropetrovsk clique together. In those days, it was crucial to be able to trust people not to accuse you of being an 'enemy of the people,' expose you as a 'traitor' and vote to expel you from the party. There was no guarantee of this, but perhaps the hope that people who had a similar biography, came from the same region, shared the same alma mater, had been protected by the same patron and bore the same responsibilities would have greater inhibitions about denouncing a comrade. It was these networks, and Khrushchev in particular, that helped Brezhnev to a rapid career also after the war. Brezhnev experienced the war himself as a simple political commissar near the front. Contrary to what his memoirs would later have us believe, he was neither directly at the front nor did he have command responsibility.[44] But once again he proved himself as an organiser of supplies, who, for example, urgently appealed for the soldiers to finally be provided with winter clothing.[45] The horrors he experienced, even three kilometres behind the front, were horrific and motivation enough to later seek a settlement with the West to avoid another war at all costs.

After Brezhnev had spent a year after the end of the war as a military man promoting the Sovietisation in Carpathian Ukraine,[46] Khrushchev ensured that when he was demobilised in the summer of 1946, he came to Zaporozhye as party leader. Here he was tasked with nothing less than the rebuilding of the famous Dnieper dam destroyed by the Germans, including the power station and the steelworks.[47] After he had mastered this hardly manageable task, Khrushchev sent him only one year later as Party Secretary to Dnepropetrovsk, which also still lay in ruins.[48] After a brief period as a CC inspector in Moscow in the early summer of 1950,[49] Stalin – on Khrushchev's recommendation – sent him as First Party Secretary to Moldova, where, just as in 1945 in Carpathian Ukraine, Soviet power with all its institutions still had to be established.[50] Brezhnev remained head of the Republic for two years before Stalin called him to Moscow. He not only appointed him to the Politburo, which had been expanded into a 'Presidium,' but also made him CC Secretary. Both posts served only Stalin's power rankings – Brezhnev lost both immediately with Stalin's death in March 1953.[51]

Party Secretary of a new type

Brezhnev was later accused, and still is, of rehabilitating Stalin after 1964. But at no time did he suffer as he did under Stalin: this began with the violence of collectivisation, continued with the loss of friends and supporters in the Great Terror, and probably reached its climax when Stalin called him at night in 1947 to demand the timely restart of the Zaporozhye Iron and Steel Works.[52] In this highly threatening situation, in which Brezhnev was expected to meet arbitrary deadlines, while he had neither sufficient material nor machinery at his disposal, he demonstrated his greatest quality: not losing his head, not shouting his people down and threatening them with prison but calmly but forcefully appealing to them to master the situation with a united effort.[53] This ability also characterised his actions later in Dnepropetrovsk and Moldova: where others indulged in Stalin-speak and demanded the unmasking of enemies of the people, Brezhnev discreetly but firmly refrained from doing so and appealed to concentrate on the factual problems. He himself got into the habit of sleeping in a camp bed in the factory in such situations and not going home until plan fulfilment could be reported.[54] He demanded the same dedication from all the other comrades involved and could also raise his voice if he had the impression that factory managers, *kolkhoz* chairmen or local party secretaries were shirking their tasks. Oleg Khlevnyuk and Yoram Gorlitsky have called this attitude of neither behaving as a despot nor serving others as a puppet, but rather acting according to clear rules and principles, that of the 'strong party secretary,' which prevailed in the 1950s.[55] Brezhnev was one of the forerunners of this new type.

106 Susanne Schattenberg

He stretched to the maximum the scope for action and discourse that he had under Stalin to avoid the rhetoric of traitors to the people. He can thus by no means be called a Stalinist. Quite the contrary, constant haste and fear gave him a heart attack in 1952 at the age of just 45.[56] He later condemned the Great Terror several times as a violation of the constitution: 'The Party has firmly denounced this practice and it should never be repeated.'[57]

What remained from the Stalin era for Brezhnev was failing health and insomnia as well as excellent organisational skills and an extensive knowledge of the wretched living conditions of the people he met in Ukraine, Moldova, and, from 1954–1956, Kazakhstan. Khrushchev had remembered Brezhnev in 1954 and sent him to Kazakhstan, first as Second Party Leader, then from 1955 as First Party Leader, to implement the Virgin Land Campaign there.[58] Living conditions were still catastrophic, an infrastructure basically non-existent and the plans still utopian, but the big difference with Stalin was that the provinces were now allowed to demand everything they needed from Moscow: people, machines, and material.

With and against Khrushchev

Khrushchev thanked Brezhnev for his great commitment and loyalty by appointing him back to Moscow in 1956 and making him CC Secretary. When Stalin's old supporters wanted to overthrow Khrushchev in 1957, Brezhnev was one of those who organised the majority for Khrushchev.[59] As CC secretary in charge of the arms industry, the glamour of the Sputnik and space flights also shone on him.[60] But he probably had his best time when he became Chairman of the Presidium of the Supreme Soviet, that is President of the Soviet Union, in 1960–1964 and travelled the world.[61] But in the meantime, his relationship with Khrushchev had deteriorated, who apparently thought his power was untouchable after the Sputnik scoop and surviving the coup. He began to tease, bully, and arbitrarily transfer his CC comrades, who had once ensured his political survival, as he saw fit.[62] It was not so much the domestic political failures or the foreign policy embarrassments that led to his removal. When Khrushchev announced before his holiday in September 1964 that the party presidium was a 'bunch of old men,' which he would blow apart on his return, they decided to act.[63] It was Brezhnev who led the mutineers, ordered Khrushchev back to Moscow from his holiday, and was consequently elected as the new First Secretary on 14 October 1964 – and General Secretary again from 1966.[64]

Ruling style: the staging of 'collective rule'

The authors of recent studies agree that Brezhnev was the most successful representative of the Soviet style of leadership.[65] This was decisively shaped by the experience under Khrushchev: under him, Brezhnev had learnt how to organise majorities – and how to lose them. The fear that he might suffer the same fate as

Khrushchev must have accompanied him all his life. Yet he had all the qualities that the CC members longed for after 40 years under Stalin and Khrushchev: he was introverted, friendly, patient, even-tempered, not inclined to extremes, and always ready to take on the concerns of others. Even his critic Roy Medvedev judged that Brezhnev did not want to be a 'leader with a hard hand.'[66] His aide Georgi Arbatov agreed: 'One of his merits was that he was not vicious and not cruel. . . . He was a generally simple person, even a democratic.'[67] To secure his rule in the long term, Brezhnev developed a 'scenario of power' that made his leadership appear as the long-awaited redemption of collective rule and consensus. 'Scenario of power' is a term introduced by Richard Wortman to explain the tsars' technique of rule, which was not based on physical violence but on imaginary worlds, rituals, and staging.[68] Under Brezhnev, too, the exercise of rule was strongly ritualised; its decisive factor was that all potential rivals were involved in the staging and became actors in the scenario themselves.[69] This type of domination was strongly performative because it manifested itself over and over again in the individual acts – unofficial meetings such as sessions, speeches and debates, votes and decisions. Brezhnev chose 'trust and care' as his scenario: the party was to follow him in the belief that he was not threatening their lives, like Stalin, nor their careers, like Khrushchev.[70] He publicly proclaimed this promise at the twenty-third Party Congress in March 1966, when he proclaimed 'trust in the cadres' and 'cadre stability' as the new guidelines of his policy.[71] The constant invocation of collective leadership may at first glance seem no different from Stalin's and Khrushchev's practice of rule, but unlike Stalin, Brezhnev did not achieve consensus through fear, and unlike Khrushchev, he did not intimidate the members of the Presidium through taunts, slurs, and vicious nicknames. Essentially, four practices were part of this scenario of trust and caring: joint editing of resolution texts, joint speech writing, plus a patronage policy that made every ouster look like a caring promotion, and finally, familiarisation in the Politburo. Brezhnev not only referred to the 'exchange of opinions in the Politburo' throughout his life and always spoke of the collective 'we,' never in the first person singular.[72] He also reactivated the editorial commissions, which were traditionally appointed by the CC plenum to edit the CC resolutions and for which Khrushchev in the end had only scorn and derision. Brezhnev not only took them seriously but acted here as a moderator who let everyone have their say. When the first discussant at the March 1965 plenary suggested deleting the entire second page of the resolution, Brezhnev merely asked cheerfully what opinions there were on the matter.[73] He found in the drafting commissions an arena in which he could demonstrate better than in the formalised and highly ritualised plenary sessions that he did not force his opinion on anyone, listened to everyone, and let everyone finish speaking. Although no more editorial commissions were set up after 1970, Brezhnev practised enough other forms in which he symbolically submitted to the will of the collective. For example, he had his own leave approved by the Politburo. On 22 June 1979, he declared that he wanted to go on holiday to the Crimea from 25 June and, if the comrades did not object, he would leave the following day. They replied

108 Susanne Schattenberg

unanimously: 'Right, Leonid Ilyich, you need to rest, the time is ripe for you to take a holiday.'[74] This was not an actual vote or discussion about the sense or nonsense of summer vacations; decisive was the ritual with which Brezhnev subordinated himself to the will of the collective.

'Labour-intensive decisions'

The demonstration of collective will was also at the forefront when all Politburo members signed all decisions together. Fyodor Burlatzky, Khrushchev's loyalist, reports: 'Under [Brezhnev], the practice of labour-intensive votes blossomed in full splendour, requiring dozens of signatures on the drafts, which in the end twisted or distorted the whole meaning of the decision taken.'[75] What sometimes caused frowns abroad[76] was, for Brezhnev, an assurance not to rise above the collective and thus be sidelined. He prevented resentment by having each of his speeches proofread beforehand. While Stalin wrote his speeches himself and Khrushchev at least provided the punchlines himself, Brezhnev made speechwriting a collective writing process. On 16 September 1965, he sent the draft for his speech at the upcoming plenum to all CC members, stating: 'I am sending you my draft speech. I ask for your comments. I am continuing to work on it. L. Brezhnev.'[77] He maintained this practice until the end of his life. Brezhnev's aide Alexandrov-Agentov recalls the joint writing as an agonising experience:

> Once I had to be present at a meeting where collectively, about 15 men in all (Politburo members and candidates, CC secretaries, one or two heads of department from the CC) were drafting the text of a letter whose task was to bring the leadership of the KPČ to its senses. It was a terrible spectacle! For several hours in a row they worked on the text, each trying to insert his opinion, which not infrequently contradicted the others.[78]

But that was precisely Brezhnev's strategy: he let his comrades argue, and only when the extremes were off the table and a centre line had been found did he interfere and add his nuances.[79] In this way, he assured himself of the loyalty of his comrades, because no one could say that his opinion had not been included. Brezhnev himself put it this way: 'Complete democracy and freedom of opinion in the discussion of any question, and iron discipline once a majority decision has been reached – that is the immutable law of our party.'[80]

Loss of power through promotion

Brezhnev's power was also based on the fact that he staged the dismissal of potential rivals and the promotion of his own entourage as consensus decisions and at the same time presented himself as a concerned party leader acting in the interests of the cadres. Typical was the way he pushed through his client as interior minister in 1966, although CC Secretary Shelepin and KGB head Semichastny presented a different candidate. Brezhnev pretended to agree with them but then invited the Politburo members to hunt at his dacha and drank and talked with them until a consensus was reached for his henchman from Dnepropetrovsk.[81] The actual loss of power often came in the guise of a formal promotion: Politburo members became deputy ministers, former ministers became influential party secretaries, and CC members were sent as ambassadors to the West. Brezhnev was scrupulous in making sure that he appeared to be a carer who was genuinely concerned about the welfare of the person who had been dismissed. When he deposed Moscow party leader Nikolai Yegorychev in 1967, he called him, 'You must please excuse me, it had to be done . . . But don't you have any worries, family or otherwise?'[82] In fact, Yegorychev's daughter had just married and was assigned a flat by Brezhnev; Yegorychev himself became ambassador to Denmark. In this way, Brezhnev ousted all his co-conspirators between 1965 and 1977. He always made sure not only that the Politburo stood behind his decision but also that the person concerned played along. Ukrainian Party leader Petro Shelest recounts how Brezhnev staged his dismissal in 1972: at the CC plenum, everyone else was huddled around Brezhnev's room during the lunch break, but he was not invited. Finally, Brezhnev called him in and said that he had been in Ukraine for ten years, that it was time for a change of scenery; if you work in one place for a long time, you lose your feeling, you start to get on people's nerves, and people get on your nerves, in short: he was needed in Moscow as deputy prime minister. Shelest remembered: ' "With great pain in my heart I said: well then, if I have no choice, do what you want." He stood up, kissed me and said "Thank you!" '[83]

Familiarity

Finally, Brezhnev relied on another means to distance himself from both Stalin's terror and Khrushchev's humiliations: he tried to appear as a friend and a family member, thus creating trust and familiarity. It began with Brezhnev telephoning his entourage and party secretaries all over the country for several hours every day, even when he was on holiday.[84] He enquired about the family as well as economic plans and party affairs, signalling that he cared about everything.[85] Every Thursday he gathered all secretaries for the CC meeting, who travelled from all over the Union to attend.[86] On the evenings before the plenary sessions of the Supreme Soviet, 15–20 regional and district secretaries always met at Brezhnev's home for an open exchange.[87] Brezhnev also allowed himself to be called 'Lyonya' by all Politburo members;[88] while this would have been unthinkable in Stalin's time and Khrushchev ended up using a swear name for everyone,[89] Brezhnev used affectionate pet names for most of them: Andropov he called – Yura, Chernenko – Kostya, to Gromyko – Andryusha, etc.[90]

110 Susanne Schattenberg

The domestic policy programme: prosperity for all

The prevailing opinion, most recently held by Leonid Mlechin, is that Brezhnev had no programme.[91] However, Brezhnev's entourage asserts that he did have goals, but they were very simple: all Soviet people should live better and no longer have to fear war.[92] His programme was mainly to continue Khrushchev's reforms. There is still much debate today about whether the late Soviet Union was a welfare state and whether the social programmes and benefits actually met the standards of a modern welfare state.[93] But no matter what criteria one tends to apply here, it was Brezhnev's declared will to secure a better standard of living for the population. 'People's prosperity' or 'people's welfare' were not just terms that Brezhnev invoked again and again but a concept that he adopted as a political guideline for the party, economic growth, and the five-year plans developed under him.[94] In a list of proverbs he kept in his office, he had underlined a quote from Albert Camus: 'The good of all comes from the happiness of each.'[95] Raising living standards remained his leitmotif, which he varied only slightly. While Brezhnev initially justified national prosperity by saying that it was an incentive for working people to work more and better, in 1970, he moved to reverse the causality and declare an adequate standard of living a prerequisite for better productivity.[96] Then, in the late 1970s, he blatantly declared the raising of the people's welfare to be the 'general line of the party.'[97] The agricultural and Kosygin's economic reforms of 1965, the lowering of the retirement age, the increase in wages and pensions, and the introduction of the five-day week served to improve the standard of living.[98] But Brezhnev went even further: according to his ideas, every Soviet citizen should live in his own flat and own a car so that he or she could drive to the countryside, to the dacha. In 1966, the Soviet government signed an agreement with Fiat to build a car plant on the Volga, which was to produce 600,000 cars a year from 1970.[99] This unconditional course towards the people's welfare is also called the 'little deal' that Brezhnev entered into with the people: he exchanged prosperity for loyalty.[100] Brezhnev called it 'developed socialism.'[101] The new policy was both pragmatism and ambition.[102] It replaced Khrushchev's reckless promise of 1962 that the Soviet people would be living under communism in 1980.[103] With 'developed socialism' Brezhnev claimed to have already reached a new stage of social development, characterised by people's demands for consumption and intensive growth of the economy: 'The main battlefield of the Soviet people for the victory of communism is the economy, the creation of the material and technical basis for communism.'[104] Brezhnev had at least two motives for raising the standard of living: first, he had seen so much misery since his childhood that he probably felt an honest need to see the population fed and warm. Second, he was aware of the consequences a poor supply situation could have. Not only had there been riots and deaths in Novocherkassk in 1962 because of rising meat prices, but the Politburo also attributed the uprisings and strikes in Hungary, Czechoslovakia, and Poland in 1956, 1968, and 1970 to the poor supply situation.[105] If Khrushchev had only touched the gold reserves after the crisis to buy grain abroad, this became the rule under Brezhnev: they bought whole breeding stations and for millions of dollars fodder, grain, cooking oil, sugar, and so on.[106] But Moscow did not only need grain and meat to keep its own population satisfied or to enable generous deliveries to the CSSR after 1968 and to Poland after 1981.[107] The proliferation of grain was also crucial for the Cold War.[108] Brezhnev warned in 1968 that while the capitalist countries accounted for 95 per cent of the world's grain exports, the socialist states, with only 7 per cent of the market, were in danger of losing influence over the decolonised countries.[109] Brezhnev understood very well that the Soviet Union was living beyond its means and regularly denounced its lagging behind the United States at the semi-annual CC plenums. But he neither wanted to limit consumption and subsidies for agriculture nor was he in a position to bring about substantial reforms. As long as Kosygin lived, he blamed the prime minister and his ministers for the failures in converting industry to intensive growth.[110]

The foreign policy programme: harmony in the East, peace with the West

'Primus inter pares'

As General Secretary, Brezhnev had no official authority to be active in foreign policy, but as leader of the CPSU, Brezhnev was the first point of contact for the chairmen in the Warsaw Pact states. The idea that the Soviet General Secretary controlled or even suppressed the other party leaders has long been disproved.[111] The inter-party relations were much more complex: there was a sensitive web of mutual dependencies. Brezhnev's relationship with the brother party leaders was like that of a patron to his clients; he treated them like the CC secretaries of the Union republics.[112] Yet he tried to avoid the impression that he was claiming a special role for himself. He used his ruling scenario here as well: he showed the same fatherly manner, was interested in the concerns of the others, listened patiently, and tried to help as much as he could. They spoke regularly on the phone and visited each other on revolutionary holidays and anniversaries or went hunting together.[113] Brezhnev thus tried to build trust and expected loyalty in return. His partners sometimes took advantage of this: they were dependent on many raw material supplies from the big brother, especially its oil and gas.[114] Repeatedly, they threatened relatively openly that if the Soviet Union did not meet their demands, they would not be able to guarantee peace and order in their countries.[115] Especially after the suppression of the Prague Spring in 1968 and the proclamation of martial law in Poland in 1981, the Soviet leadership felt obliged to provide food, energy, and funds on a large scale to pacify the respective populations. The Moscow Politburo felt virtually blackmailed by Polish party leader Wojciech Jaruzelski when he warned the Moscow comrades that without economic aid Poland would go up in flames.[116] Brezhnev was also by no means the hardliner among them. The party leaders of the GDR and Poland in

112 Susanne Schattenberg

particular, Walter Ulbricht and Władysław Gomułka, were much quicker to call for drastic measures than Brezhnev was prepared to apply them, as was shown, for example, in the case of Prague in 1968. Nevertheless, the Soviet party leader had a kind of veto power: as long as he did not agree to an invasion, the Warsaw Pact states did not act either. But he could by no means dispose of them; he always had to assure himself of their loyalty.

Thus, Brezhnev's first step after Khrushchev's ouster was to engage in lively telephone and travel diplomacy with the brother states to prevent any possible irritation.[117] But after the final failure of the rapprochement with China in 1966, Nicolae Ceaușescu's departure from the Warsaw Pact in 1968 in protest against the invasion of Prague,[118] and Tito's remaining outside the alliance despite the good personal relationship with Brezhnev, the latter had to deal with a core group of five party leaders whom he tried to win over and with whom he shaped Warsaw Pact policy as 'collective rule': it consisted of the German Walter Ulbricht, with whom he had little sympathy – whose removal by Erich Honecker in 1971 he supported, although he did not like him either –, Antonín Novotný and, after Dubček's removal in 1969, Gustáv Husák in the CSSR, whom he strongly supported, the Polish hardliner Władysław Gomułka, whom he was able to replace in 1970 with his protégé Edward Gierek,[119] and finally János Kádár for Hungary, whom he himself had helped put into office in 1956, and Todor Zhivkov for Bulgaria, who was in office longer than Brezhnev. He got on well with them and invited them individually from 1968, and together from 1971, to the Crimea every summer. Some of these party leaders also regularly went there on holiday and came to his dacha to visit him.[120] Orthodox leaders like Ulbricht, Honecker, and Gomułka or even Ceaușescu, for whom Brezhnev had no particular sympathies, came only for a few hours or a day.[121] But those he did like, such as the Hungarian Kádár, sometimes spent several days in the Crimea, exchanging ideas with Brezhnev in an unofficial setting and recovering.[122]

Prague 1968

Brezhnev saw Dubček not only as his protégé but presumably also as a kind of 'Czechoslovak Brezhnev' who replaced the unpopular, not very sociable Novotny as a youthful party hopeful.[123] For Brezhnev, the 'Prague Spring' was therefore a cadre issue: at first a positive development, which he accompanied with goodwill, then a bitter disappointment when his protégé was neither willing nor able to stand up to the 'counterrevolution.'[124] It remained a 'staff problem': the decisive factor for Brezhnev and the Politburo in Moscow was to find a man willing to replace Dubček.[125] While Ulbricht, Gomułka, and Zhivkov soon demanded a tougher stance towards Prague, Brezhnev continuously consulted with Kádár, whom he valued as a level-headed interlocutor.[126] After several bilateral and multilateral meetings, which were ultimately fruitless from Brezhnev's point of view, Brezhnev called Dubček for the last time on 13 August 1968, eight days before the invasion, and made it clear in his jovial, fatherly tone that for him it was a question of trust between two comrades: 'Sasha, I understand that you are nervous, I understand that it is a very complicated situation for you. But do you understand that I am talking to you like a friend, I want only good things for you.'[127] Although Brezhnev stuck with Dubček for the longest time, and it was not only Soviet troops who invaded Prague in 1968, the West named the doctrine after him: from then on, the sovereignty of a state ended where the interests of the Warsaw Pact were touched.[128] For Brezhnev, the 'Prague crisis' was an important turning point: on the one hand, he presumably drew the conclusion to seek even closer ties with his comrades in the socialist foreign countries and established the Crimea meetings for this purpose. On the other hand, he had thus also entered the limelight of international politics for the West and was now considered a partner to be taken seriously. Finally, this is where his addiction to pills began: the conflicts with Dubček and the fear of 'losing' the CSSR affected him so much that he increasingly resorted to sleeping pills to find peace at night.[129]

The new 'big four'

Brezhnev never missed an opportunity to emphasise that his efforts for peace, détente, and disarmament grew entirely out of his experience in the Second World War.[130] As with Khrushchev, the horror of the Second World War had left such a deep mark on him that he wanted to prevent another war at all costs.[131] Brezhnev was well aware that it would take a long time before no one would talk about the 'alleged aggressiveness of the Soviet Union' and the 'communist danger from the East' any more.[132] He himself wanted to ensure this change of times and offer himself as a new, positive projection surface. If statesmen normally represent their country as *pars pro toto*, then the challenge for Brezhnev was to present himself not as a representative of the Soviet Union but to use his own person as a distraction from the political differences. He actively worked towards being perceived not as a supreme communist but as a statesman according to the Western model or at least as a 'simple man' of flesh and blood. To this end, he sought personal contact with Western heads of state. What Brezhnev started in 1969 was a rarity in foreign policy: he set up a 'secret channel' with both Richard Nixon and Willy Brandt, which connected the statesmen on both sides, in each case excluding the government and the foreign office, only through a few confidants.[133] French President Georges Pompidou rejected a formalised channel only because relations were already so good that they could always find suitable intermediaries.[134] After Brezhnev had ensured that he was informed directly and before the ministers, he kidnapped Willy Brandt, Georges Pompidou, and Richard Nixon for one-on-one talks during their visits to Moscow in 1970 and 1972 respectively to introduce himself to them as a trustworthy 'human being.' Brezhnev openly declared that he wanted to speak as 'himself' beyond the apparatuses – the bureaucrats would only bury them in paper – and not as a diplomat.[135] He tried to further captivate all three by

114 Susanne Schattenberg

inviting them privately to Crimea and the Black Sea in 1971 and 1974 respectively. Finally, Brezhnev sought to put on a Western air about himself personally. The first time he travelled to the West, to Paris in 1971, he sent a photo of himself to AFP wearing sunglasses and a blue tracksuit on a yacht off the Crimea, looking, in his own words, 'like Alain Delon.'[136] He flaunted such hobbies and vices, which in his opinion were 'western' and were supposed to set him apart from his grey, ideologically obdurate, anti-pleasure comrades: he demonstrated his enthusiasm for cars by taking the limousines presented to him for a spin in 1973 in Bonn alone and at Camp David with Nixon staring in fear in the passenger seat;[137] at Camp David, he introduced the stewardess who was staying with him to Nixon.[138] Brezhnev ignored the fact that he sometimes violated the code of conduct for a statesman with his impetuous manner prone to physical contact. Brandt, Pompidou, and Nixon therefore did not necessarily 'read' Brezhnev as a Western statesman; but the calculation worked out that they perceived him neither as a dogmatic ideologue nor as a danger to peace but experienced him as 'warm and friendly.'[139] Thus, Nixon told the stewardess: 'Take good care of him!,'[140] after Brezhnev had confided in him that he found it much easier to find a common language with the Western statesmen than with his comrades Podgorny and Kosygin.[141]

The 'new big four,' as Brezhnev called themselves, enabled the start of negotiations on the Strategic Arms Limitation Talks (SALT I and SALT II) in 1969, which Brezhnev signed with Richard Nixon in Moscow in 1972 and with Jimmy Carter in Vienna in 1979.[142] In addition, the talks on a Conference on Security and Cooperation in Europe, which Brezhnev pushed for, started in November 1972 and led to the signing of the Helsinki Final Act on 1 August 1975.[143] With this project Brezhnev pursued nothing less than to symbolically end the Second World War with an international peace treaty and to establish a new form of cooperation in Europe. To achieve this, he was even prepared to sign the 'Basket 3' on respect for human rights.[144]

The end of détente

But what Brezhnev had once planned as his great triumph turned into the end point in two respects: first, the Basket 3 gave human rights activists throughout East–Central Europe such a boost that it eventually led to the collapse of the socialist states. Second, the new 'big four' were already no more: in 1974, first Pompidou died in office before Brandt and Nixon resigned. Brezhnev feverishly tried to establish equally close relations with their successors but fought the growing stress and sleep disorders with more and more tranquillisers, which soon rendered him incapable of acting. As he increasingly slumped under the influence of pills, appeared apathetic or acted erratically, his staff and bodyguards began to shield him from direct contact with Western heads of state. The fact that he had once referred to himself and his body to distract from the ideological system and present himself as a 'simple' man of flesh and blood now became his undoing when his body failed and went out of control. His infirmity was immediately associated with the decline of the Soviet Union, and his physically induced withdrawal from the foreign policy arena was interpreted by analysts in the West as a political departure from the former trust and Western course. Western politicians again increasingly interpreted him in the parameters of the enemy, the other, the alien, and the threatening. They saw this confirmed when Soviet troops invaded Afghanistan on 25 December 1979. Even though the invasion had been initiated by a troika consisting of Gromyko, KGB chief Andropov, and Defence Minister Ustinov because they believed that the new Afghan government wanted to switch to the US camp, the successes of the policy of détente that had begun exactly ten years earlier were finally destroyed with this step.[145]

It was above all the foreign policy disaster and the badly tarnished international image of the Soviet Union that persuaded the Moscow Politburo not to intervene in 1980/1981 in the face of the strengthening Solidarność in Poland but, instead, as Brezhnev had once done with Dubček, to persuade Wojciech Jaruzelski through good coaxing, admonitions, and warnings to get the situation under control themselves by establishing martial law.[146]

The end and outlook

Brezhnev was a moderate party leader for whom the revolution had not meant liberation but a threat, who had fled the consequences three times and had actually wanted to become an actor, who made a career in the party through Stalin's terror and actually saw himself as a 'doer' and organiser of peace and prosperity. Nevertheless, he did not go down in history with the 'Brezhnev-Nixon Doctrine' for lasting peace, as Nixon had once prophesied,[147] but remained in the memory as a hardliner who invaded Prague and Kabul. Gorbachev even gave Brezhnev's rule the label of stagnation. Yet it was Brezhnev who made the Soviet Union the unquestioned form of state and reality of life that many believed would last forever and which today is nostalgically glorified for its supposedly prosperous times and glory as a superpower.[148] In short: Brezhnev created the state for whose downfall he was held responsible. He succeeded in creating a 'social paradise' with the free Saturday, the first adequate salary of 120 roubles, and paid maternity leave: 'For the first time in the whole of history, the Soviet power said to the people: "Have a rest and did not demand enthusiasm from them. Simple loyalty was enough." '[149] Brezhnev's success and tragedy was that he found a way to pacify the traumatised society with his motto 'Let everyone live and work in peace' and in the process led the political system – not society – into stagnation. In other words, the fear from 30 years of terror was so overwhelming that dealing with it politically led to the paralysis of the CC and the Politburo. Brezhnev failed to establish a political culture in which a change of leadership would have been a healthy routine and not an existential threat. Seen in this light, his scenario of collective rule and care was paradoxically all too successful: his fellow Politburo members were afraid of a

116 Susanne Schattenberg

break-up of the well-balanced balance of power. They were more willing to grant him five months' leave a year, to relieve him of chairing the Politburo sessions, and to distribute his speech text in the CC plenum so that he would not have to read it out rather than accept his offers of resignation. Allegedly, he offered his resignation twice:[150] the first time on his seventieth birthday in 1976, when he had just struggled through the twenty-fifth Party Congress and had been through several rehabs; the second time in 1979, when he had already been president for two years and no longer felt up to the upcoming trip to Vienna to see Carter.[151] Both times the Politburo turned him down; whether Brezhnev was serious remains a matter of speculation. After all, he was badly marked by his addiction to pills and must have realised this in the lucid moments. In addition to the sleeping pill Radedorm, he took the tranquillisers Ativan and Seduxen and the highly addictive tranquilliser Eunoctin.[152] Thus, a vicious circle developed: the more pills he consumed, the harder it was for him to be awake and active during the day, the more sleeping pills he needed in the evening to fall asleep at all. Perhaps, he also fought the shame of his physical decline as someone who had always attached great importance to his appearance and had once been considered very attractive. Over the years, his doctors managed to cut him off from the uncontrolled supply of pills and put him on a fitness programme, but they were unable to achieve complete withdrawal.[153] While the personality cult that had been set in motion in 1973 became more and more widespread and brought Brezhnev not only the title of Marshal in 1976[154] but also the Lenin Prize for Literature in 1980 for his 'Memoirs,'[155] his physical decline became more and more obvious to the public. Thus, Brezhnev's addiction to fame and his inability to speak without a crib sheet became the subject of numerous jokes: 'Brezhnev opens the Olympic Games in Moscow: 1980! O! O! O! – His speaker to him: Leonid Ilyich! Those are the Olympic rings, aren't they? The text starts underneath them!'[156] Profundity was demonstrated by the joking question expressing that the Soviet Union was caught between Stalinism and stagnation: 'How many leaders does the CPSU have? – Two. One eternally alive and one eternally sick.'[157] His brother comrades in the neighbouring states also secretly mocked: Honecker only contemptuously called the General Secretary the 'General Ruin';[158] Jaruzelski told the joke circulating in the Warsaw Pact: at the parade on Red Square there had once again been a demonstration of strength: the state and party leadership had climbed the tribune under their own force.[159]

In this perspective, it is a tragedy that Brezhnev succeeded in pacifying the Politburo but not in finding a succession plan that reconciled the people with the system. Brezhnev remained a captive ruler who could only finance the minimal prosperity through gold reserves or oil and gas deliveries to the West, who initiated a new thaw with the West but could not cope with the stress and who took refuge in an addiction to pills. Willy Brandt's aide Egon Bahr therefore judged: 'The idea of going to the sauna with Brezhnev would have been absurd. No chancellor would have survived that. But without what began in 1970, neither Gorbachev nor Yeltsin would have become masters in the Kremlin.'[160]

Notes

1 Leonid M. Mlechin, *Brezhnev, Zhizn zamechatel'nykh lyudey 1325 = (1125)* (Moskva: Izdat. Molodaya Gvardiya, 2008), 387.
2 Roy A. Medvedev, *Lichnost' i epokha: Politicheskiy portret L.I. Brezhneva* (Moskva: Novosti, 1991), 5.
3 Mikhail S. Dokuchayev, *Moskva, Kreml', okhrana* (Moskva: Biznes-Press, 1995), 181.
4 Alexei Yurchak, *Everything Was Forever, Until It Was No More: The Last Soviet Generation*, In-Formation Series (Princeton: Princeton University Press, 2006), https://ebook-central.proquest.com/lib/kxp/detail.action?docID=1319175.
5 Harold G. Skilling, *Interest Groups in Soviet Politics*, with the assistance of Franklyn Griffiths (Princeton: Princeton University Press, 1971); T. H. Rigby, "The Soviet Leadership: Towards a Self-Stabilizing Oligarchy?," *Soviet Studies* (1970): 167; Thomas H. Rigby, "How strong is the leader?," *Problems of Communism* (1962); Thomas H. Rigby, *Political elites in the USSR: Central leaders and local cadres from Lenin to Gorbachev* (Aldershot: Elgar, 1990); John P. Willerton, *Patronage and politics in the USSR,* Cambridge Russian, Soviet and post-Soviet studies 82 (Cambridge: Cambridge University Press, 1992).
6 Petr A. Abrasimov, *Vspominaja proshedshie gody: Chetvert' veka poslom Sovetskogo Soyuza* (Moskva: Mezhdunarodnyye otnosheniya, 1992), 270; V. Vladimirov, "Tandem: O L. Brezhneve i K. Chernenko," *Kodry* (1990): 157; Aleksandr Murzin, "Kak pisalis' memuary: Ispoved' soflera," accessed February 11, 2022, http://leonidbrezhnev.ucoz.ru/publ/stati_zametki_intervju/kak_pisalis_memuary/2-1-0-25; Georgiy Yakovlev, "Kak sozdavalis' memuary Brezhneva," in *L. I. Brezhnev: Materiały k biografii*, ed. Juriy V. Aksyutin (Moskva: Politizdat, 1991), 290; Evgeniy I. Chazov, *Zdorov'e i vlast': Vospominaniya 'kremlevskogo vracha'* (Moskva: Novosti, 1992), 154f; Nikolaus Katzer, "Dans la matrice discursive du socialisme tardif: Les 'Mémoires' de Leonid Il'ič Brežnev," *Cahiers du Monde Russe* 54, no. 1–2 (2013).
7 Leonid I. Brezhnev, *Rabochie i dnevnikovyye zapisi: 1944–1964*, vol. 3 (Moskva: Lit, 2016).
8 John Dornberg, *Brezhnev: The Masks of Power* (London: Deutsch, 1974); P. J. Murphy, *Brezhnev: Soviet Politician* (Jefferson: McFarland, 1981); Dimitriy A. Volkogonov, *Sem' vozhdej. Galereya liderov SSSR: 4. vozhd': Leonid Brezhnev 2* (Moskva: Novosti, 1995); Rudol'f G. Pikhoya, *Sovetskiy Soyuz: Istoriya vlasti; 1945–1991* (Moskva: Izdat. RAGS, 1998); Abdurakhman Avtorkhanov, *Sila i bessilie Brezhneva: Politicheskie ètyudy* (Frankfurt/Main: Possev, 1979); Mlechin, *Brezhnev*; Sergey N. Semanov, *Dorogoy Leonid Il'ich* (Moskva: ÈKSMO, 2007); Aleksandr E. Khinshteyn, *Skazka o poteryannom vremeni: Pochemu Brezhnev ne smog stat' Putinym* (Moskva: Olma Meia Grupp, 2011); Andreï Kozovoï, *Brejnev: L'antihéros* (Paris: Perrin, 2021); Susanne Schattenberg, *Brezhnev: The Making of a Statesman* (London: I. B. Tauris & Company Ltd., 2021).
9 Leonid I. Brezhnev, *Memoirs*, 1. Engl. ed. (Oxford, New York, Toronto, Sydney, Paris, Frankfurt Main and Kronberg-Taunus: Pergamon Press, 1982), 2.
10 Nataliya Bulanova, *Kam'yans'ki etydi v stili retro*, 2nd ed. (Dnipropetrovsk, IMA-прес, 2011), 117.
11 Brezhnev, *Memoirs*, 11; Bulanova, *Kam'yans'ki etydi v stili retro*, 124.
12 Brezhnev, *Memoirs*, 5.
13 Dornberg, *Brezhnev*, 42.
14 Murphy, *Brezhnev. Soviet politician*, 8.
15 Dornberg, *Brezhnev*, 42; Medvedev, *Lichnost' i epokha. Politicheskiy portret L.I. Brezhneva*, 20.
16 O sem'e Brezhnevykh, MIK, KP-18391/D-8114, Muzey Istorii mista Kam'yans'kogo; Bulanova, *Kam'yans'ki etydi v stili retro*, 125.
17 Brezhnev, *Memoirs*, 18.

118 Susanne Schattenberg

18 Bulanova, *Kam'yans'ki etydi v stili retro*, 170.
19 O sem'e Brezhnevykh See also The Official Chronicle of the Factory, accessed February 14, 2022, www.dmkd.dp.ua/node/5562.
20 Dnepropetrovskiy Derzhavnyy Arkhiv (DDA), fond (f.) 19, opis' (op.) 6, delo (d.) 341, list (l.) 4: "Avtobiografiya Brzhžnev L.I."
21 Georgiy A. Arbatov, *Zatyanuvsheyesya vyzdorovleniye (1953–1985 gg.): Svidetel'stvo sovremennika* (Moskva: Mezhdunarodnyye otnosheniya, 1991), 356; Anatoliy S. Chernyayev, *Sovmestnyy iskhod: Dnevnik dvukh ėpokh; 1972–1991 gody* (Moskva: ROSSPĖN, 2008), 192.
22 Aleksandr E. Bovin, *XX vek kak zhizn': Vospominaniya* (Moskva: Zakharov, 2003), 253; Arbatov, *Zatyanuvsheyesya vyzdorovleniye (1953–1985 gg.)*, 356.
23 Galina P. Vishnevskaya, *Galina: Istoriya zhizni*, 5th ed. (Moskva: Soglasiye, 1996), 304.
24 DDA, f. 19, op. 6, d. 341, l. 2; Avtorkhanov, *Sila i bessilie Brezhneva*, 68.
25 Vladimir V. Karpov, "Vechernie besedy s Viktoriyey Brezhnevoy," in *Rasstreljannye marshaly, Voyennye tayny XX veka*, ed. Vladimir V. Karpov (Moskva: Veche, 2000), 407.
26 Ibid., 408; Larisa N. Vasil'eva, *Kremlevskiye zheny: Fakty, vospominaniya, dokumenty, slukhi, legendy i vzglyad avtora* (Moskva: Vagrius, 2008), 399; Mlechin, *Brezhnev*, 52.
27 DDA, f. 19, op. 6, d. 341, l. 2; Tsentr Dokumentatsii Obshchestvennykh Organizacii Sverdlovskoy Oblasti (CDOOSO), f. 4, op. 17, d. 256, l. 1oborot (ob.). Mlechin, *Brezhnev*, 53.
28 Gosudarstvennyy Arkhiv Sverdlovskoy Oblasti (GASO), f. R-160, op. 1, d. 183: Dokumenty i perepiska ob otvode zemel' . . . Bisertskogo rayona 23.1.–26.10.1929g., l. 24.
29 TsDOOSO, f. 434: Bisertskiy rayonnyy komitet VKP(b), op. 1, d. 20: Protokoly zasedaniy partiynogo aktiva plenumov i byuro raykoma VKP(b) 5.1.1929–25.12.1929g., l. 149.
30 Karpov, "Vechernie besedy s Viktoriyey Brezhnevoy," 411.
31 Brezhnev, *Memoirs*, 29.
32 DDA, f. 19, op. 6, d. 341, l. 2; Leonid L. Brezhnev, *Leonid Il'ich: Pages From His Life* (New York: Simon and Schuster, 1978); written under the auspices of the Academy of Sciences of the Soviet Union, 27.
33 A. A. Pashchenko, ed., *Dnipropetrovs'ka oblast', Istoriya mist i sil Ukrains'koy RSR 7* (Kiev: RSR, 1969), 235; Murphy, *Brezhnev. Soviet politician*, 38f; A. Kuznetsov, "I Brezhnev takoy molodoy . . . ," *Literaturnaya gazeta*, December 13, 2006, 4.
34 Surprisingly, this information is missing from his employment record, but Mlechin confirms what all the others also describe Mlechin, *Brezhnev*, 58; see also Brezhnev, *Leonid Il'ich*, 30f.
35 GASO, f. R-160, op. 1-l, d. 103, l. 16; Mlechin, *Brezhnev*, 58.
36 Reprint in Pravda, May 27, 1976; see also Brezhnev, *Leonid Il'ich*, 15.
37 DDA, f. R-5575: Narodnyy Komissariat Tyazheloy Promyshlennosti SSSR, upravleniye kadrov i uchebnych zavedeniy, Kamenskiy vecherniy metallurgicheskiy tekhnikum, 1934–1973, op. 1, d. 3: Prikazy direktora po tekhnikumu [avtograf Brezhneva], l. 63.
38 Stanislav Pshenichnyy, "Pervaya vysota Leonida Brezhneva," *Dneprovskaya Pravda*, November 4, 2006, accessed March 24, 2015, http://dneprovka.dp.ua/t1472/.
39 "IV Mis'ka partiyna konferentsiya zakinchila svoyu rabotu," *Dzerzhinets. Organ dniprodzerzhinskogo MK KP(b)U, Mis'kradi ta MRPS*, May 13, 1937; "Plenum mis'koy radi," *Dzerzhinets*, August 5, 1937.
40 DDA, f. 19, op. 2, d. 68: Stenogramma Plenuma gorodskogo partiynogo komiteta, 28.11.1937g., l. 29 ff.
41 Ibid., l. 40.
42 DDA, f. 19, op. 6, d. 341, l. 2.
43 A. Slonevskiy, "Rassakzy o Brezhneve," *Znamya Dzerzhinki*, December 20, 2012, 12; Maksim Kavun, "Leonid Brezhnev: Kar'era i zhizn' genseka," *Nedvizhimost' v dvizhenii*, April 19, 2006, 10f; Medvedev, *Lichnost' i epokha. Politicheskiy portret L.I. Brezhneva*, 28f.

44 Leonid I. Brezhnev, *Trilogy: Little Land. Rebirth. The Virgins Lands* (Moscow: Progress, 1980), 44.
45 Tsentral'nyy Arkhiv Minoborony Rossii (TsAMO), f. 33, op. 682524, d. 12, l. 168ob., accessed February 8, 2017, http://liders.rusarchives.ru/brezhnev/docs/nagradnoi-listna-zamestitelya-nachalnika-politupravleniya-yuzhnogo-fronta-brigadnogo-komissara; Andrey A. Grechko, "Gody voyny: Chast' pervaya. Surovyye ispytaniya," accessed February 16, 2022, http://militera.lib.ru/memo/russian/grechko_aa2/04.htmlhttp://milit era.lib.ru/memo/russian/grechko_aa2/04.html.
46 Brezhnev, *Trilogy*, 99; Brezhnev, *Leonid Il'ich*, 80; Brezhnev, *Rabochie i dnevnikovyye zapisi*, 24, 26, 30; Katrin Boeckh, *Stalinismus in der Ukraine: Die Rekonstruktion des sowjetischen Systems nach dem Zweiten Weltkrieg* (Wiesbaden: Harrassowitz, 2007), 126; Vasyl Markus, *L' incorporation de l'Ukraine subcarpathique à l'Ukraine soviétique 1944–1945* (Louvain: Centre Ukrainien d'Études en Belgique, 1956), 30; Vikentiy Shandor, *Carpatho-Ukraine in the Twentieth Century: A Political and Legal History* (Cambridge, MA: Distributed by Harvard University Press for the Ukrainian Research Institute at Harvard University, 1997), 263; František Němec, *The Soviet Seizure of Subcarpathian Ruthenia* (Toronto: Anderson, 1955), 83.
47 Derzhavnyy arkhiv Zaporiz'koy oblasti (DAZO), f. 157, op. 1, d. 1473: Protokol No. 9, zasedaniya plenuma Zaporozhskogo gorkoma KPU, 24.12.1946g., l. 2; Brezhnev, *Trilogy*, 108.
48 Ibid., 184.; DDA, f. 19, op. 5, d. 203: Protokol i stenogramma XVIII Plenuma Dnepropetrovskogo obkoma, 21.11.1947g., l. 2; f. 18, op. 3, d. 324: Stenogramma XVII Plenuma Dnepropetrovskogo gorkoma, December 9, 1947g., l. 195.
49 Leonid I. Brezhnev, *Rabochie i dnevnikovyye zapisi, 1964–1982*, 1168; Brezhnev, *Leonid Il'ich*, 103.
50 Arhiva Organizatiilor Social-Politice a Republicii Moldova (AOSPRM), f. 51, op. 9, d. 94: Stenogramma i protokol zasedaniya V Plenuma TsK KP Moldavii, 4.–6.7.1950g,; I. I. Bodyul, *Dorogoy zhizni: Vremya, sobytiya, razdum'ya* (Chisinău: Cusnir, 2002), 49; Mlechin, *Brezhnev*, 84; Aleksandr Gavrilyuk, "Teper' muzhik skazhet . . .: Iz zhizni nomenklatury," in Aksyutin, *L. I. Brezhnev*, 262; Medvedev, *Lichnost' i epokha. Politicheskiy portret L.I. Brezhneva*, 60.
51 Oleg V. Khlevnyuk, ed., *Politbyuro TsK VKP (b) i Sovet Ministrov SSSR: 1945–1953* (Moskva: ROSSPĖN, 2002), 88–91; Rossiyskij Gosudarstevnnyy Arkhiv Sotsial'no-Politicheskoy Istorii (RGASPI), f. 3, op. 8, d. 17, l. 2–4, accessed February 16, 2022, http://liders.rusarchives.ru/brezhnev/docs/protokol-1-zasedaniya-prezidiuma-tsk-kpss-o-raspredelenii-obyazannostei-mezhdu-sekretaryami-tsk; Mlechin, *Brezhnev*, 95.
52 Brezhnev, *Trilogy*, 150.
53 DAZO, f. 157, op. 1, d. 1631: Originaly Zasedaniya Plenuma Zaporozhskogo Gorkoma KPU, 28.4.1947g., attachment to file, pp. 1, 3.
54 Brezhnev, *Trilogy*, 149.
55 Oleg V. Khlevnyuk, "Regional'naya vlast' v SSSR v 1953 – konce 1^950kh godov: Ustoychivost' i konflikty," *Otechestvennaya istoriya* 3 (2007); Yoram Gorlizki, "Too Much Trust: Regional Party Leaders and Local Political Networks Under Brezhnev," *Slavic Review* 69, no. 3 (2010); Yoram Gorlizki and Oleg V. Chlevnjuk, *Substate Dictatorship: Networks, Loyalty, and Institutional Change in the Soviet Union* (New Haven and London: Yale University Press, 2020).
56 Chazov, *Zdorov'e i vlast'*, 11.
57 RGANI, f. 2, op. 3, d. 429, l. 20.
58 APRK, f. 708, op. 27, d. 29: Stenogramma zasedaniy IX Plenuma KP Kaz 5.–6.2.1954g., l. 32; Saulius Grybkauskas, *Governing the Soviet Union's National Republics: The Second Secretaries of the Communist Party* (Abingdon, Oxon and New York: Routledge, 2021), 76.

120 Susanne Schattenberg

59 Sergei Khrushchev, *Nikita Chrushchev: Trilogiya ob ottse*, 3rd ed. (Moskva: Vremya, 2010), 438.
60 RGANI, f. 80, op. 1, d. 1200, l. 46; f. 3, op. 12, d. 356, l. 15; accessed February 16, 2022, http://liders.rusarchives.ru/brezhnev/docs/postanovlenie-prezidiuma-tsk-kpss-o-brezhneve-li-29-marta-1958-g.
61 RGANI, f. 80, op. 1, d. 1200, l. 49; GARF, f. R-7523, op. 78, d. 76: Materialy o poyezdke t. Brezhneva v Gvineyu, Ganu i Marokko (obzor pechati), l. 34: Izvestiya, February 9, 1961: 'Shchastlivogo puti'.
62 Vladimir Semichastnyj, *Bespokoynoye serdce*, Moj 20. vek (Moskva: Vagrius, 2002), 204; Petro J. Shelest, . . . *Da ne sudimy budete: Dnevnikovyye zapisi, vospominaniya chlena Politbyuro TsK KPSS* (Moskva: Edition q, 1995), 204; see all files with the title 'repliki' in RGANI, f. 2, op. 1, d. 44 (July 1953), d. 60 (September 1953), d. 88 (March 1954), and so on until the last one d. 742 (July 1964).
63 Khrushchev, *Nikita Chrushchev*, 1035; RGASPI, f. 666: Petr Efimovich Shelest: op. 1, d. 26: Avtobiograficheskiye zametki 1964–1966, l. 14.
64 Shelest, . . . *Da ne sudimy budete*, 201; Semichastnyj, *Bespokoynoye serdce*, 351.
65 Ian Thatcher, "Brezhnev as Leader," in *Brezhnev Reconsidered*, ed. Edwin Bacon and Mark Sandle (Houndmills: Palgrave Macmillan, 2002), 32; Edwin Bacon and Mark Sandle, eds., *Brezhnev Reconsidered* (Houndmills: Palgrave Macmillan, 2002), 13; William Tompson, *The Soviet Union Under Brezhnev*, Seminar Studies in History (Harlow: Pearson Longman, 2003), 17; Donald Raleigh, "Russia's Favorite: Reevaluating the Rule of Leonid Il'ich Brezhnev, 1964–1982," *Russian Studies in History* 52, no. 4 (2015); Guest editor's introduction.
66 Roy A. Medvedev, "Vo vtorom eshelone," in Aksyutin, *L. I. Brezhnev*, 26.
67 Georgiy A. Arbatov, "Iz nedavnego proshlogo," in Aksyutin, *L. I. Brezhnev*, 85.
68 Richard S. Wortman, *Scenarios of Power: Myth and Ceremony in Russian Monarchy*, 2 vols., Studies of the Harriman Institute, Columbia University (Princeton, NJ: Princeton University Press, 1995); From Peter the Great to the death of Nicholas I, p. 4.
69 Susanne Schattenberg, "Trust, Care, and Familiarity in the Politburo: Brezhnev's Scenario of Power," *Kritika* 16, no. 4 (2015).
70 Georgiy K. Shakhnazarov, *S vozhdyami i bez nikh* (Moskva: Vagrius, 2001), 231.
71 RGANI, f. 1, op. 5, d. 1: XXIII s'ezd KPSS 1966 stenogramma pervogo zasedaniya, otchetnyy doklad L.I. Brezhneva, 29.3.1966g., l. 228; Tompson, *The Soviet Union Under Brezhnev*, 22.
72 RGANI, f. 2, op. 1, d. 787: Sentyabr'skiy Plenum 1965g., Protokol No. 12, l. 19; f. 2, op. 1, d. 809: Stenogramma vtorogo zasedaniya Dekabr'skogo Plenuma 1965g., l. 66; f. 2, op. 1, d. 820: Stenogramma zasedaniya Martovskogo Plenuma 1966g., l. 2; f. 2, op. 3, d. 21: Stenograficheskyy otchet Mayskogo Plenuma 1966g., l. 308.
73 RGANI, f. 2, op. 1, d. 773: Materialy k protokolu No. 11. Stenogramma zasedaniya komissii po vyrabotke proyekta postanovleniya Plenuma TsK "O neotlozhnykh merakh dal'neyshego razvitiya sel'skogo khozyaystva SSSR," 25.3.1965g., l. 23.
74 RGANI, f. 89, perechen' 25, d. 4: Ob otpuske L.I. Brezhneva, Politbyuro, June 22, 1979g., l. 1.
75 Fedor M. Burlatskiy, "Brezhnev i krushenie ottepeli," in Aksyutin, *L. I. Brezhnev*, 113.
76 Muḥammad Ḥ. Haikal, *The Road to Ramadan* (London: Collins, 1975), 94.
77 RGANI, f. 2, op. 1, d. 790: Materialy k protokolu No. 12, l. 1.
78 Andrej M. Aleksandrov-Agentov, *Ot Kollontay do Gorbacheva: Vospominaniya diplomata, sovetnika A. A. Gromyko, pomoshchnika L. I. Brezhneva, Yu. V. Andropova, K. U. Tsernenko i M. S. Gorbacheva* (Moskva: Mezdunarodnyye Otnosheniya, 1994), 249.
79 Bovin, *XX vek kak zhizn'*, 144; Karen N. Brutenc, *Tridcat' let na staroj ploščadi* (Moskva: Meždunar. otnošenija, 1998), 241, 247.
80 RGANI, f. 1, op. 5, d. 1: XXIII s'ezd KPSS 1966 stenogramma pervogo zasedaniya, otchetnyy doklad L.I. Brezhneva, March 29, 1966g., l. 229.
81 Semichastnyj, *Bespokoynoye serdce*, 393f.

82 Citing Burlatskiy, "Brezhnev i krushenie ottepeli," 115; Nikolay Yegorychev, "'U nas byli raznyye vzglyady': Iz interv'iu korrespondentu 'Ogonka' L. Pleshakovu," in Aksyutin, *L. I. Brezhnev*, 204.
83 Shelest, . . . *Da ne sudimy budete*, 518.
84 Fëdor Burlacky, *Khrushchev and the First Russian Spring* (London: Weidenfeld & Nicolson, 1991), 217; Medvedev, *Lichnost' i epokha. Politicheskiy portret L.I. Brezhneva*, 279; Mikhail Gorbachev, *Zhizn' i reformy*, 2 vols. (Moskva: Novosti, 1995), 180; Shelest, . . . *Da ne sudimy budete*, 179, 191.
85 Shakhnazarov, *S vozhdyami i bez nikh*, 232.
86 Mlechin, *Brezhnev*, 194.
87 Juriy M. Churbanov, *Moy test' Leonid Brezhnev* (Moskva: Algoritm, 2007), 84.
88 Shelest, . . . *Da ne sudimy budete*, 199.
89 Zapis' vystupleniya chlena prezidiuma i sekretarya TsK KPSS tov. M.A. Suslova na plenume tsentral'nogo komiteta KPSS, in Andrey N. Artizov, ed., *Nikita Khrushchev 1964: Stenogrammy plenuma TsK KPSS i drugiye dokumenty* (Moskva: Izdat. Materik, 2007), 256.
90 Vladimir T. Medvedev, *Chelovek za spinoy: Vospominaniya nachal'nika lichnoy okhrany Brezhneva i Gorbacheva* (Moskva: Russlit, 1994), 120.
91 Mlechin, *Brezhnev*, 436.
92 Ibid.
93 George W. Breslauer, *Khrushchev and Brezhnev as Leaders: Building Authority in Soviet Politics*, 1. publ. (London: Allen & Unwin, 1982); Galina M. Ivanova, Stefan Plaggenborg, and Lukas Mücke, *Entstalinisierung als Wohlfahrt: Sozialpolitik in der Sowjetunion 1953–1970* (Frankfurt am Main: Campus Verlag, 2015); Stefan Plaggenborg, *Experiment Moderne: Der sowjetische Weg* (Frankfurt and New York: Campus Verlag, 2006); Lukas Mücke, *Die allgemeine Altersrentenversorgung in der UdSSR, 1956–1972* (Stuttgart: Steiner, 2013), 81.
94 Brezhnev, *Rabochie i dnevnikovyye zapisi, 1964–1982*, 43.
95 RGANI, f. 80, op. 1, d. 330, l. 42.
96 RGANI, f. 2, op. 3, d. 215: Protokol No. 15 Dekabr'skogo Plenuma, December 7, 1970g., l. 41.
97 RGANI, f. 2, op. 3, d. 467: Stenogramma pervogo zasedaniya Iyul'skogo Plenuma, July 3, 1978g., l. 5f.
98 RGANI, f. 2, op. 3, d. 78: Protokol No. 6, zasedaniye Sentyabr'skogo Plenuma, September 26, 1967g., l. 10–14.
99 RGANI, f. 2, op. 1, d. 45: Dekabr'skij Plenum, stenogramma pervogo zasedanija, December 12, 1966g., l. 40; S. V. Zhuravlev, *AvtoVAZ mezhdu proshlym i budushchim: Istoriya Volzhskogo avtomobil'nogo zavoda, 1966–2005* (Moskva: RAGS, 2006), 46; Lewis H. Siegelbaum, *Cars for Comrades: The Life of the Soviet Automobile* (Ithaca: Cornell University Press, 2008).
100 James R. Millar, "The Little Deal: Brezhnev's Contribution to Acquisitive Socialism," in *Soviet Society and Culture: Essays in Honor of Vera S. Dunham*, ed. Terry L. Tompson and Richard R. Sheldon (Boulder, CO: Westview Press, 1988).
101 Leonid I. Brezhnev, "Pjat'desjat let velikikh pobed sotsializma," in *Voprosy upravleniya ekonomikoy razvitogo socialisticheskogo obshchestva: Rechi, doklady, vystupleniya*, ed. Leonid I. Brezhnev (Moskva: Polit. Literatury, 1976), 147.
102 Joachim Zweynert, "'Developed Socialism' and Soviet Economic Thought in the 1970s and Early 1980s," *Russian History* 41 (2014).
103 Mark Sandle, "Brezhnev and Developed Socialism: The Ideology of Zastoj?," in Bacon and Sandle, *Brezhnev Reconsidered*.
104 Brezhnev, "Pjat'desjat let velikikh pobed sotsializma," 147.
105 RGANI, f. 2, op. 3, d. 215: Protokol No. 15 Dekabr'skogo Plenuma, December 7, 1970g., l. 42.

122 Susanne Schattenberg

106 CIA, "Intelligence Memorandum: The View from the Kremlin Three Months After the Summit, Washington, September 13, 1972," accessed February 16, 2022, https://history.state.gov/historicaldocuments/frus1969-76v15/d45; Chernyayev, *Sovmestnyy iskhod*, 21, 185.

107 Wojciech Jaruzelski, *Hinter den Türen der Macht: Der Anfang vom Ende einer Herrschaft* (Leipzig: Militzke, 1996), 264; Fond Gorbacheva, f. 5, op. 1, kartochka 20662, l. 2, 4.

108 RGANI, f. 2, op. 3, d. 121: Protokol No. 9 Oktyabr'skogo Plenuma, October 30–31, 1968g., l. 26.

109 RGANI, f. 2, op. 3, d. 121, l. 25.

110 RGANI, f. 2, op. 3, d. 168, l. 36.

111 Laurien Crump, *The Warsaw Pact Reconsidered: International Relations in Eastern Europe, 1955–69* (New York: Routledge, 2015), 22, 203.

112 Shelest, . . . *Da ne sudimy budete*, 460.

113 Brezhnev, *Rabochie i dnevnikovyye zapisi, 1964–1982*, 352.; RGANI, f. 80, op. 1, d. 30, l. 34.

114 Ibid., 1097, 1101; RGAÉ, f. 4372, op. 66, d. 87: Zapisi besed predsedatelya Gosplana SSSR i ego zamestiteley s predstavitelyami zarubezhnykh stran, Feb.–Nov. 1965, l. 5 f.; Jaruzelski, *Hinter den Türen der Macht*, 48, 275.

115 RGANI, f. 5, op. 30, d. 489, l. 13–15; Shelest, . . . *Da ne sudimy budete*, 436; Jaruzelski, *Hinter den Türen der Macht*, 426.

116 "Dokumenty 'Komissii Suslova': Sobytiya v Pol'she v 1981g," *Novaya i noveyshaya istoriya*, 1994, 1, 100; Jaruzelski, *Hinter den Türen der Macht*, 430.

117 Brezhnev, *Rabochie i dnevnikovyye zapisi, 1964–1982*, 45ff. RGANI, f. 80, op. 1, d. 329: Zapiski i spravki otdelov TSK KPSS, ministerstv i vedomstv po mezhdunarodnym voprosam . . ., l. 16; "Rukopisnye zametki L. Brezhneva vo vremya razgovorov s rukovoditelyami bratskikh partiy," October 29, 1964g.

118 Crump, *The Warsaw Pact Reconsidered*, 202–4.

119 Bovin, *XX vek kak zhizn'*, 217.

120 Brezhnev, *Rabochie i dnevnikovyye zapisi, 1964–1982*, 513, 648, 655, 660–62; Klaus Wiegrefe, "Honecker und Brežnev auf der Krim: Eine Aufzeichnung über das Treffen vom 19. August 1976," *Vierteljahrshefte für Zeitgeschichte* 41, no. 4 (1993); Hans-Hermann Hertle and Konrad Jarausch, eds., *Risse im Bruderbund: Gespräche Honecker-Breshnew 1974 bis 1982* (Berlin: Links-Verlag, 2006).

121 E. Gerek, "Edvard Gerek o Leonide Brežneve," *Literaturnaja gazeta*, September 26, 1990, 14.

122 Brezhnev, *Rabochie i dnevnikovyye zapisi*, 424, 446 RGANI, f. 80, op. 1, d. 330, l. 41.

123 Olivier Orban, *Kremlin – PCF: Conversations secrètes* (Paris: Orban, 1984); Brezhnev in conversation with the French Communist Party leader Waldeck Rochet in Moscow on July 16, 1968, 63.

124 Bovin, *XX vek kak zhizn'*, 173; Jan Pauer, *Prag 1968: Der Einmarsch des Warschauer Paktes; Hintergründe, Planung, Durchführung* (Bremen: Ed. Temmen, 1995), 46.

125 Susanne Schattenberg, "'Sascha, ich würde Dir gern glauben, aber versteh auch Du mich . . . ': Breschnew, Dubček und die Frage von Kadern und Vertrauen im Konflikt um den Prager Frühling 1968," *Historische Anthropologie* 21, no. 2 (2013).

126 RGANI, f. 80, op. 1, d. 981, l. 4, 26ob., 34ob., 64ob., 77.

127 Dokument 57: Telefongespräch L.I. Brežnevs mit A.S. Dubček vom August 13, 1968, in Stefan Karner, ed., *Prager Frühling: Dasinternationale Krisenjahr 1968*, Bd. 2 Dokumente (Köln: Böhlau, 2008), 335.

128 S. Kovalev, "Suverenitet i internattsional'nyye obyazannosti sots. stran," *Pravda*, September 26, 1968.

129 Chazov, *Zdorov'e i vlast'*, 74; Shelest, . . . *Da ne sudimy budete*, 382.

Leonid Brezhnev **123**

130 Donald Raleigh, "'Soviet' Man of Peace: Leonid Il'ich Brezhnev and His Diaries," *Kritika* 17, no. 4 (2016).
131 Bovin, *XX vek kak zhizn'*, 255.
132 RGANI, f. 2, op. 3, d. 251, l. 78; Willy Brandt, *Begegnungen und Einsichten: Die Jahre 1960–1975*, Knaur 576 (München: Droemer Knaur, 1978), 448.
133 Valentin M. Falin, *Politische Erinnerungen* (München: Droemer Knaur, 1993), 87.
134 Archives nationales Paris, 5 AG 2/1018, Second tête-à-tête entre le Président de la république et M. Brejnev, Octobre 26, 1971, Elysée, 16:15–20:15, p. 24.
135 Archives nationales Paris, 5 AG 2/1018, Entretien entre le Président de la république et M. Brejnev, Kremlin, Octobre 13, 1970, 10:30–11:40, p. 1; Henry Kissinger, *Memoiren, 1968–1973*, 2 vols. (München: Bertelsmann, 1979), 1281; Edward C. Keefer, ed., *Soviet-American Relations: The Détente Years, 1969–1972*, Department of State Publication 11438 (Washington, DC: United States Government Printing Office, 2007), 834.
136 Vladimir Musael'yan, "Brezhnev, kotorogo ne znali," *Kollektsiya Karavan Istoriya* 7 (2015): 149.
137 Falin, *Politische Erinnerungen*, 245; Richard M. Nixon, *Memoiren* (Köln: Ellenberg, 1978), 584f.
138 Viktor M. Sukhodrev, *Jazyk moy – drug moy: Ot Khrushcheva do Gorbacheva*, 2nd ed. (Moskva: TONChU, 2008), 323f.
139 Ibid; Willy Brandt, "Vertrauensvolle Gegnerschaft: Der Spiegel, November 15, 1982," in *Berliner Ausgabe 9*, ed. Willy Brandt (Bonn: Dietz, 2009), 385; Richard M. Nixon, *The Memoirs of Richard Nixon* (London: Arrow Books, 1979), 716–17.
140 Sukhodrev, *Jazyk moy – drug moy*, 324.
141 Ibid., 331.
142 Arvid Schors, *Doppelter Boden: Die SALT-Verhandlungen 1963–1979*, vol. 27 (s.l.: Wallstein, 2016).
143 Michael C. Morgan, *The Final Act: The Helsinki Accords and the Transformation of the Cold War* (Princeton and Oxford: Princeton University Press, 2018).
144 Anatoliĭ F. Dobrynin, *Sugubo doveritel'no: Posol v Vashingtone pri shesti prezidentakh SShA, 1962–1986 gg*, Izd. 2-e (Moskva: Mezhdunarodnye otnosheniia, 2008), 344; Juriy V. Dubinin, *Diplomaticheskaya byl': Zapiski posla vo Frantsii* (Moskva: ROSSPĖN, 1997), 208.
145 Archiv der sozialen Demokratie (AdsD), Willy Brandt Archiv (WBA), inventory A 9, folder 7: Inoffizielle Übersetzung, An Brandt, without date [after Afghanistan-invasion].
146 "Telefonat Breschnews mit Kania am 21. Juli 1981," in Michael Kubina, ed., *'Hart und kompromißlos durchgreifen': Die SED contra Polen 1980/81; Geheimakten der SED-Führung über die Unterdrückung der polnischen Demokratiebewegung*, Studien des Forschungsverbundes SED-Staat an der Freien Universität Berlin (Berlin: Akad.-Verlag, 1995), 332; Brezhnev, *Rabochie i dnevnikovyye zapisi, 1964–1982*, 1087.
147 Dobrynin, *Sugubo doveritel'no*, 301.
148 Yurchak, *Everything Was Forever, Until It Was No More*.
149 Konstantin Kozlov, "Otdykhay, strana!," *Liter*, April 17, 2008, 10.
150 Kuznetsov, "I Brezhnev takoy molodoy," 4; Aleksandrov-Agentov, *Ot Kollontay do Gorbacheva*, 273.
151 Aleksandr Kolesnichenko, "Kak popast' v istoriyu i ankedot: Leonid Il'ich byl odnim iz samykh 'riskovykh' sovetskikh vozhdey," *Argumenty i fakty*, May 26, 2010, Rasskaz Aleksandra Ryabenko, 29.
152 Mikhail Kosarev, "K 75 godam Leonid Il'ich sovsem rasslabilsya: Beseda nashego korrespondenta Pavla Korobova s vrachem Mikhailom Kosarevym," *Vlast'*, November 11, 2002, 72; Mlechin, *Brezhnev*, 554.

124 Susanne Schattenberg

153 Chazov, *Zdorov'e i vlast'*, 138f; Mlechin, *Brezhnev*, 584f; Brezhnev, *Rabochie i dnevnikovyye zapisi, 1964–1982*, 617, 724; Kosarev, "K 75 godam Leonid Il'ich sovsem rasslabilsya," 72.
154 RGANI, f. 89, perechen' 42, document 67: Zasedaniye Politbyuro, 27.4.1976g., l. 3.
155 Leonid I. Brezhnev, *'Vo imya dela partii, dela naroda': Vručenie Leninskoj premii General'nomu Sekretarju TsK KPSS Predsedatelyu Prezidiuma Verkhovnogo Soveta SSSR L.I. Brezhnevu, 31.3.1980g* (Moskva, 1980), 12f.
156 A. S. Golubev, ed., *Istoriya SSSR v anekdotakh: 1917–1991* (Smolensk: Smyadyn', 1999), 154.
157 Ibid., 135.
158 Chernyayev, *Sovmestnyy iskhod*, 167; Vyacheslav E. Kevorkov, *Der geheime Kanal: Moskau, der KGB und die Bonner Ostpolitik* (Berlin: Rowohlt, 1995), 179.
159 Jaruzelski, *Hinter den Türen der Macht*, 63.
160 Egon Bahr, *Zu meiner Zeit*, 3. Aufl. (München: Blessing, 1996), 296f.

7

NICOLAE CEAUŞESCU

Interpreting a national-Stalinist

Francesco Magno

Introduction

On 21 August 1968, an excited crowd occupied the old Palace Square in Bucharest, waiting for a sign from its leader. On the previous night, the Soviet tanks had entered Prague to end Alexander Dubcek's attempts to build 'socialism with a human face,' highlighting once more the Soviet Union's dominance over its satellites. Suddenly, Nicolae Ceauşescu peeped at the other members of the Central Committee gathered around him on the balcony from which he would address the crowd. They were much older than him; their grey hair and wrinkled faces made the 50-year-old Ceauşescu look even younger and more energetic. Perfectly disguising his internal fears, the general secretary of the Romanian Communist Party fiercely condemned the Soviet invasion of Prague, defining it as 'a big mistake and a severe threat to European peace.'[1] Waving his arm up and down and emphatically pointing his finger towards a distant and invisible enemy, Ceauşescu stigmatised the Soviet meddling in Czechoslovak internal affairs. He never took his eyes off the crowd, which he seemed to control with the simple movement of his hand. When he proclaimed the strenuous fight of the Romanian people to defend – if threatened – its independence, the crowd erupted in a roar. It was Ceauşescu's finest hour. The writer and future dissident Paul Goma admitted that listening to Ceauşescu on that day, he felt Romania had found a veritable leader who 'appealed not to communists, but to . . . citizens; to defend, not the party, but the country.'[2]

Twenty-one years later, on 21 December 1989, on the same balcony, looking at the same square, the scenario was very different. Now wrinkles furrowed Ceauşescu's face; nobody was standing beside him. His wife Elena and the other comrades stayed distant as if they wanted him to handle the crowd alone. The 71-year-old Ceauşescu wore a heavy black coat and a fur hat, which made him look

DOI: 10.4324/9781003426165-7

126 Francesco Magno

clumsy. He could not disguise his anxiety. Instead of looking directly at the crowd, he read his speech from a piece of paper held in a trembling hand. 'A warm and revolutionary welcome to the participants, and best of luck in each field of your activity.' Despite the awkward attempt to create empathy with the crowd, he had no control over the people below him. Suddenly, a gunshot was heard from the middle of the square. The most powerful man in Romania looked almost mummified as chaos unfolded before him while Elena tried to take control of the situation.[3]

Nicolae Ceauşescu's political experience is symbolically enclosed between the two balcony speeches. In 1968, he was a maverick within the Soviet bloc, the only one who expressively stood against Moscow privately and publicly. The West looked at him as a moderate, someone who could be used to undermine communist unity. He was the first communist leader to establish diplomatic relations with West Germany. In 1967, he declared Romania's neutrality regarding the Six-Day War, setting himself apart from his traditional allies.

In 1989, however, Ceauşescu had become a Cold War relic in a post-Cold War world. The Berlin Wall had fallen apart a month and a half before his speech. All over eastern Europe, communist regimes were crumbling, and the old élites were refashioning themselves in new social–democratic clothes. During the 1980s, Romania had been the only socialist state – together with Albania – which did not intensify contacts with the West; on the contrary, trying to repay Romania's external debt, Ceauşescu moved away from that Western world which he had tried so hard to attract at the end of the 1960s. With his fur hat and his speeches from the balcony, the old *Conducător* (Leader) was anachronistic. Not surprisingly, the day after the broken speech, he and his wife ran away from Bucharest to escape raging demonstrators ready to assault the Central Committee building. Arrested shortly thereafter, the two were sentenced to death on Christmas morning, after a show trial.

In the Romanian public discourse, the two speeches represent two sharply distinct phases. The first, between 1965 and the first half of the 1970s, was characterised by moderation, openness to the West, and rebellion against Soviet dominance in eastern Europe. The second phase, until 1989, was defined by growing nationalist rhetoric, strict control over the population through the secret police (the infamous *Securitate*), and absurd economic and social policies.

What caused the change? Why did, all of a sudden, an alleged-enlightened communist turn into one of the most renowned tyrants of Cold War Europe?

For some, the explanation lies in a 1971 trip he made to China and North Korea. Looking at how Mao and Kim il-Sung controlled and were idolised by the masses, Ceauşescu thought he could replicate the model in Romania.[4] For others, it was Elena's influence and her greed for power that radicalised Nicolae's rule.[5] Other observers believe that, like many politicians later turned into dictators, Ceauşescu was corrupted by absolute power.

Though all the above explanations are plausible and partially explain changes in Ceauşescu's behaviour and policies, they fail to highlight the *file rouge* connecting the first and the second speech from the balcony of the Central Committee building. Moreover, the idea of the two Ceauşescu's, a young 'good' leader opposed to an old 'bad' tyrant, hampers every objective analysis and interpretation of the Romanian communist era, reducing it to Ceauşescu's growing madness and megalomania.

If we look at Ceauşescu's rule in its entirety, however, we can grasp an inner coherence. If we place his figure in the broader context of Romanian history, even the late degeneration becomes understandable, analysable, and more complex than pure megalomania. Nicolae Ceauşescu was not just a Cold War product but the fruit of a long history made of several – and often contradictory – cultural influences and political contingencies.

This chapter aims to highlight the factors that shaped Ceauşescu's leadership, transforming a humble cobbler into one of the most infamous European dictators. The best way to achieve this goal is to enlarge the perspective, simultaneously analysing the role played by Cold War dynamics and the legacies of interwar Romanian history and Romanian political culture. Only by keeping these factors together, Ceauşescu and his peculiar way of being a leader become interpretable, going beyond simplistic narratives which emphasise just the grotesque side of his 24 years of rule. The political climate of interwar Romania, the marginality of the Communist Party, the relationship between communism and nationalism, and the ambiguous impact of Khrushchev's deStalinisation speech left an indelible mark on Ceauşescu. The combination of these factors helps us explain his rule, including some of its worst degenerations, and give it coherence, abandoning the ideas of the two Ceauşescus (the good one of 1968 and the bad of 1989).

The argument put forward is that Nicolae Ceauşescu embodies the unresolved issues of Romanian political history: aspirations to modernisation, the troubled relationship between cities and countryside, the weakness of leftist thought, the centrality of nationalism, and the inferiority complex of small states and their fear of disappearance. Ceauşescu's rule is simultaneously a product of these issues and an attempt to go beyond them.

Therefore, I will focus extensively on Ceauşescu's youth and early career to highlight, in the chapter's last sections, to what extent the events and the atmospheres he experienced between the 1930s and the 1950s can help us interpret his figure and rule.

A humble cobbler at the service of class struggle

Nicolae Ceauşescu was born on 26 January 1918, the third of ten children, in Scorniceşti, a desolate village in southern Romania, one of the country's poorest areas. The Ceauşescus looked like a typical family of rural Romania. The householder Andruţa worked in the fields the whole day, and at night he did not disdain the company of a bottle and a mistress. His wife, Licsandra, Nicolae's mother, cared about the house and the children. The whole family lived in a two-room wooden house, which was still bigger than many others nearby.

128 Francesco Magno

In late communism, the official party's propagandists portrayed the Ceaușescus as an extremely poverty-stricken family, striving every day to guarantee a meal to the children. This narrative was instrumental in shaping the image of the leader who became familiar with class consciousness from a very early age. According to the official tale, the young Nicolae began to develop revolutionary instincts during his childhood in Scornicești, looking at the degradation of Romanian peasants' life. In the official autobiography he wrote for the party in 1949, Nicolae declared that the family owned ten hectares of land, a medium property for Romanian interwar standards. However, as Ceaușescu's biographer Lavinia Betea pointed out, 'according to the 1930 census, the only one carried out during the interwar period, three-quarters of rural properties consisted of maximum 5 ha, and only 5.5% owned between 10 and 20 ha.'[6] Consequently, the Ceaușescus were far from indigent. Even the presence of strong proletarian class consciousness in 1920s Scornicești is improbable. Universal suffrage had been conceded to peasants only after the First World War as a reward for their military efforts; the countryside lacked political culture and basic knowledge of political and institutional mechanisms.

Thus, the Ceaușescus were not communists, nor were they indigent. Nevertheless, it would be wrong to consider them wealthy. In 1920s southern Romania, owning land did not necessarily translate into high incomes. Cultivation techniques were rudimentary, and peasants lacked a profit mentality. They ignored basic principles of modern agriculture, such as crop rotation, and did not have any proper location for storage.[7] The collapse of the price of wheat that followed the 1929 world crisis deteriorated peasants' economic conditions even further.

Under these circumstances, it is not particularly surprising that in 1930 Andruța and Licsandra sent the 11-year-old Nicolae to work in Bucharest, where the older sister Niculina had already moved. Indeed, during the interwar period, Romania was experiencing the first mass migration from the countryside to the cities. As for many other teenagers of peasant origins, for Nicolae leaving the family represented the chance of a better future.

In the early 1930s, Bucharest was thriving. After the victory in the war and the annexation of lands that had previously belonged to the Habsburg (Transylvania and Bukovina) and the Russian (Bessarabia) empires,[8] Romania aspired to become a regional power, and Bucharest reflected these aspirations. The city had started to develop geographically and demographically before the war, but after the conflict, the population growth rates boomed. From 348,000 inhabitants in 1916, the population grew so fast as to reach almost one million in 1941.[9] The capital was growing too fast, the competition in the job market was ruthless, and it was hard for newcomers with few resources to gain satisfactory living standards. Nevertheless, thanks to Niculina's help, Nicolae found a job as a cobbler apprentice.

According to his autobiography, Nicolae joined the communist youth union *Uniunea Tineretului Comunist* (UTC) in 1933. Officially, he was co-opted by his employer, but the details of his adhesion to the communist cause remain unclear. At that time, the Romanian Communist Party (RCP) resembled more of a religious sect than a political group. Born in May 1921, when the then-Socialist Party general assembly voted for the transformation into the Communist Party and for the adhesion to the Third International, the RCP had in Gheorghe Cristescu, known as *Plăpumarul* (literally 'the blanket maker') its first secretary. However, he was soon marginalised as he challenged Moscow over the future of Bessarabia. Indeed, the Soviet Union claimed its sovereignty over the region, which since 1812 had been part of the Russian Empire, not recognising the union with the Kingdom of Romania that had occurred on 27 March 1918. After Cristescu's dismissal, the RCP surrendered to the Soviet requests, and that prevented it from gaining ample popular support and political legitimacy. The annexation of Transylvania, Bukovina, and Bessarabia had represented the fulfilment of the national project, namely the union under the same statehood of the lands inhabited by Romanian speakers. For public opinion, denying its legitimacy and embracing the Soviet Union's dogmas implicitly meant condemning Romania to marginality and everlasting subjugation to foreign powers. The general hostility towards the communists increased as the RCP did not limit itself to discursive acceptance of the Soviet narrative but acted concretely to undermine Romanian sovereignty. Communist activists, with Soviet support, undertook frequent terrorist attacks in Bessarabia and fostered popular uprisings. As a result, at the end of the same year, the government led by the National Liberal Party outlawed the RCP which from that moment on operated clandestinely. The communist message managed to find its way only within isolated clusters, such as the railway unions, or among mavericks attracted by the Marxist message. Thus, the RCP became an entity formed by small, secretly operating groups with scarce coordination and weak leadership. Indeed, after Cristescu, the RCP had only non-Romanian leaders approved by the Kremlin throughout the interwar period.

When he joined the party at the age of 14, however, Ceaușescu should not have been too aware of the party's ambiguities. What impressed Nicolae and convinced him to embrace the communist cause was the bloody repression of the Bucharest railway workers' strike in February 1933, one of the founding events of communist epics. On that occasion, the Romanian army violently dispersed the workers who had occupied the factories of the national railway company on strike because of the lowering of wages. Seven people died, and 44 were injured. Fifteen hundred were arrested and sent to Jilava, a prison not far from Bucharest, where the authorities used to lock communists and other people convicted of political crimes.[10] One of the strike's masterminds was Gheorghe Gheorghiu-Dej,[11] Ceaușescu's political mentor and predecessor at the head of the party, an electrician active in railway workers' unions.

In June 1934, Ceaușescu organised donations for the workers arrested at the railway factory and gathered letters of protest against the army. Discovered by the police, he was arrested and interrogated but never revealed the identities of his accomplices. Released shortly thereafter, less than three months later, he was arrested again for joining the meetings of the so-called Antifascists Committee

130 Francesco Magno

(*Comitetul National Antifascist*), an organisation under the Comintern patronage, which had as its primary goal to unite political forces opposed to the radical right. After spending house arrest in Scorniceşti, Nicolae was appointed as leader of the UTC in the Prahova district in southern Romania.

In January 1936, he experienced a new arrest after the police found communist brochures and publications in his house.[12] For the first time, Ceauşescu went to trial. He was judged by a military court, which found him guilty of distributing illegal material and conspiracy and condemned him to two and a half years in prison. It was the first direct jail experience for the 18-year-old Nicolae, a mandatory step for every aspiring revolutionary leader. The first months must have been hard for Ceauşescu, who resisted fiercely as required by the communist rules. According to his cellmate, Toma A. Toma, he was introverted and never shared intimate feelings. Relatives did not pay him any visit; only party mates sometimes sent some packages.[13]

Once the court rejected his appeal in August 1936, the authorities sent him to Doftana in southern Romania, another prison dedicated to political criminals. According to the Romanian historian Cristina Diac, the choice of placing together in the same location the communist activists strengthened their comradeship and commitment to the cause. In jail, even those who, at that time, did not have an unshakable Marxist faith became loyal communist soldiers.[14] This was Ceauşescu's case. He entered the prison as a young agitator but walked out as a mature party servant.

In Doftana, he met all the future leaders of communist Romania: Vasile Luca, Alexandru Draghici, Chivu Storica, and, above all, Gheorghe Gheorghiu-Dej, his real mentor. Spending time in jail with Dej changed Ceauşescu's perspective on communism and class struggle and, on a more general level, it changed his life. During detention, Gheorghiu-Dej acted as the undisputed leader of the communist group behind bars. He struggled with authorities to improve prisoners' living standards; after protracted negotiations, he obtained newspapers and books and continued to organise the revolutionary activity. Gheorghe Apostol, a young communist confined to Doftana and one of Nicolae Ceauşescu's main opponents for the RCP's leadership in 1965, described Dej as a man 'who found time and had the patience to have friendly conversations with all the prisoners. . . . Everyone recognized his merits.'[15]

Doftana's detention left an indelible mark on Ceauşescu's life not only because of his political meetings. During the confinement, he was involved in what other communist prisoners called an 'inappropriate relationship.' Rumours circulated about a homosexual affair with Smil Marcovici, one of the RCP's founders, 25 years older than Nicolae. Marcovici's homosexuality was well known among party members, as well as his appreciation for younger lovers. It is still unclear how willingly Ceauşescu accepted Marcovici's attention. The whole affair remains, still today, obscure. According to Dumitru Popescu, an RCP's Central Committee member during Ceauşescu's rule, what happened in Doftana explained Nicolae's

Nicolae Ceauşescu **131**

dependence on his first – and only – girlfriend. 'With patience, comprehension and tenderness,' Elena pushed Nicolae to abandon 'customs he had learnt in the darkness of prison, forcing him to move back to heterosexual love.'[16]

Ceauşescu met Elena Petrescu shortly after his release from Doftana in December 1938. They made their relationship public during the summer of 1939 after months of dating. Like Nicolae, Elena came from a peasant family and moved to Bucharest in search of a better future. She met Nicolae through her brother Gheorghe, a member of the Communist Party. The first phase of the relationship with Elena coincided with the beginning of the Second World War and a period of dramatic changes, which soon affected Ceauşescu's life.

In 1938, after a bloodless coup, King Carol II Hohenzollern-Sigmaringen seized power, transforming Romania into an authoritarian state which had Mussolini's Italy as its primary model. Yet international events accelerated the fall of the so-called Royal Dictatorship. In August 1939, Nazi Germany and the Soviet Union signed the Molotov–Ribbentrop Pact. According to the Secret Protocol attached to the final agreement, the two powers established their spheres of influence in eastern Europe; consequently, the Soviet Union would have retaken control of Bessarabia and northern Bukovina. On 26 June 1940, the Romanian ambassador in Moscow received an ultimatum through which the Soviets claimed the restitution of the two areas. Carol II had to accept Soviet requests and proclaim the end of Romanian sovereignty over the two regions. The loss of Bessarabia and Northern Bukovina enhanced anti-communist feelings and brought stricter control over RCP's covert activities.

Nicolae Ceauşescu fell victim to this climate. Betrayed by one of his associates, he was arrested in July 1940 for distributing flags and banners to comrades. From prison, he observed the end of the Royal Dictatorship,[17] Carol II's escape, his substitution with his son Mihai, the installation of Antonescu's authoritarian government, and Romania's entrance into the Second World War on the side of Nazi Germany. In jail he met once again with Gheorghiu-Dej and other former cellmates.

When analysing Ceauşescu's government, it is important to pay enough attention to the influence of the time spent in detention on his later style of rule. Especially during his last stay in prison between 1940 and 1944, Ceauşescu absorbed and internalised peculiar models. The first was the idea of subjugation to an undisputed leader whose power is based on an unshakable legitimacy. In jail, this kind of leader was Gheorghiu-Dej. The second fundamental principle he learnt was cohesion. To survive the harshness of imprisonment and carry on in the class struggle, comrades had to stick together, each devoted to his task. On this idea of cohesion, he later founded his interpretation of the party and society.[18] This last arrest symbolically put an end to Ceauşescu's youth. An era that marked him politically and personally and enormously influenced his future behaviour.

Outlawed in 1924, the Romanian Communist Party was a small formation, extremely dependent on the Soviet Union and whose leading positions were

132 Francesco Magno

occupied by the Comintern functionaries. Consequently, Romanian communists were never able to develop their own cultural identity or, in other words, to adapt communism to Romanian peculiarities. Superficial Stalinism remained their primary reference. Nicolae Ceauşescu grew up in this political and cultural atmosphere.

From a personal point of view, he never got rid of the paranoia of the people forced to act in secret, with the constant fear of being discovered and punished. The years of political activism at the service of a party marginalised by institutional politics had strengthened the underdog mentality typical of peasants coming to the big city with few resources and nothing to lose.

In Gheorghiu-Dej's shadows

Ceauşescu was released on 5 August 1944, 18 days before the end of Antonescu's government and Romania's geopolitical and military turnaround. On 20 August, the Red Army started a new offensive on the Iaşi-Chisinau line, obtaining a clear victory and breaking through the country. On 23 August,[19] King Mihai dismissed Ion Antonescu and had him arrested. He began official talks with the Allies for an armistice in the following hours. Subsequently, he appointed a new government, led by General Constantin Sănătescu, endorsed by all the parties that had opposed Antonescu, including the RCP. In the new scenario, the communists became essential because of their ties with the Soviet Union.

Not surprisingly, a few days after Antonescu's arrest, communist activists who had managed to escape to the Soviet Union in the early stages of the war came back to Romania. The most prominent figure among them was Ana Pauker, a woman of Jewish descent who had fled the country in 1941 and spent the war years in the Soviet Union, where she had strengthened her connections with the Soviet leadership. She became the leader of the new RCP's Ruling Committee, which also included Gheorghe Gheorghiu-Dej and Nicolae Ceauşescu. He was entrusted with the party's youth organisation, the aforementioned UTC. Indeed, not only did he have experience in youth union activities, he was also legitimised by six years in prison during the Carol and Antonescu dictatorships. The features of his relationship with Ana Pauker in those troubled months are unclear, even though he later defined her return to the country as 'a disgrace.'[20]

The communist representative in the new government was Lucreţiu Pătrăşcanu, a lawyer from a wealthy family, educated in Germany, who had embraced the communist cause in the 1930s. He became the new Minister of Justice. Dej, Pauker, and Pătrăşcanu represented three different ways of being a communist. While Pauker had been active for years in the communist international movement and worked for the Comintern, Dej was an uneducated electrician who had learnt about class struggle through unions' activism. He did not have international connections and had never visited the Soviet Union. Pătrăşcanu was more an intellectual than a party activist. His communism was academic and doctrinaire; he was an upper-middle-class professional, not just in his family roots but also in his public behaviour. Not surprisingly, he was the only communist capable of negotiating with the king and the other political leaders.

Given the above, it is easy to understand why Dej remained Ceaușescu's primary reference. Nicolae could not boast Pauker's direct experience of the Soviet Union or Pătrășcanu's intellectual background. With Dej, on the contrary, Nicolae shared the humble origins and years of working clandestinely and in detention. In the troubled months which followed the armistice with the Allies signed on 12 September, however, the sharp differences within the Communist Party were overshadowed by the common ambition to gain absolute power. In the RCP's rise to power, the Soviet Union's help proved fundamental. The presence of the Red Army on Romanian soil put pressure on the king. In 1945, he was forced to form a new government within which the communists held key posts, such as the Ministry of Internal Affairs, the Ministry of Justice, and the Ministry of Infrastructure and Public Transports.

The direct control of the police, the secret services, and the judiciary allowed the communists to gradually eliminate political opponents. Many opposition leaders were sentenced to life in prison, accused of collaboration with Antonescu and the Nazis during the war. Others were accused of treason just because they had tried to flee the country. Elections were rigged, giving the RCP's majorities unthinkable for a formation that, in 1945, numbered only a thousand members. The last obstacle to absolute power was the king, who was forced to abdicate on 30 December 1947. A week before, on 23 December, Nicolae and Elena married in Bucharest. The Ceaușescus sealed their union right when the RCP was about to eliminate its last enemy.

Once absolute power was gained, the time had come to solve once and for all the matter of the party leadership. Two factions faced one another. On one side, the so-called Muscovites, namely those who had spent the war years in the Soviet Union, led by Ana Pauker. On the other, Gheorghiu-Dej and his prison mates. Despite Pauker's experience in the Soviet Union, in the end, Stalin preferred Dej. Pauker's Jewish descent may have influenced the Soviet leader, who appreciated Dej's political trajectory in the clandestine movement and his 'healthy' proletarian roots. The party's congress of February 1948[21] officially sanctioned the new balance of forces. Dej was elected as the party's general secretary while Ana Pauker was appointed secretary for agriculture, a position deprived of concrete power.

She was forced to work closely with Nicolae Ceaușescu, appointed deputy minister for agriculture in May. He was born in the countryside and knew the agricultural world much more than Pauker. He later mocked her by saying that 'she couldn't even tell the difference between the wheat and the sickle.'[22] Nevertheless, the two had to work together in the complicated process of land collectivisation. Pauker would have preferred a slow approach to the matter.

First and foremost, the party had to focus on mechanisation and productivity and then on the creation of collective farms. Ceaușescu, on the contrary, had as

134 Francesco Magno

his first goal the elimination of the rich peasants (*chiaburi*, the Romanian *kulaki*). Eventually, Dej used Pauker's hesitation to accuse her of 'rightist deviationism' and marginalise her. In February 1953, she was arrested and released only thanks to Molotov's mediation. Ana Pauker spent the rest of her life under house arrest until she died in 1960.

Even if, in 1950, Ceaușescu abandoned the agricultural sector to hold the post of deputy minister of the army, collectivisation remained one of his main concerns throughout the decade. He was often sent to different localities to supervise the process and, when required, to suppress rebellions. In 1957, in Vadu Roșca, a little village in Eastern Romania, he commanded the military units that mercilessly suppressed a peasant uprising.[23] According to the official numbers, on that occasion, nine people died.[24]

The harshness of collectivisation reflected the atmosphere of terror of those years. Indeed, during the 1950s, Romania became one of the harshest regimes worldwide. Hundreds of thousands of people were arrested with the final goal of eliminating the whole pre-war élite. The prison of Sighet, a city in northern Romania close to the Hungarian border, hosted the leaders of interwar political parties, Greek and Roman Catholic Church bishops, and other prominent figures of the cultural or judicial world.[25] Most of them died there because of the harsh conditions of imprisonment.

Victims of communist terror were not just political opponents and representatives of the bourgeois. External repression went hand in hand with internal purges. In 1954, after years in detention, Lucrețiu Pătrășcanu was killed, as Dej feared that, after Stalin's death, the new Soviet leadership could have seen in him a suitable leader for the new course.[26] Just as Dej was destroying what had been left of pre-war Romania, Nicolae Ceaușescu climbed the party's hierarchical ladder. His proximity to Dej and the years spent in prison with him saved Nicolae from the purges and paved the way for his ascension to leadership. In 1954, Dej made him a member of the Politburo, a veritable step forward for his career. He took advantage of his position to strengthen his connection with the leader even further, distinguishing himself, especially during the 1956 Hungarian uprising. Indeed, Dej feared that the revolution could extend to Transylvania, home to a vast Hungarian community. Therefore, he sent Ceaușescu to Cluj to ensure that the local students remained loyal to the party. His efforts in those days proved fundamental for saving the regime's stability and were appreciated by Dej, who took advantage of the Hungarian events to strengthen his power.

Indeed, Dej's position had become more fragile after the twentieth Congress of the Soviet Communist Party. Instigated by Khrushchev's condemnation of Stalin, some party members started to accuse him of a cult of personality. He feared the Soviets could endorse a change in Romania, closer to the new Soviet leadership. The Hungarian revolution came at the right moment, proving fundamental for his political survival. He offered the Soviets full Romanian support in the repression of the rebellion, condemning the 'fascist' forces which were jeopardising the working-class revolution. He received Moscow's gratitude and managed to put aside the claims for internal changes. In other words, he gained time to rethink Romania's relationship with Moscow and to build a new legitimacy for the regime.

Deprived of the Soviet endorsement that he had enjoyed under Stalin, Dej could find new legitimacy only within his country. The simplest way to bring the Romanian people and the Communist Party closer was nationalism. The party's propagandists elaborated a new version of the recent history which, as Romanian political scientist Dragos Petrescu correctly argues, exhumed two standard features of Romanian political history: fear of Moscow and distrust towards Budapest.[27] In the new official narrative, Dej and his former cellmates were presented as genuine defenders of the Romanian people against Ana Pauker and the other Muscovites who wanted to transform Romania into a mere Soviet satellite. Moreover, Gheorghiu-Dej often insisted on the 'Romanianness' of Transylvania, recovering one of the primary *topoi* of nineteenth-century Romanian nationalist discourse. It is worth underlining that this turnaround served mainly to save Dej's position. It was far from a re-evaluation of the recent past or condemnation of Stalinism. On the contrary, it was a way to disguise it under new forms.

New interpretations of recent history represented the premise for a concrete political shift, which occurred in 1964, when the party issued an official document stating:

> It is the exclusive right of each communist party to elaborate independently its political line and specific objectives, as well as the ways and methods to reach them. . . . There is no 'parent' party and 'offspring' party. . ., but there is the large family of communist and workers parties having equal rights.[28]

The 1964 acceleration arose from a new clash with the Soviets regarding economic policies. Indeed, in the early 1960s, Moscow had promoted a new 'Division of Labor' among socialist countries: each had to specialise in one particular economic sector and supply the whole bloc with its output. According to the Soviet programme, Romania and Bulgaria would become the primary agricultural suppliers of communist eastern Europe. The Soviet idea went against Dej's plan of industrial development and modernisation. As an orthodox Stalinist, he believed in industrialisation by all means; Romania could not have become a modern socialist state without a solid national industry. That explains why, until his death, he fostered nationalism and anti-Soviet sentiment. He was clever enough to understand that the only way to legitimise the regime and to carry out his plans in the post-Stalin era was to partially recover the themes of nationalism, which had been successful throughout contemporary Romanian history.

Ceauşescu was alongside Dej during the elaboration of the new doctrine, internalised it, and continued to apply it when he succeeded him. His national Stalinism was anything but original. On the contrary, it was the continuation of Dej's independent policy.

136 Francesco Magno

Stalinism disguised

Gheorghe Gheorghiu-Dej died on 19 March 1965. After a few days of negotiations among party dignitaries, Ceauşescu was chosen as his successor. His knowledge of the entire party's structure was a fundamental asset for him and did much to secure him the endorsement of the local sections. In fact, since 1958, he had been the head of the so-called Organizing Department *Secţia Organizatorică*, (SO), which dealt with the party's internal organisation nationally and locally. The SO was in charge of the appointments of local secretaries and decided upon promotions and wages. This post had marked a watershed in Ceauşescu's political trajectory. According to one of the most prominent communist ideologues Alexandru Bârlădeanu, leading the SO allowed Ceauşescu to pave his way to the leadership and explain his success in 1965 after Dej's death. He had access to the personal files of RCP's members; he knew their weaknesses and, consequently, he could blackmail them all. He acquired debts of gratitude with the ones he promoted, and when the time came, he did not hesitate to collect the debt.[29]

In the spring of 1968, in one of his first resounding acts as leader, Ceauşescu rehabilitated Lucreţiu Pătrăşcanu and other party members imprisoned during Dej's rule and shifted the blame of the regime's degeneration onto his predecessor. Surprisingly, Ceauşescu repudiated his model and mentor, blaming him for the terror of the 1950s, the political assassinations, and the deportations, showing unexpected political cynicism as he did so. The incredible turnaround was not due to an alleged desire for liberalisation. Blaming the defunct leader for past crimes had become a custom in the Soviet Bloc, Khrushchev's denunciation of Stalin being the most paradigmatic example. Ceauşescu's real aim was to clear the field from his main competitor for the leadership, Alexandru Draghici, who, during the 1950s' terror, was minister of internal affairs and de facto chief of the secret police. By rehabilitating Pătrăşcanu and denouncing the abuses committed during his trial, Ceauşescu eliminated his primary internal opponent and refashioned himself as a new type of leader. Draghici was excluded by the government while the other party's dignitaries accused by Ceauşescu of misbehaviours in the Pătrăşcanu case declared their subjugation to the new leader to keep their privileges and avoid trial. Not surprisingly, the Romanian historian Adrian Cioroianu defines Pătrăşcanu's rehabilitation as a disguised political purge.[30] Even the artistic and cultural liberalisation can be interpreted with his will to distance himself from the past. His criticism of 'vulgar sociologism' and 'socialist realism' in literature did not arise from a sincere desire for artistic freedom but from the will to 'undermine the traditional leading group.'[31]

What is important to stress is that, even though he wanted to present himself as a new leader, Ceauşescu did not deviate from Dej's policies. Independence from Moscow and the rhetorical display of nationalism continued to be the beacon of the RCP even after 1965. In a speech delivered in May 1966, he showed continuity with his predecessor by denouncing Soviet interpretations of the Romanian national question. In particular, Ceauşescu stigmatised the interwar RCP's passive acceptance of Soviet claims on Bessarabia. He defined the decisions taken at that time as 'deeply erroneous,' as they 'called for the dismemberment of the national State and the Romanian people's disintegration.'[32]

The balcony speech mentioned at the beginning of this piece and the fierce condemnation of the invasion of Czechoslovakia by the Soviet Union and the Warsaw Pact's allies represented a further step in that direction. The speech did not result from the appreciation towards Alexander Dubcek's reforms but from the necessity to reaffirm Romania's independence and autonomy. [33]

In the West, however, nobody seemed to notice Ceauşescu's instrumental use of the Prague Spring. After the 21 August speech, he became a veritable political star. Heads of state invited him for official visits, and investors started to imagine Romania as a new profitable market. In 1969, Richard Nixon visited Romania. It was the first official visit of a US president in the communist bloc, a reward for Ceauşescu's display of independence.[34] Ceauşescu, on his side, was extremely glad to sign commercial agreements with Western businessmen, as they allowed him to escape Soviet plans to transform Romania into a mere agricultural supplier for the whole Eastern bloc. Indeed, as a good, orthodox Stalinist, he could not conceive economic development without constructing a competitive national heavy industry, and the West was instrumental in achieving this goal. Agriculture served exclusively to finance industrial development.

Economic growth and improvement of living standards contributed to strengthening the image of the Romanian leader as an example of moderate socialism. Yet signs of the opposite were far from invisible. A few months before the balcony speech, when asked by reform-orientated party colleagues to recognise the role of the market in economic relations, Ceauşescu responded by reiterating the prominence of the planned economy and the central role of heavy industry in the country's development.[35]

Despite the tentative signs of cultural liberalisation and the Interior Ministry's reorganisation after Draghici's removal, the secret police (the sadly famous *Securitate*) was still active and pervasive. In 1965, the notorious Decree Law 12 'On the Medical Treatment of Dangerously Mentally Ill Persons' was issued and thereafter used to lock political dissidents (or presumed such) in psychiatric hospitals. In the early 1970s, when Ceauşescu was praised worldwide for his stance towards the Soviets, 'special psychiatric hospitals' were created all over the country. The most notorious was in Ştei, a city in Western Romania at the time named *Dr. Petru Groza* as a tribute to the prime minister of the first communist cabinet in 1945.[36]

In 1966, Ceauşescu promulgated the notorious Decree 770, which recriminalised abortion, repealing a 1957 law that had liberalised it. As Jill Massino correctly recalls Ceauşescu, like Stalin before him, considered a large workforce essential to economic development and national sovereignty. . . . Ceauşescu's demographic policies were rooted in a desire to increase the workforce and create a vigorous, self-sufficient nation.[37] Women were victims of all kinds of abuses: gynaecological exams in the workplace, strict police control in hospitals, and imprisonment.[38] In

138 Francesco Magno

no other country of the Eastern bloc women experienced something comparable. In the same year, *Time* magazine dedicated its cover to Nicolae Ceaușescu. Above his face, the title read 'Life Under Relaxed Communism.'[39]

Degeneration (or rediscovering the roots)

In the summer of 1971, Ceaușescu went on a trip to East Asia. He visited China, North Korea, Vietnam, and Mongolia. Images of his reception in Pyongyang are astonishing. On the way from the airport to the city centre, the open car carrying Ceaușescu and Kim il-Sung was accompanied by a spectacular choreography. White-dressed Korean women waved sinuously yellow and purple scarfs while behind them, men held the Korean and Romanian flags and the portraits of the two leaders.

A few days after his return, on 6 July, Ceaușescu delivered a speech to the RCP's Executive Committee in which he stressed the necessity to increase political education among the population and 'continuously strengthen the party's leading role in all the political and educational matters.'[40] That meant enhancing the party's presence in the peripheries and, above all, in schools and universities to avoid deviation from the official doctrine. The speech marked the end of the timid liberalisation of the 1960s and inaugurated a personality cult that peaked in the following decade.

For years scholars debated the 1971 turnaround. Was it really the trip to communist Asia that changed Ceaușescu's attitude? While most historians of communist Romania concede that Mao and Kim il-Sung could have inspired Ceaușescu's cult of personality, it is now commonplace to interpret the 1971 speech as something Ceaușescu was planning for years. According to the Polish historian Adam Burakowski, Ceaușescu started thinking about tightening up the party's control on society after a students' demonstration occurred in December 1968, which brought him to blame the higher education system, incapable of adequately indoctrinating students.[41] Cezar Stanciu, on the other hand, stresses the importance of the Polish riots of December 1970 and their influence on Ceaușescu. He feared that a sharp separation between the party and society could have brought protests similar to those which pushed the Kremlin to withdraw its support for Władysław Gomulka and endorse his substitution with Edward Gierek.[42] Beyond the different interpretations, it is essential to emphasise that the 1971 turning point did not symbolise the end of Ceaușescu's liberal phase and the birth of a crazy tyrant. Even in the 1960s, his goal was to construct a socialist society of industrial workers led by the Communist Party.

In the 1970s, however, the internal and external scenarios were changing. Between 1969 and 1971, various socialist countries experienced leadership changes: besides Gierek in Poland, new figures emerged in Czechoslovakia (Gustáv Husák) and East Germany (Erich Honecker). These changes put pressure on Ceaușescu, enhanced his fear of losing power, and probably reawakened the sense of paranoia and uncertainty which characterised his youth as a young agitator. Moreover, the atmosphere of *détente* between the two blocs made the presence of a communist maverick superfluous. Claims of independence progressively lost the strength they had in the 1960s.

To this we must add the beginning of the economic crisis. Indeed, economic growth stopped, mainly because of Ceauşescu's stubborn obsession with heavy industry. While other eastern European countries were starting to differentiate their economies, laying the foundations of a proto-consumerist society, Ceauşescu prioritised state-led industrial development, denying any opening to the market. His Stalinist orthodoxy prevented him from accepting the economic changes already affecting the Communist bloc, keeping him anchored to the superficial Marxism he had learnt in prison in the 1930s. Unlike Hungary, where the local Communist Party managed to control society by granting good living standards and consumerism, Ceauşescu had to adopt what Katherine Verdery defines as a 'symbolic-ideological mode of control.'[43] Unable to provide consumer goods, he had to secure people's subjugation by creating social cohesion around common symbolic values. The most powerful bearer of symbolic meaning was the nation. Nevertheless, claims of independence from the Soviet Union and autonomous rule were no longer sufficient. To cement society around him, Ceausescu had to recover the traditional nationalist *topoi* of pre-communist history and include them in a broader narrative culminating with his rise to power.

Historians rewrote national history.[44] For the official narrative, the Communist Party had won the centuries-old struggle of the Romanian people for their self-determination. A *file rouge* connected Ceauşescu with the Dacian kings fighting the Romans, the medieval Wallachian and Moldovan princes who had faced the Turks, the national movement of the nineteenth century, and the army that had fought in the First World War to unite Transylvania and Bessarabia with the rest of the country.[45] Not surprisingly, since the 1970s, the interwar anti-Hungarian feelings re-emerged powerfully, encouraged by Ceausescu's support. Indeed, he often emphasised the superiority of the Romanian civilisation to the Magyar (or Slavic) one. While the former, he claimed, arose from the union between Dacian and Roman culture, the latter was essentially nomadic.[46]

During the 1970s and the 1980s, the cult of personality reached grotesque peaks. More and more often, portraits and propagandistic banners represented Ceauşescu – and not rarely also his wife – together with sixteenth-century Prince Vlad Ţepes, commonly referred to as 'the Impaler,' or with Ştefan cel Mare (Stephen the Great), the sixteenth-century Christian prince of Moldova. For the new official history, Ceauşescu succeeded where previous leaders failed: he gave dignity to the Romanian people and freed them from slavery. Not surprisingly, he started to present himself as a monarch. In 1974, he assumed the role of President of the Republic, and right after the appointment, he received a sceptre as a symbol of his absolute rule. The Spanish painter Salvador Dalì, amused by the ceremony pictures, sent an ironic telegram to the Romanian leader, congratulating him for his sceptre.

Incredibly, the Romanian press did not grasp the sarcastic tone of the telegram and published it the next day.

Vladimir Tismăneanu links the ridiculous evolution of Ceauşescu's cult of personality to his 'pariah syndrome.' Ceauşescu suffered from a sort of inferiority complex typical of people who spent their youth at the margins of society. Moreover, he felt a sense of awe towards his predecessor, Gheorghe Gheorghiu-Dej, who had distinguished himself during his prison years as a veritable leader. Ceauşescu lacked Dej's charisma and authority; consequently, his weird cult of personality would represent a way to equalise his mentor.[47]

According to the Romanian historian Florin Constantiniu, Ceauşescu's cult of personality derived from the 1970s composition of the Communist Party. Incapable of adapting to industrial work, hundreds of peasants who had moved to the cities started to work for the RCP as activists. Lacking proper Marxist education, they centred their propagandistic messages around the leader.[48]

Beyond the grotesque degeneration, it is more important to understand why Ceauşescu's cult of personality drew so much from the traditional nationalist discourse developed since Romania's independence. The theme has been much debated among historians. Katherine Verdery argues that Ceauşescu was almost forced onto the terrain of nationalism by intellectuals, who progressively imposed it as the 'master symbol,' the only one capable of putting aside all the other discourses. Ceauşescu became the leading representative of this nationalist resurrection, 'but he did not do so from a position of dominance over its meaning.'[49] It was not Ceauşescu who entrenched nationalism in the Romanian cultural discourse. The post-war communist takeover and the following decade of terror did not manage to extirpate the roots of nationalist discourse, which had been so strong during the interwar period, stirred by the post-First World War annexation. Anti-Russian and anti-Hungarian feelings continued to pervade large sectors of the cultural world and eventually found a relief valve after Dej's declaration of independence of 1964. Therefore, Ceauşescu absorbed something which already existed. Verdery goes as far as to say that 'the party's own national exaggeration reflects, precisely, the effort that was required to assert some authority over the national idea.'[50] Romanian historian Cristian Vasile takes a different stance, arguing that for Dej and Ceauşescu, nationalism served mainly to find political legitimacy and widespread consensus at times of a tense relationship with Moscow.[51] It was always the party which set the cultural agenda and controlled how the nationalist discourse was purveyed.

Surely, Ceauşescu tried to channel nationalist feelings into his project, which always was the transformation of Romania into a modern communist country. He never forgot the lessons learnt during the clandestine period and never changed his inner self. Consequently, during Ceausescu's rule, what happened in Romania was not a conscious ethnicisation of the regime, as has been advocated for decades by Romanian historians educated between the 1960s and 1980s. Despite the frequent use of the nationalist discourse, the *Conducător* remained a devoted communist throughout his life.

The dramatic 1980s

The Iranian revolution of 1979 and the following oil price increase had a huge impact upon the Romanian economy. In fact, in the second half of the 1970s, Romania had invested in refineries and petrochemical factories that could not work without an enormous amount of oil. Rather than abjure his faith and beliefs, shutting down the factories and relocating labour, Ceauşescu decided to ask for foreign loans to save his industrialisation plans. Simultaneously, however, the US Federal Reserve increased interest rates to fight inflation, deepening the debt crisis in many countries. In 1981, Romania owed international creditors three billion dollars.[52] Faced with international hostility after his requests to reschedule payments, Ceauşescu felt that Romanian economic sovereignty was being threatened by outside forces. From this fear arose the choice to make the early payment of the foreign debt the absolute priority of the next five-year plan. Imports had to be cut, whereas the export of domestic production would have to finance the debt payment. Nevertheless, since the Romanian industrial output was not competitive in Western markets, and agricultural goods hardly entered the western European markets because of the protectionist Common Agricultural Policy of the European Economic Community, the only buyers of Romanian products were African and Asian countries. Unexpectedly enough, bearing in mind Ceauşescu's attitudes in the late 1960s, Romania by 1989 was diplomatically closer to the Third World than to the West.

The effects on the population of the austerity policies of the 1980s were dramatic. The already-low consumption rates decreased even further. Chronic shortages of food and other essential goods became the norm, and electricity and public lighting were rationed. The rage of the Romanian people increased looking at Ceauşescu's crazy expenses, such as the 'People's House' (*Casa Poporului*), an enormous building in the Bucharest city centre which had to symbolise the greatness of the leader.

People wondered what happened to the brave Ceauşescu of 1968, who had stirred patriotism and pride. The answer is that he never changed. Repaying the foreign debt had the same significance as condemning the Soviet invasion of Czechoslovakia in 1968: the defence of Romanian sovereignty. His modernisation ideas in 1989 were precisely the same as those in 1968 – industrialisation by all means. He always retained the principles learnt in prison and at Dej's service in the 1950s. Not surprisingly, he deplored Mikhail Gorbachev's attempts to reform the Soviet Union. For Ceauşescu, *perestroika* was a historical mistake, a fatal distancing from what he believed was socialist orthodoxy.

The bloody 1989 revolution that marked the end of his rule resulted mainly from the suffering of the 1980s. Everything started on 16 December, in Timişoara, with a small demonstration against the forced relocation of a Hungarian pastor suspected of espionage. It evolved, first, into a mass protest and then an open rebellion against the regime. Ceauşescu underestimated the events. He could not conceive the hatred

142 Francesco Magno

of his people. That same year, Romania had repaid its foreign debt entirely, and a bright future seemingly lay ahead. Finally, the austerity was over, and Romania, in his opinion, could thrive again, freed from the chains of the foreign powers.

Therefore, despite the dramatic news coming from Timişoara, he left for Iran, where he had to discuss important commercial deals, leaving Elena in charge of the situation. Back from Teheran, on 20 December, he appeared on national television, labelling the Timişoara demonstrators as 'terrorists' and 'anti-national.'[53] The next day, on 21 December, he delivered the speech mentioned at the beginning of this chapter. Only at that moment he finally realised just how serious the situation was. On the morning of 22 December, after discovering that his minister of defence had committed suicide and that raging demonstrators were ready to assault the Central Committee, Ceausescu left the capital by helicopter. His political experience ended just like it started: clandestinely, trying to avoid arrest. As Lavinia Betea recalls, Nicolae and Elena ran away 'without documents, money or food; a couple of hours before, they had a country.'[54] He hoped to lead the counter-revolution from the countryside but did not find any support. The radio had broken the news of their escape, and the army sided with demonstrators; his destiny was sealed. He was arrested in Târgovişte, a small city in Southern Romania, a few hours after the helicopter left the Central Committee building. Three days later, they were sentenced to death after a show trial. Ceauşescu's last moments were coherent with the rest of his life. In front of the military jury, he firmly declared that the only jury he recognised was the General Assembly of the Communist Party. Even in the last tragic moment of his life, he remained faithful to himself.

The tragic events of December 1989 have been televised worldwide, but the details of what really happened remain obscure. Too many people died even after Ceauşescu's arrest, and the responsible are still mysterious. Who gave the order? Who had an interest in bloodshed? A new study recently published claims that a *Securitate* special corps, trained to deal with insurrections and foreign occupations, tried to carry out a counter-revolution. According to the authors, the continuity of secret services personnel in post-communist Romania hindered fair investigations.[55]

Conclusions

Every year, on 26 January, a small group gathers at Nicolae Ceauşescu's grave to celebrate his birthday.[56] It is not really clear what they miss about communism: youth, job security, pensions, Marxism, or a mixture of them all.

In recent years, several polls have shown that a non-neglectable part of the Romanian people considers Nicolae Ceauşescu one of the best politicians in Romanian history. According to a 2014 opinion poll commissioned by the newspaper *Adevărul*, more than 24 per cent of Romanians considered Ceauşescu the best president Romania had ever had.[57] They probably forgot the pervasiveness of the Securitate, food shortages, and the grotesque cult of personality. Nevertheless, the polls data reflect the electoral history of post-communist Romania. Parties and leaders mixing radical

Nicolae Ceaușescu **143**

nationalism and social paternalism had enormous success and remained influential. Not surprisingly, in the aforementioned poll, behind Nicolae Ceaușescu, we find his successor, Ion Iliescu, another communist. Iliescu made a career within the Communist Party before being marginalised by Ceaușescu, who feared his ambition. After the arrest of Nicolae and Elena, he resurfaced, proclaiming himself the leader of the revolution. He repudiated Ceaușescu – just like Ceaușescu did with Dej – but not the communist experience as a whole. He just dressed the issues and the ambiguities Ceaușescu had embodied in new clothes suitable for the new epoch. Modernisation, the relationship between cities and the countryside, the features of the Romanian national identity, and the place of Romania in Europe continued to be a fundamental matter of dispute in the 1990s and remain so today.

Ceaușescu tried to solve the problems of Romania by combining Marxist theory and nationalism. His tragic trajectory represented the failures of two of the main ideologies of the twentieth century and a warning for future leaders.

Notes

1 The 1968 speech is readily available online, accessed September 30, 2022, www.you tube.com/watch?v=u9NUQgSeaVA.
2 Quoted in D. Petrescu, "Building the Nation, Instrumentalizing Nationalism: Revisiting Romanian National-Communism, 1965–1989," *Nationalities Papers* 4 (2009): 530.
3 Accessed September 30, 2022, www.youtube.com/watch?v=wWIbCtz_Xwk&t=74s.
4 On December 15, 2020, the most important Romanian newspaper, *Adevărul,* published an article about the 1971 visit in East Asia titled "The Trip That Screwed Romania in the 1970s. Ceaușescu's Megalomania Stirred by the Asian Spark," accessed October 24, 2022, https://adevarul.ro/stiri-locale/botosani/calatoria-care-a-nenorocit-romania-in-anii-70-2065372.html.
5 In 2018, the Romanian national television broadcast a documentary about Elena and her influence on Ceausescu's late degenerations, titled "The Female Pharaoh," accessed October 24, 2022, www.youtube.com/watch?v=RrHu-hbDLVg.
6 L. Betea, *Ceaușescu si epoca sa,* (Bucharest: Corint, 2021), 22.
7 B. Murgescu, *România și Europa. Acumularea decalajelor economice (1500–2010)* (Iași: Polirom, 2010), 230.
8 During the war Romania had sided with France, Great Britain, and tsarist Russia, aiming primarily at annexing Transylvania, at the time belonging to the Austro-Hungarian Empire. The outburst of the Bolshevik revolution and the crisis which Russia experienced thereafter allowed Romania to take control also of Bessarabia. After the war, Romania doubled its size and population, acquiring also a conspicuous number of non-Romanian ethnics.
9 J. R. Lampe, "Interwar Bucharest and the Promises of Urbanism," *Journal of Urban History* 3 (1983): 267.
10 E. Neagoe-Pleșa, "Gheorghe Gheorgiu-Dej și procesul ceferiștilor (1933–1934)," in *Comuniștii înainte de comunism: Procese și condamnări ale ilegaliștilor din România,* ed. A. Cioroianu (Bucharest: Editura Universității din București, 2014), 91.
11 Gheorghe Gheorghiu had already been for months under strict surveillance of the Romanian secret services, then known as *Siguranța.* When he moved to the Transylvanian town of Dej to work in the local factories, the *Siguranța* added the suffix Dej to his surname, to distinguish him from other Gheorghiu under investigation working in other factories all over the country.

144 Francesco Magno

12 Betea, *Ceauşescu*, 77–83.
13 C. Diac, "Nicolae Ceauşescu: tânăr, rebel şi ilegalist. O cotitură a destinului: Arestarea şi procesul din anul 1936," in *A fost odată ca niciodată. Partidul comunist român 1921–2021. Pentru o istorie dezinhibată a viitorului luminos*, ed. A. Cioroianu (Iaşi: Polirom, 2021), 180.
14 Ibid., 182.
15 G. Apostol, *Eu şi Gheorghiu-Dej* (Bucharest: Paco, 2011), 50.
16 L. Betea, C. Diac, F. R. Mihai, and I. Ţiu, *Viaţa lui Ceauşescu vol. I. Ucenicul Partidului* (Bucharest: Adevărul, 2012), 183.
17 Carol II left the country after the so-called Second Vienna Award. The agreement, arbitrated by Nazi Germany and Fascist Italy, had given Northern Transylvania to Hungary. The tide of popular discontent and the growing hostility of the army forced the king to put an end to his authoritarian experiment.
18 P. Campeanu, *Ceauşescu: Anii numaratorii inverse* (Iaşi: Polirom, 2002), 51.
19 During the communist era, the 23 August became Romanian national holiday.
20 Betea, *Ceauşescu*, 149.
21 At the 1948 Congress, after the merge with the Social-Democratic Party, the Romanian Communist Party changed its name to Romania Workers' Party (*Partidul Muncitoresc Român*). The word 'communist' returned in the party's official denomination only in 1965.
22 Quoted in R. Levy, *Ana Pauker: The Rise and Fall of a Jewish Communist* (Berkeley: University of California Press, 2001), 90.
23 G. Kligman and K. Verdery, *Peasants Under Siege: The Collectivization of Romanian Agriculture 1949–1962* (Princeton: Princeton University Press, 2011), 132.
24 Accessed October 28, 2022, www.memorialsighet.ro/tarani-din-vadu-rosca-vrancea-impuscati-la-4-decembrie-1957-timpul-revoltei-taranesti/.
25 D. Deletant, *Romania Under Communism: Paradox and Degeneration* (London: Routledge, 2019), 183.
26 On the Pătrăşcanu case, see L. Betea, *Lucreţiu Pătrăşcanu: Moartea unui lider comunist* (Bucharest: Curtea Veche, 2006).
27 D. Petrescu, "Community-Building and Identity Politics in Gheorghiu-Dej's Romania 1956–64," in *Stalinism Revisited: The Establishment of Communist Regimes in East-Central Europe*, ed. V. Tismăneanu (Budapest: CEU Press, 2009), 414.
28 Quoted in Ibid., 420.
29 L. Betea, C. Diac, F. R. Mihai, and I. Tiu, *Viata lui Ceauşescu, vol. II. Fiul Poporului* (Bucharest: Adevarul, 2013), 35.
30 A. Cioroianu, *Pe umerii lui Marx. O introducere in istoria comunismului romanesc* (Bucharest: Curtea Veche, 2005), 399.
31 V. Tismăneanu, *Stalinism for All Seasons: A Political History of Romanian Communism* (Berkeley: University of California Press, 2003), 193.
32 Quoted in W. van Meurs, *The Bessarabian Question in Communist Historiography. Nationalist and Communist Politics and History-Writing* (New York: Columbia University Press, 1994), 242.
33 On Ceauşescu's attitude towards the Prague Spring, see L. Betea, ed., *21 August 1968. Apoteoza lui Ceauşescu* (Bucharest: Corint, 2018).
34 P. Pechlivanis, "Between Detent and Differentiation: Nixon's Visit to Bucharest in August 1969," *Cold War History* 3 (2017): 241.
35 Tismăneanu, *Stalinism for All Seasons*, 198.
36 D. Deletant, *Ceauşescu and the Securitate. Coercion and Dissent in Romania, 1965–1989* (London: Routledge, 2015), 94–95.
37 J. Massino, *Ambiguous Transition: Gender, the State, and Everyday Life in Socialist and Postsocialist Romania* (New York: Berghahn, 2019), 261.
38 Ibid., 262.

Nicolae Ceauşescu **145**

39 *Time Magazine*, March 18, 1966.
40 N. Ceauşescu, *Propuneri de măsuri pentru imbunătaţirea activităţii politico-ideologice, de educare marxistst-leninista a membrilor de partid, a tuturor oamenilor muncii* (Bucharest: Editura Politica, 1971), 8.
41 A. Burakowski, *Dictatura lui Nicolae Ceauşescu, 1965–1989: Geniul Carpaţilor* (Iaşi: Polirom, 2011), 157.
42 C. Stanciu, "The End of Liberalization in Communist Romania," *The Historical Journal* 4 (2013): 1080–81.
43 K. Verdery, *National Ideology Under Socialism. Identity and Cultural Politics in Ceauşescu's Romania* (Berkeley: University of California Press, 1991), 86.
44 On Romanian historiography during Ceausescu's rule, see F. Zavatti, "Between History and Power: The Historiography of Romanian National-Communism (1964–1989)," *Cuadernos de Historia Contemporánea* 42 (2020): 39–58.
45 L. Boia, *Istorie şi mit în conştiinţa românească* (Bucharest: Humanitas, 2011), 354–66.
46 U. Korkut, "Nationalism Versus Internationalism: The Roles of Political and Cultural Elites in Interwar and Communist Romania," *Nationalities Papers* 2 (2006): 145.
47 Tismăneanu, *Stalinism for All Seasons*, 25–26.
48 F. Constantiniu, *O istorie sinceră a poporului român* (Bucharest: Univers Enciclopedic, 2011), 506.
49 Verdery, *National Ideology*, 124.
50 Ibid., 126.
51 C. Vasile, *Viaţa inteletuală şi artistică în primul deceniu al regimului Ceauşescu 1965–1974* (Bucharest: Humanitas, 2014), 21.
52 C. Ban, "Sovereign Debt, Austerity, and Regime Change: The Case of Nicolae Ceauşescu's Romania," *East European Politics and Societies* 4 (2012): 758.
53 Accessed October 28, 2022, www.youtube.com/watch?v=zi9eyF20Kf4.
54 Betea, *Ceauşescu*, 769.
55 A. Ursu and R. Thomasson, *Trăgători şi mistificatori. Contrarevoluţia Securităţii în decembrie 1989* (Iaşi: Polirom, 2019), 20. On the continuity of personnel and practices in the Romanian secret services, see also M. Oprea, *Moştenitorii Securităţii* (Iaşi: Polirom, 2014).
56 One of this gathering is perfectly described by the Croatian writer Slavenka Drakulic in her book *Café Europa: Life After Communism* (London: Penguin, 1999).
57 Accessed October 25, 2022, www.hotnews.ro/stiri-politic-17692358-nicolae-ceauscu-considerat-cel-mai-potrivit-presedinte-care-avut-romania-urmeaza-ion-iliescu-traian-basescu-sondaj.htm.

8

THE RISE AND FALL OF RICHARD NIXON AS A GLOBAL LEADER

Umberto Tulli

Towards the end of his life, Richard Nixon drew a balance of his years at the White House:

> I will be known historically for two things. Watergate and the opening to China ... I don't mean to be pessimistic, but Watergate, that silly, silly thing, is going to rank up there historically with what I did here.[1]

He was not pessimistic at all in making this statement. Watergate obscured much of what he had realised as President, especially in international affairs. By the time of his resignation in August 1974, with the lowest approval rating for a sitting president (a mere 24%), Nixon had achieved several unprecedented advances in foreign policy: détente with the Soviets and international agreements to limit the nuclear race; a redefinition of global financial relations; the end of the Vietnam War; an unprecedented agreement in the Middle East between Egypt and Israel; the opening to the People's Republic of China; and a new – albeit short-lived – domestic consensus regarding foreign policy. While this record can be accurately characterised as one of the 'most pro-active and dynamic of the Cold War presidencies,' as scholar Asaf Siniver wrote, it was nevertheless subject to criticism and, to some extent, proved ephemeral and short-lived.[2] Moreover, most of these initiatives were not radically new. For example, although the Johnson administration was entrapped in the ongoing military escalation in Vietnam, it had been diligently searching for an exit strategy from such a conflict. Similarly, Nixon's détente with the Soviets was based on policy the Kennedy administration had initiated in the aftermath of the Cuban missile crisis. Although it was proactive, Nixon's foreign policy was less revolutionary than generally credited, in terms of both means and ends. What made it truly new was the political discourse surrounding it, which was developed by the White House.

DOI: 10.4324/9781003426165-8

The rise and fall of Richard Nixon as a global leader **147**

Finally, Nixon's record on foreign affairs remains hard to assess because it was primarily a joint effort in terms of its design and implementation, because President Nixon had to share the stage with his National Security Advisor, and later Secretary of State, Henry Kissinger. Indeed, just as Watergate overshadowed Nixon's initiatives, Kissinger overshadowed the President in the conduct of American foreign policy.

Scholars still debate who – between the two – was the strategist and the main architect of American foreign policy during what has been labelled the 'Nixinger' era. The literature on their personalities, relationship, foreign policy achievements, and shortcomings is almost limitless. They were the odd couple of American foreign policy during the Cold War. Richard Milhous Nixon was a controversial figure in American politics since his early experiences as a communist-hunting member of Congress in the late 1940s. In just a few years, he rose to become Eisenhower's Vice-President and the Republican candidate for the 1960 presidential election. Defeated by John F. Kennedy in one of the closest races for the American presidency, Nixon was defeated once again in 1962 by Pat Brown in the gubernatorial race for California. Following the loss, Nixon promised to withdraw from American politics: 'You won't have Nixon to kick around anymore because, gentlemen, this is my last press conference,' he declared the day after the defeat. While temporarily out of politics, Nixon never concealed that foreign policy had become a true passion for this American Quaker, who firmly believed that the United States should take advantage of whatever opportunity presented itself. As many direct collaborators and aides recalled, Nixon's intelligence and political skills were extraordinary and second only to his arrogance, disdain, insolence, and distrust of others.[3] For a man with such a complicated personality, his political strategy consisted of many recurring patterns; ambiguous and convoluted ideas supported by straightforward rhetoric and a view of politics as a zero-sum enterprise. Most of these features were rediscovered once he entered the White House, although his political stance softened from radical and uncompromising anticommunism and conservatism to a more centrist position. According to the President himself, his vision was based on political realism with a hint of idealism. Such a vision was expressed in the coda of his memoirs *In the Arena*: 'idealism without pragmatism is impotent. Pragmatism without idealism is meaningless. The key to effective leadership is pragmatic idealism,' an indication that discernment of reality must be coupled by a concrete appreciation of the existing tools and a vision of what one wishes to achieve.[4]

By the time of his political ascendancy, Kissinger had created an aura of being a heterodox Cold War intellectual: an exponent of a tradition of European-style political realism unfamiliar to the United States. To Kissinger, the ideology of anticommunism was irrelevant because, as Walter Russell Mead wrote years ago, 'the United States and the Soviet Union' were simply 'two great powers like Prussia and Austria.'[5] A German–American Jew who completed a doctoral programme at Harvard, Kissinger moved across academia and federal agencies, becoming a prominent and well-known expert on foreign affairs and foreign policy during the

148 Umberto Tulli

1950s and 1960s and whose pessimistic vision about the future of the West was well known. Kissinger himself fuelled this perception. In one famous interview, he reaffirmed his ideas about the unavoidable decline of the United States and the West in general, because 'every civilization of the past had ultimately collapsed.'[6]

Rendering their working relationship even more unlikely, Kissinger had contributed to Nelson Rockefeller's primary campaign within the Republican Party against Nixon. During those months, he never concealed his personal dislike of, and even hostility towards, Nixon. Kissinger was reported to consider Nixon a sort of demagogue, a 'disaster' for the Republican Party, 'and thank God he can't be elected president or the whole country will be a disaster.'[7]

Despite these misgivings, most scholars agree that the relationship between Nixon and Kissinger worked unexpectedly well. This may be attributable in part to the fact that both men considered themselves outsiders to the foreign policy establishment. Additionally, some common features of their political styles contributed in forging this unlikely alliance. Both men had a penchant for unilateral and bold actions; a deep distrust of bureaucracy and even hostility towards Congress; a determination to exclude many Cabinet members from relevant decisions; a willingness to unbound American primacy in world affairs; and, above all, a preference for secrecy, backchannelling, and grandiose coup de théâtre. Finally, both Nixon and Kissinger realised that they should overcome new limits and problems that no Cold War president had faced before: the brand new decline in American power and the erosion of the domestic consensus that had sustained American Cold War policies for about 20 years. Indeed, the evolving nature of the international system and the apparent decline of the United States vis-à-vis friends and foes alike represented the fundamental challenge faced by the Nixon administration.[8]

This chapter will argue that President Nixon succeeded in juggling these unprecedented problems and in defining a new foreign policy for the United States. Much of this was made possible by his personal alliance with Kissinger and their leadership styles, which contributed to the Nixon administration's grandiose achievements (peace with honour in Vietnam, détente with the Soviets, and the opening to China) as a fait accompli, far from public scrutiny. Yet there were two prices to pay. Too often, President Nixon was forced to share the stage with his National Security Advisor. There were, of course, exceptions. The opening to China, for example, was Nixon's brainchild and was initially opposed by Kissinger. For this reason, Nixon was determined to conclude it. It would help the President reaffirm his primacy vis-à-vis Kissinger. Second, in implementing all of these initiatives, Nixon isolated his staff and allies, both at home and abroad. His penchant for secret backchannels alienated Congress and, in the long run, the American public. His claim that idealism in foreign policy had to give way to realism soon led to accusations of amorality and even immorality. His international actions left behind allies, producing a sort of paradox: the Nixon administration developed a better working relationship with adversaries and enemies rather than with traditional allies. Thus, the very same features that helped him relaunch American foreign policy contributed to his decline as a global leader.

When Richard Nixon entered the White House, disappointment over the United States's inability to win the Vietnam War had turned into general embarrassment. In his inaugural address, he declared that the time had come for the United States to get out and lead the world 'out of the valley of turmoil and onto the high ground of peace.' Pacification was his top priority, both at home and abroad. Domestically, since his inaugural address, he pledged to listen to everyone and to adopt a style of presidential communication that would convey realistic goals and concrete solutions, instead of high-sounding and bombastic promises or what he defined as the 'fever of words' that affected the United States over the previous years.[9] Such a stance, which maybe reflected by his Quaker heritage, demonstrated the need to create pacification and new unity among American citizens. Yet, both at home and abroad, many were still debating the legal and political basis for the American intervention and concluded that the war was illegal and a demonstration that, after all, the United States was an imperialist country. Others were questioning the war's moral foundation and, more generally, that of American Cold War foreign policy. Both were considered flawed because, as scholar Trevor McCrisken wrote, 'The United States was using its immense power in ways inconsistent with the principles, the values and the ethical standards of the American people.'[10] To political scientist and future National Security Advisor Zbigniew Brzezinski, the war was 'the Waterloo of the WASP elite' and its foreign policy consensus.[11] It was time to identify new directions for American foreign policy and to elaborate a new consensual doctrine to sustain American engagement with the world. At one of the extremes of this debate, many conservatives criticised the Democratic establishment for its inability to win a war in a remote Third World country and, by extension, they lashed out at the supposedly self-defeating moderation of containment. They advocated for a more muscular foreign policy that would not leave the initiative to the Soviets, as they believed containment had done since its inception. At the opposite extreme, the 'New Left' found in the Vietnam War both a natural consequence of Cold War logic and a demonstration of the imperial hubris of American foreign policy. With revolutionary rhetoric, the 'New Left' proposed a heterogeneous panoply of initiatives that encompassed the rejection of any form of militarism, called for nuclear disarmament, and espoused the vague notion of Third-Worldism. Between these two extremes, different solutions were proposed. To the now-discredited Cold War Warriors, the solution to the crisis of containment included the reaffirmation of containment itself and its fundamental pillars: a new moral, political, and military American leadership to confront Soviet communism. To the contrary, much of the Democratic establishment embraced what became the buzzword of the decade: interdependence. To them, the Cold War and its unambiguous categories had become too rigid to usefully make sense of an increasingly pluralistic world in which new international actors, ranging from transnational movements to international institutions, played an important role, and new international problems were

150 Umberto Tulli

emerging. To cope with these global transformations – they argued – the United States should work towards negotiated and collective solutions and re-evaluate the positive role of international regimes and organisations.[12]

A more conservative proposal for the future direction of American foreign policy was elaborated by Republican President Richard Nixon, who entered office in 1969, and his National Security Advisor, Henry Kissinger. Nixon and Kissinger did not deny that an increasingly pluralistic world was developing. 'The post-war order of international relations – the configuration of power that emerged from the Second World War – is gone,' they wrote to Congress in 1971. 'With it are gone the conditions which have determined the assumptions and practice of United States foreign policy since 1945.' To them, a new multipolar international system was progressively emerging, one in which the economic growth of western Europe and Japan, the rise of a Chinese alternative within the communist world, and Soviet nuclear parity with the United States were fostering the relative decline of American power.[13] To cope with these emerging challenges, the Nixon administration promised a 'new structure of peace,' which was based on détente with the Soviets, the opening to China, and the formulation of an exit strategy from Vietnam. These were the fundamental underpinnings of Nixon and Kissinger's 'elusive grand design.'[14] But these initiatives also revealed a major contradiction. However grandiose their slogans on multipolarism were, their understanding of international affairs remained defined by Cold War categories. Any international event was analysed through traditional Cold War bipolar prisms and judged for its impact on the Cold War. This analytical dimension almost automatically slipped into a prescriptive one. Bipolarism was a political perspective to (re)impose onto international relations. International stabilisation and order would become their buzzwords.[15]

To realise what was presented as an ambitious plan, the Nixon administration relied on a realistic approach to world affairs to promote international stability and order and to freeze the power hierarchy in the international system. Realism, an approach to international relations theory that neglects ideals and values and claims to promote and protect national interests and national security, was the guiding principle of the Nixon administration. On this point, the administration's polemics with the supposed traditional idealism that inspired American foreign policy since Woodrow Wilson were inflexible: Nixon and Kissinger wanted to eradicate Wilsonianism and idealism from the American tradition of foreign affairs and promote the real national interest that – as the President explained to the *New York Times* – 'should be narrowly constructed to exclude moral commitments or causes that do not promise a clear, direct, predictable payoff in increased security or prosperity for the nation.'[16]

The mechanism through which the administration promised to conduct a realistic foreign policy was identified through the linkage. Linkage became a new buzzword to comprehend and describe Nixon's foreign policy. According to the administration, problems were interconnected and, given the administration's basically bipolar understanding of world affairs, should be evaluated in connection with what the Soviet Union could gain or lose from them. Kissinger and Nixon believed that linkage, making progress in negotiations in one area dependent upon progress in another area, was the best tactic to achieve several goals in international relations, especially in the evolving dialogue with the Soviet Union. The President himself defined linkage in a letter to the Secretary of Defense, Melvin Laird, soon after his inauguration. Theorising that 'the great issues are fundamentally interrelated,' Nixon wrote: 'We must seek to advance on a front at least broad enough to make clear that we see some relationship between political and military issues.' The Soviets, he continued, 'should be brought to understand that they cannot expect to reap the benefits of cooperation in one area, while seeking to take advantage of tension or confrontation elsewhere.'[17]

Against this backdrop, the President's personality itself contributed to shape his approach to world affairs. Nixon's political strengths were his encyclopaedic knowledge of American politics and its mechanism; his great intelligence, and his unbounded determination to realise his political purposes. As political scientist Fred Greenstein wrote, he 'had a keen insight into the psychology of others, and an instinctive capacity to discern the possibilities for actions.'[18] By the same token, his introverted and contradictory personality presented some strong weaknesses. Known since the 1950s as 'Tricky Dick,' Nixon never concealed he was fierce and irascible and had little patience with democratic and bureaucratic procedures. Shared by Kissinger, Nixon's radical hostility was a fundamental pillar of his approach to American diplomacy. With its parochial interests, ideological bias, and the primacy of routine and procedures over creativity, the State Department's bureaucrats and diplomats prevented the development of a consistent foreign policy. Centralisation of decision-making soon became a mantra. To overcome resistance from personnel at the State Department, one of the first decisions adopted by Nixon was a radical reform of the foreign policy machinery that bypassed the State Department in favour of the National Security Council. In his first report to Congress, Nixon described the new NSC mechanisms as a simplification that would ensure that

> clear policy choices reach the top, so that the various positions can be fully debated in the meeting of the Council. . . . I refuse to be confronted with a bureaucratic consensus that leaves me no options but acceptance or rejection, and that gives me no way of knowing what alternatives exist.[19]

While one may doubt that Nixon was patient enough to debate all positions, there is no doubt that this mechanism would have eliminated checks and interferences, allowing Kissinger and his staff direct access to the President. In short, Kissinger became indispensable to the President, outflanking the Secretary of State and long-time friend of the President, William P. Rogers; Secretary of Defense Melvin Laird; as well as the bureaucracy of both of their departments. By the same token, such a mechanism both reflected and exacerbated Nixon's personality and style of

152 Umberto Tulli

leadership: his decision to surround himself with particular associates and staff, such as Kissinger, strengthened his reluctance to engage openly with both Congress and the bureaucracy.

Finally, Nixon's foreign policy was based on a constant concern for the public image of the United States, both internationally and domestically. Both Nixon and Kissinger felt that their new course should be sold to, and approved by, the American public. While many have argued that both the President and his National Security Advisor were contemptuous and disinterested in democratic procedures, arrogant towards Congress and American citizens (an argument that was subsequently reinforced by the Watergate scandal), the White House was constantly aware that domestic support was crucial to the success of its foreign policy. Nixon was 'almost paranoid' about the administration's public appearance, as Nathan and Oliver noted.[20] For this reason, the President himself, Kissinger, and many others in the administration used grandiose and bold slogans to describe their international actions, which contributed to the overselling of their achievements and, in the end, eroded the public support such a strategy was intended to build. On this specific point, there was also a unique tension between the President and his National Security Advisor. Since entering office, Nixon worried that Kissinger could upstage him. After all, in February 1969 – just one month after Nixon had entered the White House – *Time* magazine celebrated Kissinger as the intellectual pivot of the administration, the one who could reverse the course of American foreign policy: 'Bonn, Paris and London may disagree on a score of issues, but they are in happy unanimity in their respect for him; even Moscow is not displeased.' After all, the article claimed, Kissinger 'knows more foreign leaders than many State Department careerists.'[21] Kissinger's prolonged shadow over the President's actions in foreign affairs remained constant. For this reason, Nixon was particularly worried that his National Security Advisor could eclipse him. For a man with such a complicated personality, as the President had, his leadership strategy consisted of many recurring patterns: ambiguous and convoluted ideas supported by straightforward rhetoric; a view of politics as a zero-sum enterprise; the constant search for stages to affirm his credentials as a global leader; and as the actual person in charge of America's foreign policy. Overseas trips, and press conferences on those occasions, offered Nixon such a stage. After a visit to many western European Countries in February 1969, which generated positive news coverage, Nixon announced a ten-day world tour, with stops in Guam, the Philippines, Indonesia, Thailand, Vietnam, India, Pakistan, Romania, and England. Yet the first stop was on the USS *Hornet* to welcome and greet Apollo 11 astronauts returning from their lunar exploration. In an early demonstration of his penchant for theatrics and self-centredness, he celebrated

> the greatest week in the history of the world since the Creation, because as a result of what happened in this week, the world is bigger, infinitely, and also, as I am going to find on this trip around the world, and as Secretary Rogers will

The rise and fall of Richard Nixon as a global leader **153**

find as he covers the other countries in Asia, as a result of what you have done, the world has never been closer together before.[22]

While the linkage between the Apollo 11 mission and Nixon's diplomatic mission was clear only to the President, the stakes were definitely high. Disengagement from Vietnam was at the top of the presidential agenda. Yet Nixon also had other purposes for his diplomatic voyage, especially his stops in Pakistan and Romania. The former could be useful to reach the Soviets and other Eastern bloc countries. The latter could become an intermediary to reach the Chinese and offer a backchannel to explore the rapprochement with Beijing.

The following day, President Nixon held an initial off-the-record news conference to 'impress himself on the press, the public, and the world as a visionary leader intent on changing U.S. dealings with Asia' and gain exclusive credit for accomplishing it.[23] Nixon said very little in his prepared remarks, beyond some platitudes about persisting American economic and political interests in the region. He wanted to reassure listeners that once the war in Vietnam was over, the United States would remain in the region to assure peace and stability, without embarking on major new military commitments. Indulging on this point in his dialogue with journalists, Nixon assured them that his administration was determined to continue playing 'a significant role' in the region to strengthen the United States's ties with allies and contain belligerent Chinese, North Korean, and North Vietnamese attitudes. Yet he also clarified this point: 'We must avoid that kind of policy that will make countries in Asia so dependent upon us that we are dragged into conflicts such as the one that we have in Vietnam.' The press immediately celebrated these remarks as the promise of an end to substantial American military involvement in Asia. 'The Guam doctrine,' as it was immediately labelled, was perceived as a major departure from what any other president had done before, even though President Johnson and Democratic presidential candidate Hubert Humphrey would share the same views. Nevertheless, public opinion was satisfied with the promises that there would be 'no more Vietnams' and the United States would help combat future communist insurgencies 'but not fight the war for them.'[24] To Nixon, the positive news coverage of his speech nevertheless had a bad aftertaste. He was not satisfied that the policy was associated with Guam instead of himself. After all, as vague and nonspecific as this label was, it could have obscured how much of his original ideas were in the speech, leaving enough room to credit Kissinger. Accordingly, he urged his staff to identify it as 'the Nixon Doctrine' to ensure he remained under the spotlight for this apparently new foreign policy towards Asia.[25]

The Nixon administration succeeded in presenting every single decision in foreign affairs as a great achievement and a radical departure from previous administrations' actions, even when this was not the case. This was, for example, what happened with the Vietnam War. As Jeffrey Kimball argued, Nixon's Vietnamisation of the conflict originated before Nixon took office among the anti-war movement, Congressional doves, and President L.B. Johnson's official representatives,

154 Umberto Tulli

and it was even discussed during the 1968 electoral campaign.[26] Nevertheless, Nixon's slogans, and his ability to keep preparations and negotiations for the American de-escalation and withdrawal out of public scrutiny, cemented the idea that the withdrawal of American troops from Vietnam – while simultaneously delegating security responsibilities to the South Vietnamese – in conjunction with winning the war and reaching an honourable peace, was its administration's trademark. Moreover, Vietnamisation was not the primary component of Nixon's strategy, which included détente with the Soviets and triangular diplomacy (with the Soviets and the Chinese); negotiations with the Vietnamese communists; expanded military operations; and the application of what Nixon regarded as the 'madman theory': as the President confided to his Chief of Staff, H.R. Haldeman,

> I want the North Vietnamese to believe I've reached the point where I might do anything to stop the war. We'll just slip the word to them that, for God's sake, you know Nixon is obsessed about communism. We can't restrain him when he's angry – and he has his hand on the nuclear button and Ho Chi Minh himself will be in Paris in two days begging for peace.[27]

The definitive withdrawal was far more complex and less magnificent than the administration was willing to admit and concluded only after the 1973 Paris Peace Accords. In the end, there was no victory. There was no 'peace with honour.' There was no 'decent interval' between the withdrawal and the South Vietnamese collapse (Saigon fell in 1975, with the Americans still there). Even though it was not what the administration had hoped for and promised, the national nightmare was over.

Vietnam was a perfect application of linkage. Without discussions, negotiations, and backchannels with the Soviet Union and China, the administration would never have defined an exit strategy from the Vietnamese quagmire. It was also part of the comprehensive détente with the Soviet Union. Far from representing the end of the Cold War, détente was an attempt to rationalise, stabilise, and renew bipolar confrontation, recognising that it was possible to introduce some areas of dialogue and cooperation with the Soviets within a framework that remained substantially competitive. For this reason, détente was based on an attempt to de-emphasise the ideological warfare that was joined to America's Cold War while promoting a form of 'containment by other means' suitable for an age of strategic, economic, and political limits, as the 1970s were perceived. Through negotiations with the Soviets, détente aimed to strengthen American security and promote its interests. The dialogue with the Soviets was meant, among other things, to stabilise the Cold War division into blocs to impose a new discipline within the Western alliance at a moment when many Western allies were protesting American hegemony, to elaborate an exit strategy from the Vietnamese quagmire, to reduce the financial burden of containment, and to prevent the spread of Soviet-inspired communism to new areas of the world.[28]

Détente was probably the 'least adventurous' of Nixon and Kissinger's initiatives, because it simply formalised an ongoing process that was started by Kennedy and followed by Johnson. Nevertheless, it was the architrave of the United States's foreign policy in the 1970s and the one which demonstrated that realism and secrecy were the perfect tools to reaffirm American leadership in the world. Beginning in 1972, the United States and the Soviet Union signed a variety of documents and treaties, encompassing a broad range of topics and issues, such as scientific and technological cooperation, space exploration, a 12-point declaration on 'Basic Principles of Mutual Relations between the United States and the Soviet Union,' a commitment to reducing conventional forces, and the summoning of a multilateral conference on security and cooperation in Europe. The very essence of negotiations, and indeed the very essence of détente, was nuclear weapons. During President Nixon's historic visit to Moscow, he and Brezhnev signed the Interim Agreement on the Limitation of Strategic Arms (SALT), which froze the number of nuclear weapons each country could have.[29] SALT negotiations were the quintessential expression of the administration's preference for secrecy and hostility towards bureaucracy. A secret backchannel between Kissinger and Soviet Ambassador Anatoly Dobrynin, which ran parallel to the official negotiations conducted by the Arms Control and Disarmament Agency, became the primary means through which the United States negotiated arms control (as well as other issues), sheltering the accords from congressional pressures, bureaucratic and procedural slowdowns, and information leaks.[30]

Détente also aimed to rebuild domestic consensus over foreign policy. To accomplish this, Nixon and Kissinger proposed a 'centrist national security agenda,' which combined security imperatives with the need to contain 'massive military retrenchment (left) and massive military escalation (right).'[31] Prior to becoming a policymaker, Kissinger the professor wrote: 'the acid test of a policy . . . is its ability to obtain domestic support.'[32] To accomplish this, Kissinger the policymaker developed political discourse that presented détente as a new policy that would ensure international stability, a reduction of American burdens, and a new structure of peace, as he pompously claimed. Selling détente to the American public became a pivotal mission for the White House, which was achieved almost immediately. Nixon and Kissinger succeeded in portraying détente as a dramatic reduction in both the risk of a nuclear war and Cold War tensions with the Soviet Union.[33]

The last, and most innovative, piece of the diplomacy of détente was the opening to the recognition of the People's Republic of China. It was also the initiative in which Nixon was able to carve out a leading role, far from Kissinger's prolonged shadow over American foreign policy. Nixon started toying with the idea of developing a dialogue with 'Red China' already in 1967. In a well-known article in *Foreign Affairs*, Nixon cautiously explained that the United States 'simply cannot afford to leave China forever outside the family of nations, there to nurture its fantasies, cherish its hates and threaten its neighbors' and should pull 'China back into the world community,' proceeding 'with both an urgency born of necessity

156 Umberto Tulli

and a patience born of realism, moving step by calculated step toward the final goal.'[34] Once in office, he moved swiftly to follow his intuition. While repeating his view that 'we do not want 800,000,000 [people] living in angry isolation. We want contact,' and that likely 'no change' would arrive in the short term, he instructed the NSC to prepare a study on US policy towards China.[35] Kissinger was more reluctant. Never terribly interested in Asian issues, the National Security Advisor focused on Europe and relations with the Soviet Union. After February 1969, he told his deputy Alexander Haig: 'Our leader has taken leave of the reality. He has just ordered me to make this flight of fantasy come true.'[36] For months, Kissinger remained suspicious. In a meeting in May 1969, for example, he wondered

> whether an isolated China, so long as it caused no major problems, is necessarily against our interests. A China that was heavily engaged throughout the world could be very difficult and a dislocating factor. Why is bringing China into the world community inevitably in our interest?[37]

However, he had no choice but to go along with Nixon's wishes. In time, Kissinger came to accept the President's arguments. Three arguments, in particular, explained the importance of establishing diplomatic relations with China according to the President.

First, the escalation of the Sino-Soviet tension during the spring and the summer of 1969 opened a window of opportunity for a bold initiative. The disagreement between the Soviet Union and China had grown over the years, resulting in some military clashes along the Ussuri River in 1969. During an NSC meeting in August 1969, President Nixon clarified that it was 'against our interests to let China be smashed in a Sino-Soviet war.'[38] On this point, the convergence between the United States and China was evident. Both Mao Zedong and Prime Minister Zhou Enlai viewed their country's isolation on the world stage with concern. Formal recognition by the United States would have provided crucial help in this regard and in counterbalancing the Soviets. Thus, if Nixon thought of the opening to China in terms of triangular diplomacy that was intended to produce effects on bipolar relations on the Soviet Union, Mao and Zhou did exactly the same.

Second, the opening of China was also imagined with Vietnam in mind and the (quite wrong) assumption that the Soviets and the Chinese could exert direct influence over the North Vietnamese. The Nixon administration believed that Beijing could have placed pressure on Hanoi to resolve the Vietnam War and permit the United States to reach 'peace with honor.'

Third, considerations about economic policy and electoral politics played a role. Since the late 1800s, the United States had begun to consider the limitless potential of the Chinese market. Decades later, such a dream seemed to be materialising, finding wide support in the American business community and the American public.[39] Finally, as Richard Nixon's brainchild, which was partially opposed by Kissinger, the opening to China was meant to reaffirm Nixon's primacy in the conduct

The rise and fall of Richard Nixon as a global leader **157**

of international affairs and place the President – not his Advisor – in the spotlight. As Secretary of State Rogers noted, 'a higher-level meeting with the Chinese . . . would be a major international event, receiving the widest public attention and with widespread and substantial international and domestic political effects.[40]

Through diplomatic mediations, table tennis matches, and private exchanges between Nixon and Zhou, a secret mission to Beijing was agreed upon. From July 9 to 11, 1971, Kissinger would fly to China, as Nixon's personal representative, to pave the way for the official President visit to the People's Republic of China. Very few people in the US administration had been informed about Kissinger's visit until it was over. Beyond the delicacy of the mission, all of this secrecy was yet another demonstration of the scant forbearance the President had with the bureaucracy, Congress, or allies, as well as his passion for theatrics and bombastic announcements. Within days of Kissinger's mission, Nixon announced to an astonished world:

> Premier Chou En-lai and Dr Henry Kissinger, President Nixon's Assistant for National Security Affairs, held talks in Peking from July 9 to 11, 1971. Knowing of President Nixon's expressed desire to visit the People's Republic of China, Premier Chou Enlai, on behalf of the Government of the People's Republic of China, has extended an invitation to President Nixon to visit China at an appropriate date before May 1972. President Nixon has accepted the invitation with pleasure.[41]

The date of President Nixon's visit to China had been defined by Kissinger and Zhou Enlai in Beijing on 20 October 1971, at their first meeting, but it was not formally announced until the end of November that same year.

In 1972, Richard Nixon was re-elected to the White House. During the electoral campaign, there were few doubts about his chances. Nixon's foreign policy record contributed to his uncontainable victory. Moreover, the public discourse he and Kissinger developed about their achievements – progress in ending the Vietnam War, the SALT treaty with the Soviet Union, and the opening of China – appeared capable of building a new and much-needed domestic consensus on foreign policy. Many Democrats welcomed Nixon and Kissinger's achievements, including more stable contacts with the Soviets, the SALT Treaty, the 1972 US–Soviet trade treaty, and growing scientific and economic contacts. To Nixon and Kissinger, these achievements represented a deep break with the discredited policy of containment and could eventually permit both a demilitarisation of American foreign policy and a shift of resources in favour of domestic priorities. Equally successful was the diplomatic opening of China. Although it was conceived as a strictly bipolar initiative to push the Soviets towards a more cooperative attitude towards American disengagement from Vietnam and détente in general, Nixon's visit to Beijing envisaged better trade relations with the potentially nearly limitless Chinese market. And, of course, most Americans openly supported negotiations to

158 Umberto Tulli

end the Vietnam War. Over the following months, the signing of the Paris Peace Treaty, which definitively ended the American nightmare in Vietnam, and a new agreement to limit the nuclear race (the so-called Vladivostok agreement in 1974) seemed to confirm this trend.

Enthusiasm towards Nixon and his foreign policy was short-lived, however. Well before the clouds of the Watergate scandal hung over the presidency, forcing Nixon's resignation, many grew sceptical of the White House's realism, secrecy, and amoral approach to foreign affairs. Theatrics and drama surrounding achievements, preceded by secrecy and unilateralism during their preparations and negotiations, came at the expense of a lasting consensus at home and strong relations with allies and led to more general distrust in the President.

Centralisation and secrecy may have been productive and conducive to many impressive outcomes in foreign policy. Nevertheless, they entailed several problems. Years later, former Secretary of State William Rogers criticised Nixon and Kissinger's reform of the NSC. He attacked Kissinger for having become 'too much a policy maker,' thus eroding Rogers's own role and power, and claimed that the NSC should have had more regular meetings and eventually involved the Secretary of the Treasury. Moreover, Rogers was impressed by the degree to which Nixon was 'antagonistic to the State Department' and its bureaucracy – the very same bureaucracy that was called upon to implement the President's decision. Indeed, being put at the margins, the State Department apparatus became increasingly sceptical at this new course in foreign affairs.[42]

Congressional reactions at Nixon's style were even more radical. Having been placed in the margins of foreign policy for years, a resurgent Congress took the lead in challenging the White House over foreign affairs. Critics of Nixon claimed that the presidency had chosen isolation, secrecy, and an autocratic style, and that it was imperial. Above all, many in Congress began to feel that American foreign policy had abandoned its traditional values. Members of Congress focused on the apparent lack of morality at the White House. So, while the American nightmare in Vietnam was ending, many in Congress began to ponder whether Nixon's strategy to end the war was morally and politically acceptable. When it was disclosed that the United States was already carrying out bombings over Cambodia and Laos in 1969, Congressional actions first led to the adoption of the Cooper-Church amendment, which cut off funds for Nixon's incursions into Cambodia and later, to the adoption of the 1973 War Powers Act, over President's Nixon veto. It reassessed Congressional authority in declaring and provided some specific limits to the President's authority to deploy US troops abroad. The President could commit troops only under specific circumstances: a congressional declaration of war, specific legislative authorisation, or a defensive reaction to protect US troops under direct or imminent attack.[43] This was the prelude to a major Congressional offensive on human rights. The Congressional human rights surge was based on the rejection of Kissinger's alleged amoral foreign policy. Human rights became common ground for both liberals and 'neo-internationalists,' who asked the American government to rediscover its traditional values and define a foreign policy for growing global interdependence and for conservatives and neoconservatives, who wanted to abandon détente with the Soviet Union and relaunch a traditional policy of containment. The convergence between these two groups contributed to the erosion of Nixon's foreign policy. After opposing any strong commitment to the promotion of human rights, which had no place in a realistic foreign policy and was at odds with the conservative nature of the 'Nixinger' foreign policy, and failing to address Congressional pressures on this issue, the President and his National Security Advisor 'left it to Congress to implement a reactive punitive and unilateral approach,' as historian B. Keys wrote.[44]

Abroad, Nixon found more friends in Moscow and Beijing rather than in the capitals of Allied countries. The 'week that changed the world,' as Nixon pompously defined his trip to China, provoked much chagrin among American allies in Asia. Taiwan felt abandoned by Nixon. Japan's Prime Minister, Satō Eisaku, learnt about the news 'only minutes before it was announced' and, like many others in Japan, he felt betrayed by Nixon's new course towards China. Japan would be equally shocked by Richard Nixon's unilateral decision to delink the dollar from gold, striking a blow to the Bretton Woods system.[45] Western Europeans' reaction to Nixon's economic policy was no different. To them, not only was such a decision one-sided, it was also a threat to the very survival of the European common market.

Economic tensions were not the single issue in the strained transatlantic alliance during the Nixon presidency. While many western Europeans welcomed détente with the Soviets, they often objected to their marginality in such a rapprochement and battened down the hatches by intensifying their own rapprochement to the Soviet Union and central and eastern Europe. Although parallel to American–Soviet détente, this form of intra-European détente was also in opposition to the more conservative dialogue that was developing between Moscow and Washington. It sought to strengthen cooperation and dialogue between the two Europes and eventually 'dissolve the Blocs, a little bit' as French President Georges Pompidou confessed to the German Chancellor Willy Brandt.[46] The fiasco surrounding the 'Year for Europe' in 1973 was perhaps the moment when European hostility towards the United States was clearest. Noting the worsening of transatlantic relations, the Nixon administration unilaterally identified 1973 as the American 'Year of Europe,' which should have led to a new Transatlantic Partnership, new common institutions, and a solemn renewal of the Atlantic Declaration. Yet such an initiative prompted the countries of the European Community to engage in a bold attempt to develop a sort of embryonic common foreign policy to counterbalance the United States and in search of a proper political identity in international relations.[47]

Exceptional times of crisis, as the 1970s were perceived by most Americans, called for exceptional leaders or, at least, for leaders who were able to develop exceptional political discourse about their foreign policy decisions and actions. Nixon and Kissinger succeeded in presenting their foreign policy as a bold and

160 Umberto Tulli

groundbreaking departure from what previous administrations had done. This was also the case in those areas in which Nixon and Kissinger built their strategies – the exit strategy from Vietnam and détente with the Soviets – on existing initiatives. Yet by infusing a dose of realism into foreign policy and privileging theatrics and secrecy in negotiations over the involvement of bureaucrats, diplomats, and Congress, Nixon and Kissinger were able to present their achievements as more revolutionary than they actually were. Even the opening to China – the boldest and most innovative action developed by the administration, and the only one in which Richard Nixon was actually in charge of foreign policy, stepping out of Kissinger's shadow – did not produce any radical change in the short run. Nevertheless, no one could deny that Nixon's visit to Beijing was, as the President claimed, the week that changed the world. Tactical changes were significant, but the overall priorities, strategies, and goals remained much the same as the previous administration.

The outcome was that the administration oversold its foreign policy and created exalted expectations in the minds of the public. Nixon's style contributed to this outcome. Oscillating constantly between secrecy and hostility towards the bureaucracy and Congress and his determination to make bold political and diplomatic moves, his autocratic style at conducting foreign affairs soon became a target for his opponents. Thus, critics of the administration began to lash out at Nixon's foreign policy features, such as its secrecy and lack of any moral concerns. During the 1976 presidential campaign, political scientist Zbigniew Brzezinski invited the Democratic candidate Jimmy Carter to harshly attack the legacy of the Nixon administration's foreign policy initiatives, even in those areas that had 'achieved occasional brilliant successes,' because the United States has been 'relatively shortsighted and unsuccessful in the field of foreign policy.' The Nixon administration had 'misled the Congress and the Country, emphasizing secrecy and surprises rather than consultation and consideration both for the people, the Congress, and our major friendly allies.'[48] With Nixon out of the game, the focus of Carter's criticism became Kissinger and his 'Lone Ranger' style of diplomacy, which also fitted perfectly to Nixon. Ironically, this expression, which was first used by Kissinger to describe his and Nixon's foreign policy in 1972, had contributed to their popularity in Nixon's first years in office.

Notes

1 Monica Crowley, *Nixon in Winter* (New York: Random House, 1998), 159.
2 Asaf Siniver, *Nixon, Kissinger, and US Foreign Policy Making: The Machinery of Crisis* (Cambridge and New York: Cambridge University Press, 2009).
3 Fred I. Greenstein, *The Presidential Difference: Leadership Style From FDR to Barack Obama* (Princeton: Princeton University Press, 2009), 91–98.
4 Richard M. Nixon, *In the Arena: A Memoir of Victory, Defeat, and Renewal* (New York: Simon & Schuster, 1990).
5 Walter Russell Mead, *Special Providence: American Foreign Policy and How It Changed the World* (New York: Routledge, 2002), 72.

The rise and fall of Richard Nixon as a global leader **161**

6 The interview of Henry Kissinger by James Reston is in *the New York Times*, 13 October 1974. See also Dana Allin, *Cold War Illusions: America, Europe, and Soviet Power, 1969–1989* (London: Palgrave Macmillan, 1995), 30. A somehow different portrait, which underlines the contradiction between such a pessimistic view and the optimistic ideas about American capabilities to overcome limits, is in Mario Del Pero, *The Eccentric Realist: Henry Kissinger and the Shaping of American Foreign Policy* (Ithaca and London: Cornell University Press, 2009), 67–70.

7 Quoted in Siniver, *Nixon, Kissinger, and U.S. Foreign Policy*, 40.

8 On Kissinger and Nixon: Coral Bell, *The Diplomacy of Detente: The Kissinger Era* (New York: St. Martin's Press, 1977); Seymour Hersh, *The Prince of Power: Kissinger in the Nixon White House* (New York: Summit Books, 1983); Walter Isaacson, *Kissinger: A Biography* (New York: Simon & Schuster, 1992); William Bundy, *A Tangled Web: The Making of Foreign Policy in the Nixon Presidency* (New York: Hill and Wang, 1998); Richard C. Thornton, *The Nixon Kissinger Years: The Reshaping of American Foreign Policy*, 2nd ed. (St. Paul, MN: Paragon House, 2001); Jussi M. Hanhimaki, *The Flawed Architect: Henry Kissinger and American Foreign Policy* (New York: Oxford University Press, 2004); Jeremy Suri, *Henry Kissinger and the American Century* (Cambridge, MA: Belknap Press of Harvard University Press, 2007); Frederik Logevall and Andrew Preston (eds.), *Nixon in the World: American Foreign Relations, 1969–1977* (New York: Oxford University Press, 2008); Robert Dallek, *Nixon and Kissinger: Partners in Power* (New York: HarperCollins, 2009); Del Pero, *The Eccentric Realist*; Barbara Keys, "Henry Kissinger: The Emotional Statesman," *Diplomatic History* 35, no. 4 (2011): 587–609.

9 First Inaugural Address of Richard Milhous Nixon, January 20, 1969, http//:avalon.law.yale.edu/20th_century/nixon1.asp.

10 Trevor B. McCrisken, *American Exceptionalism and the Legacy of Vietnam: US Foreign Policy Since 1974* (Basingstoke and New York: Palgrave Macmillan, 2003), 26; Jeremy Suri, *Power and Protest: Global Revolution and the Rise of Detente* (Cambridge, MA: Harvard University Press, 2003).

11 Simon Serfaty, "Brzezinski: Play It Again, Zbig," *Foreign Policy* 32 (Fall 1978): 3–21.

12 Del Pero, *The Eccentric Realist*, 39–42; John Ehrman, *The Rise of Neoconservatism: Intellectuals and Foreign Affairs* (New Haven, CT and London: Yale University Press, 1995), 33–62.

13 Richard Nixon, "Second Annual Report to the Congress on United States Foreign Policy," in *Public Papers of the Presidents of the United States: Richard Nixon, Containing the Public Messages, Speeches and Statements of the President, February 25, 1971* (Washington, DC: US Government Printing Office, 1972), 231–32.

14 Jussi M. Hanhimäki, "An Elusive Grand Design," in Logevall and Preston, *Nixon in the World*, 25–44.

15 Del Pero, *The Eccentric Realist*, 43–75; Hanhimäki, *The Flawed Architect*; Dallek, *Nixon and Kissinger*. See also, Logevall and Preston, *Nixon in the World*.

16 George F. Will, *The New York Times*, December 23, 1973.

17 Letter from President Nixon to Secretary of Defense Laird, February 4, 1969, *Foreign Relations of the United States, 1969–1976*, vol. I (Foundations of Foreign Policy, 1969–1972), accessed October 2022, https://history.state.gov/historicaldocuments/frus1969-76v01/d10.

18 Greenstein, *The Presidential Difference*.

19 Richard M. Nixon, "First Annual Report to Congress on United States Foreign Policy for the 1970s, February 18, 1970," in *Public Papers of the Presidents of the United States (henceforth PPPUS): Richard Nixon, 1970* (Washington, DC: U.S. Government Printing Office, 1971), 122.

20 James A. Nathan and James K. Oliver, *United States Foreign Policy and World Order* (Boston: Little Brown and Company, 1976), 360.

162 Umberto Tulli

21 "Kissinger: The Uses and Limits of Power," *Time Magazine*, February 14, 1969.
22 President Nixon's Remarks to Apollo 11 Astronauts Aboard the U.S.S. Hornet Following Completion of Their Lunar Mission, July 24, 1969, accessed October 2022, www.presidency.ucsb.edu/documents/remarks-apollo-11-astronauts-aboard-the-uss-hornet-following-completion-their-lunar.
23 Dallek, *Nixon and Kissinger*.
24 President Nixon's Informal Remarks in Guam With Newsmen, July 25, 1969, Guam, accessed October 2022, www.presidency.ucsb.edu/documents/informal-remarks-guam-with-newsmen.
25 Dallek, *Nixon and Kissinger*, 144.
26 Jeffrey Kimball, "The Nixon Doctrine: A Saga of Misunderstanding," *Presidential Studies Quarterly* 36, no. 1 (2006): 59–74.
27 Quoted in Rick Perlstein, *Nixonland: The Rise of a President and the Fracturing of America* (New York: Simon & Schuster, 2008), 419.
28 On the nature of détente, see Anders Stephanson, "Fourteen Notes on the Very Concept of the Cold War," *H-Net Diplomatic History List (H-Diplo)*, June 24, 1996, accessed October 2022, https://issforum.org/essays/PDF/stephanson-14notes.pdf. On détente conservative nature and its aims: John L. Gaddis, *Strategies of Containment: A Critical Appraisal of Postwar American National Security Policy* (Oxford and New York: Oxford University Press, 1982).
29 Raymond L. Garthoff, *Détente and Confrontation: American-Soviet Relations From Nixon to Reagan* (Washington, DC: The Brookings Institution, 1994), 146–223.
30 Richard A. Moss, *Nixon's Back Channel to Moscow Confidential Diplomacy and Détente* (Lexington: University of Kentucky Press, 2017).
31 Julian E. Zelizer, "Détente and Domestic Politics," *Diplomatic History* 33, no. 4 (September 2009): 633–52.
32 Henry A. Kissinger, *A World Restored: The Politics of Conservatism in a Revolutionary Age* (New York: Grosset & Dunlap, 1964), 326.
33 Phil Williams, "Détente and US Domestic Politics," *International Affairs* 61, no. 3 (July 1985): 431–47; Dan Caldwell, "The Legitimization of the Nixon-Kissinger Grand Design and Grand Strategy," *Diplomatic History* 33, no. 4 (September 2009): 633–52.
34 Richard Nixon, "Asia After Viet Nam," *Foreign Affairs*, October 1967.
35 Memorandum from President Nixon to his Assistant for National Security Affairs (Kissinger), February 1, 1969, and National Security Memorandum 14, February 5, 1969, both in *Foreign Relations of the United States, 1969–1976, Vol. XVII, China, 1969–1972* (hereinafter, FRUS online, vol. 13) The first document is https://history.state.gov/historicaldocuments/frus1969-76v17/d3; the second document is accessed October 2022, https://history.state.gov/historicaldocuments/frus1969-76v17/d4.
36 Margaret MacMillan, "Nixon, Kissinger, and the Opening to China," in Logevall and Preston, *Nixon in the World*, 107–25.
37 Minutes of the Senior Review Group Meeting, May 15, 1969, *Foreign Relations of the United States*, vol. 13, accessed October 2022, https://history.state.gov/historicaldocuments/frus1969-76v17/d13.
38 Henry Kissinger, *The White House Years* (Boston: Little, Brown, 1979), 182.
39 Mario Del Pero, *Libertà e Impero. Gli Stati Uniti e il mondo, 1776–2016* (Roma-Bari: Laterza, 2016), 359–60.
40 Memorandum from Secretary of State Rogers to President Nixon, March 10, 1970, *Foreign Relations of the United States*, vol. 13, accessed October 2022, https://history.state.gov/historicaldocuments/frus1969-76v17/d72.
41 Remarks to the Nation Announcing Acceptance of an Invitation to Visit the People's Republic of China, July 15, 1971, accessed October 2022, www.presidency.ucsb.edu/documents/remarks-the-nation-announcing-acceptance-invitation-visit-the-peoples-republic-china.

The rise and fall of Richard Nixon as a global leader **163**

42 Joan Hoff, "A Revisionist View of Nixon's Foreign Policy," *Presidential Studies Quarterly* 26, no. 1 (Winter 1996): 107–29.
43 Robert D. Johnson, *Congress and the Cold War* (New York: Cambridge University Press, 2006).
44 Barbara Keys, "Congress, Kissinger, and the Origins of Human Rights Diplomacy," *Diplomatic History* 34, no. 5 (November 2010): 823–51. See also Barbara Keys, *Reclaiming American Virtue: The Human Rights Revolution of the 1970s* (Cambridge, MA: Harvard University Press, 2014); Umberto Tulli, "'Whose Rights Are Human Rights?' The Ambiguous Emergence of Human Rights and the Demise of Kissingerism," *Cold War History* 12, no. 4 (2012): 573–93.
45 Robert S. Ross, "U.S. Relations with China," in *The Golden Age of the U.S.–China – Japan Triangle, 1972–1989*, ed. Ezra F. Vogel, Yuan Ming, and Tanaka Akihiko (Cambridge, MA: Harvard University Press, 2002); Thomas W. Zeiler, "Nixon Shocks Japan, Inc," in Logevall and Preston, *Nixon in the World*, 289–308. A different evaluation is in Midori Yoshii, "The Creation of the Shock Myth: Japan's Reaction to American Rapprochement with China, 1971–1972," *The Journal of American – East Asian Relations* 15 (2008): 131–46.
46 Federico Romero and Silvio Pons, "Europe Between the Superpowers, 1968–1981," in *Europe in the World International Arena During the 1970s*, ed. A. Varsori and G. Migani (Brussels and New York: Peter Lang, 2011), 85–97.
47 Silvia Pietrantonio, "The Year That Never Was: 1973 and the Crisis Between the United States and the European Community," *Journal of Transatlantic Studies* 8, no. 2 (2020): 158–77.
48 Zbigniew Brzezinski to Jimmy Carter, Foreign Policy Speech: An Agenda for the Future, Jimmy Carter Presidential Library (Atlanta, GA), 1976 Presidential Campaign, Box 17, F.1.

9

MOHAMMAD REZA SHAH PAHLAVI

A moderniser challenged by Islamists
and Leftists

Pejman Abdolmohammadi

Introduction

Mohammad Reza Shah Pahlavi (1900–1980) is one of the most relevant political personalities of the twentieth century. He was the last Shah (King) of Iran
(Persia) in the twentieth century and reigned from 1941 until 1979. His reign was
overthrown during the Iranian Revolution led by Ayatollah Ruhollah Khomeini.
Consequently, from 1979 onwards Iran became an Islamic Republic and remains
so today.

Mohammad Reza Shah's life was influenced by relevant international events
such as the Second World War, the Cold War, the Arab-Israeli War, and the two
energy crises of the 1970s. Moreover, on the domestic level, he had to face the rise
of the National Front, led by Mohammad Mosaddeq, the penetration of the Soviets
in Iran through the Communist Party of Tudeh and finally the rise of political Islam
led by Shiite clergy and also by the so-called Islamic intellectuals.

His main effort was to modernise the country. He had a good level of success in
modernising Iran economically, culturally, and socially while on the political front
he was unsuccessful in creating a pluralistic political system. The political life of
the Shah can mainly be divided into two main phases: the first one starts from his
coronation as the new King of Persia in 1941 until the 1953 coup d'état against
Mosaddeq's government while the second phase follows from 1953 until the 1979
revolution.

Contrary to the main historiography which in the last four decades has described
the Shah, mainly following a sort of ideological cliché, as a pro-Western and Impe-
rialistic authoritarian figure, this chapter considers the Shah's legacy based on three
main pillars: secularism, modernism, and nationalism, highlighting particularly his
vision and his independent spirit in foreign policy. The chapter analyses the Shah's

DOI: 10.4324/9781003426165-9

Phase 1 (1941–1953): *the coronation of the young Shah*

The leadership of the young Mohammad Reza Shah started in 1941, when he replaced his father, Reza Shah. After ascending the throne, he started to conduct a new political agenda in Iran. First, he started to be more moderate than his father by making the secularisation process more inclusive and pluralistic. For example, he abolished the main restrictions to which political opponents were previously subject and opened up the possibility of them returning to participate in the public life of the country. Several young intellectuals, who had not been able to take part in the constitutional movement at the beginning of the century, now began to undertake political and social initiatives and write articles in which they disclosed their thoughts on a variety of previously forbidden subjects. In addition, the Shiite clergy, which had remained on the sidelines for all the previous years, returned to exercising its religious and political role within the mosques and confessional schools.[1]

The Shah promoted a new balance of power in the domestic sphere of Iran based on a cautious liberal openness,[2] presenting a new window of opportunity for advocates of democratic change. At the cultural level, the Shah's main aim was to involve as many thinkers, intellectuals, and politicians to build up a more modern cultural elite.

Also, at the institutional level, under the Shah's young leadership, the parliament acquired more autonomy and new parties were born, so that a partial pluralism also started to be affirmed at the political level. This openness, on the one hand, benefitted the political life of the country, but on the other, it damaged its existing socio-economic development which the previous reign of Reza Shah had begun. This new political freedom led to the birth of various parties and set forth a current of ideological and political alignments, including those of the extremists.[3] For example, in addition to the formation of secular, communist, nationalist, and conservative parties, it also allowed the birth of the Islamic fundamentalist movement of Fadayan-e Islam (those who sacrifice themselves for Islam).

Having regard to the religious tendencies of a part of Iranian society, the Shah tried to gain the trust of the Shiite clergy, revoking the anti-clerical laws adopted by his father. He returned several lands that had been confiscated by the state from the clergy, abolished the law that prohibited the use of the veil for women, and recognised the authority of some Grand Ayatollahs present in the holy city of Qom. This opening towards the religious world continued with the decision of the first government of the new Shah, in the mid-1940s, to separate the two sexes in schools and to introduce the 'Islamic religion' into the curriculum. These accommodating policies towards the Shiite religious world made the clergy return to the country's political scene. It is apparent, therefore, that in the first phase of his monarchy, the Shah

166 Pejman Abdolmohammadi

wished to be more inclusive than his father had ever been. Evidently, he wanted to have more segments of the society in alliance with the Iranian royal institution.[4]

Ruhollah Khomeini wrote and published his first political text, *Kashf-e asrar* (The Revelation of Secrets), two years into the reign of Mohammad Reza Shah, in 1943. Allowing the publication of this critical text towards the founder of the Pahlavi dynasty showed how the Shah had decided to adopt a non-authoritarian political line. Ironically, however, as will be noted later, the evolution of the political context of Iran led him to return partially to the positions adopted by his father before him. This became especially true in the second phase of his reign when he applied restrictions on his opponents and imposed political censorship once more – actions which helped to cause the rebellion of the disparate component parts of the opposition to the Pahlavi monarchy.

Besides, Khomeini, also Mohammad Mosaddeq,[5] a prominent Iranian politician, found the political space to be back in the political arena once again. Mosaddeq had been forced out of politics during the 1920s because of his opposition to Reza Shah.[6] In 1943, however, Mosaddeq presented himself as an independent candidate in the parliamentary elections and received the most votes of all the candidates in the capital.[7]

Clearly, the new liberal policy of the Shah gave space to various political and religious personalities and movements to play a role in the country. One of the unexpected consequences of this policy was an increasing political instability in Iran. The terrorist attack against the Shah in 1948 was one of the first signs of this situation. During a student ceremony at the University of Tehran a young man tried to assassinate him by firing several shots at him. The aggressor was killed immediately, and it was not possible to understand from which political side this action had come. From that moment onwards, the Shah changed his attitude to domestic politics.

He had no hesitation in increasing his power: the Communist Party Tudeh was considered 'hostile' to the monarch, so it was proclaimed an outlaw organisation. As a result, some personalities from the political world and the press were arrested, the Shiite religious leader Ayatollah Kashani was sent into exile, and finally, the Shah decided to convene a Constituent Assembly to modify some parts of the Constitution and ask for the dissolution of the parliament, calling the voters to the polls. The Constituent Assembly modified the legislative body – which was previously unicameral – by establishing a national assembly and a senate. In reality, the introduction of the senate expressed the Shah's intention to better control legislative activity. The senate was considered an instrument closer to the monarchy and was designed to counterbalance the weight of the national assembly (Majles-e Melli).

With the new decade of the 1950s, the Shah had to face new challenges. The most important one was the rise of the political coalition of the National Front (Jebhe-ye Melli), which was led by the nationalist Mosaddeq and the Islamist Kashani.[8] The National Front in its first official declaration supported the following political line: reform of the electoral law with the aim of transforming the parliament from being a formal legislative body into an effective institution; revision of laws regarding press censorship, so that free expression was guaranteed; revision of curfew laws to limit the power of the state to repress opponents; and greater protection for parliamentarians to make them free to express their positions. The Front did not want to be considered a party but only a grand coalition made up of people from different political families.[9] The coalition included both parties from the national democratic camp and parties with communist and Islamic leanings.[10] In reality, the National Front represented two different strands of Iranian society: on the one hand, the traditional middle class (merchants, small entrepreneurs, the clergy) and on the other the new middle class (Islamic intellectuals, some civil servants, and young graduates). In essence, the first group saw in Islam the right law for human life and considered religious scientists as the preservers of the shariatic tradition and especially of Twelver Shiism. In their opinion, Islam would have solved all the problems of the Iranians. The second group, on the contrary, consisted of a large part of those who wanted to confine religion to the private sphere of the individual (without recognising it as having any public role) and to adopt laws according to the secular model.[11]

This was the first serious political challenge towards the Shah's leadership. The National Front represented a notable part of the society and moreover, through the leadership of Mosaddeq and Kashani, both prominent and charismatic figures of their time, it began attracting more consensus and support than the Shah. As such, it was perceived by the Shah as a threat to his legacy and authority.

The nationalisation of oil became one of the first political battles between the Shah and Mosaddeq's National Front. One of the most relevant issues of the 1940s and 1950s in Iran were the oil contracts: since the discovery of black gold in Iran in 1908, the British had enjoyed, through the foundation of the Anglo Iranian Oil Company (AIOC), the advantage of establishing an exclusive trading relationship with Iran, such that the British oil company had become beneficiaries of Persian oil. The world geopolitical situation, however, was in a transitional phase: the powerful British Empire, after the Second World War, had lost its dominance while the Soviet Union and the United States had become the two unrivalled superpowers. These changes also adversely influenced the commercial relations that the British Empire had hitherto established with the various states in the first half of the twentieth century. The nationalisation of oil soon became a major political issue both within Iranian society and on the international scene: the population began to demonstrate and the workers of the oil company went on strike in support of the proposed parliamentary bill; meanwhile, the British were incensed by the possibility of Iranian oil nationalisation and exerted pressure on the Shah to block this law.[12]

Despite a year of controversy and discussions, which had seen the Shah and Prime Minister Razm Ara inclined to resolve the issue in a pro-British way, the National Front refused to give up its quest for nationalisation of the oil reserves. Razm Ara, considered pro-British, was assassinated in March 1951 by the fundamentalist movement of Fadayan-e Islam. The killing of the prime minister

168 Pejman Abdolmohammadi

was indicative of the frustration and anger of the opposition groups. The Shah, who had invested heavily in Razm Ara to bargain with the British, found himself alone against the supporters of nationalisation. As a result, the parliament, taking advantage of the situation, appointed Mosaddeq prime minister and the law on the nationalisation of oil was approved and implemented.

Mosaddeq was primarily concerned with making the oil law operational while the United Kingdom threatened Iran with dire consequences and asked all countries to boycott its oil. All the British experts left Khuzestan and the British government turned to the United Nations Security Council, asking for the intervention of the international body to resolve the case. In October 1951, Mosaddeq himself went to the United Nations in New York and defended the cause of Iran. His intervention was very persuasive and led the Security Council to pronounce itself in favour of Iran, the nationalisation of oil being considered a purely domestic matter.[13]

Mosaddeq returned victoriously to Iran in mid-November 1951, but the economic and political situation (both domestic and international) was changing against him. On an economic level, the effect of the British embargo was beginning to be felt. Iranian oil production, which was estimated at 660,000 barrels per day in 1950, had dropped to 20,000 barrels. This had generated a sharp increase in unemployment and inflation, leading the country into a situation of stagnation. The economic crisis provoked middle-class discontent and weakened the backbone of the National Front.[14]

Mosaddeq, in addition to having lost the internal support of the traditionalists and having to face the economic crisis, was faced with a very complicated international scenario. The Conservatives, under the leadership of the ageing Winston Churchill, had emerged victorious in the British parliamentary elections of 1951. The new prime minister wanted to regain his country's privileged position in Iran and persuaded the US administration to implement a plan aimed at eliminating the Mosaddeq government even though the Truman administration had previously supported the Iranian premier, considering him a national-democratic anti-communist. Mosaddeq, having lost the support of the Islamists, had, however, softened his position towards the pro-Soviet Communist Party Tudeh.[15] This openness, albeit very timid though it was, led the American administration – which was in a transitional phase, between the end of the Truman presidency and the beginning of the Eisenhower administration – to suspect the anti-communist line of the Iranian prime minister. As Kenneth M. Pollack, the director of Persian Gulf affairs in the US National Security Council, points out, Mosaddeq's big mistake was to threaten the Americans, if they didn't support Iran's case against the United Kingdom, with a possible rapprochement that could be formed between Iran and the Soviet Union.[16]

Following this declaration, the Americans resolved to follow Churchill's suggestions: the Mosaddeq government must fall so that the Shah could regain all his power, thereby guaranteeing Iran's membership in the Western bloc. Starting in June 1953, the CIA, supported by the British, launched the 'Ajax' operation to destabilise the Iranian government. As a result, an organised coup d'état took place

Mohammad Reza Shah Pahlavi **169**

led by a part of the Iranian army and supported by both the British and United States intelligence services. Needless to say, a part of the population, who were supporters of the Shah, supported this coup d'état.[17]

Following the coup, the Shah, who had temporarily left Iran, returned home and began a period of restoration. He undertook, first of all, to re-establish his power, forming a new government led by General Zahedi (one of the main actors who had led the *Ajax* coup d'état) and making the role of parliament meaningless. From then on, the parliament was transformed into a formal body dependent on the Shah. The Communist Party Tudeh and the constituent parties of the National Front were outlawed and their leaders persecuted. Mohammad Reza Shah wanted to be sure that what happened with the Mosaddeq government, which had taken control of the country away from him, could never happen again.[18]

In the aftermath of the 1953 coup, during the Eisenhower administration and the government of General Fazollah Zahedi, the average annual US economic aid jumped from $9.7 million (pre-1953) to $64.5 million. The US presence replaced the British one in 1954: a 50/50 agreement between the newly born Iranian National Oil Company on one side and the five American 'sisters' of oil was reached for Iranian oil extraction, production, and marketing. Moreover, the growing Iranian economy was able to purchase weapons and military assistance from the United States in an ever-increasing way up from a total of $17.6 million (pre-1953) to $60 million at the end of the 1950s on an annual basis.[19] The Shah's political alliance worked, and he managed to regain power, and his leadership of the country was consolidated.

With Mosaddeq's political eclipse, Iranian secular thinking was 'suspended' and replaced by Islamic components fuelled by anti-Western sentiment. In other words, the ascent of Khomeinism in the late 1970s cannot, in fact, be understood without examining Mosaddeq's demise, and it is very likely that if his government had continued in Iran there would have been no Khomeinism and thus no Islamic Republic. To advance political Islam, these religious movements sought out new platforms, and in certain cases, they were even willing to fuse Islam with nationalist and Marxist beliefs. Religious forces were no longer playing a defensive political game in this situation as they had in the past. Instead, to forward their goal, they created an ambitious political vision that incorporated aspects of political modernisation, like the use of mass politics.

The so-called Islamic intellectuals (Roshanfekran-e Dini), whose most notable representatives were Jalal-e Al-e Ahmad, Mehdi Bazargan, Ali Shariati, and Abolhassan Bani Sadr, emerged in the late 1950s. This new generation of elites envisioned an interventionist and revolutionary Islam to accomplish its goals to mobilise the masses against the domestic power represented by the Shah and in defiance of the external threats represented by the imperialist powers. They did so by drawing inspiration from Quranic principles.[20]

After the removal of the National Front, the Shah was forced to engage with the Islamic Front. Although the Shah's attention during the 1950s and early 1960s was

170 Pejman Abdolmohammadi

mainly on modernising Iran both economically and culturally, he made the mistake of not paying sufficient attention to the growing Islamist ideology. Instead, his major concern lay with the spectre of communism and a sort of nationalism linked to Mosaddeq.

Phase 2: the Shah in the post-1953 period

In the second phase of his rule, Mohammad Reza Shah, like his father, began an effort at authoritarian modernisation. The political system of the country was still not institutionalised enough to support such an ambitious undertaking. Iran was not founded on a robust military organisation that could serve as the nation's backbone, in contrast to nations like Egypt and Turkey with their more stable or effective top-down modernisation systems. Iran lacked both a strong administrative state like those found in Japan or Germany and a political system centred on a stable, institutionalised single party like those found in communist states. Furthermore, because the modernisation primarily concentrated on the economic and social fields and disregarded the desire for political pluralism, it yielded only partial successes.

The Shah started to limit and socially control the leftist and nationalist forces while not focusing on controlling the political Islamist forces. Thus, the Islamic religious movements began progressively to occupy notable spaces in the opposition, competing with leftist political parties by standing up for and advancing many of the same ideals as them, including social justice and equality (in Farsi: *Edalat va Barabari*). During the 1960s and 1970s, spokesmen for Islamic forces were not only defending traditional Islamic principles but also putting up political projects and entering the political sphere. This development aided political Islam's radicalisation and social ascent in Iran and gave it the opportunity to align itself with secular groups that shared its aims, particularly those of the Marxist movement.

The Shah, for example, devoted himself to the elaboration of an internal security policy, establishing in 1957 'the Organization for internal security and intelligence' or the well-known and notorious secret police called SAVAK. This newborn organisation was interested in the clandestine activities of internal opposition groups, with particular reference to the Communist Party which the Shah greatly feared.[21] His relationship with the traditional religious world improved, and various religious authorities such as Ayatollah Borujerdi and Behbahani were accepted at receptions with ease. Even in private life, the Shah proved to be a believing and practising Muslim. On several occasions, he went to Mecca on pilgrimage or visited the holy cities of Karbala in Iraq and Mashhad and Qom in Iran, showing respect for the Islamic religion and Shiite orthodoxy. In reality, the Shah also saw in Islam a political ideology that could have hindered the communist one; the Islamist forces thus increased their power and became part of the political forces of the country.

The Shah's leadership in the late 1950s became stronger, and he focused also on its foreign policy. He improved diplomatic relations with the United States and Israel, opposing the Soviet bloc and the Arab world. He wanted to turn Iran into a military superpower in the Middle East, and to achieve his goal he needed the support of the United States. This support, due to the geopolitical position of Iran (neighbouring the then-Soviet Union) in the context of the Cold War, was not long in coming. The Shah's Iran became a faithful ally of the West and a point of balance in the Middle East. Military aid provided by the United States to Iran between 1953 and 1961 rose to about $500 million and led to Iran significantly expanding its military power. In the early 1960s, the Shah seemed to have achieved his main goal, which was full control of the country.

The achievement of relative domestic security and the change in the international political direction of the United States, with the election of the Democrat John F. Kennedy, led the Shah to inaugurate a new phase of reforms. Relations with the White House were important, and Kennedy, unlike his predecessors, as well as on military issues, placed the emphasis on sociopolitical changes, aimed at achieving a democratic civil society. The reformist tendencies of the new US president also influenced Iran. The Shah decided to replace his prime minister with Amini, the former Iranian ambassador in Washington and a diplomat on friendly terms with the American administration. Amini appointed several reformist ministers linked to the National Front and drafted various bills aimed at reforming a large part of the economic, social, and political spheres of the country. Nonetheless, the Shah was dissatisfied with the lack of a formal American guarantee towards Iran, since the United States never became an effective member of the Baghdad Pact. Having discarded multilateral negotiations, the Shah decided to negotiate bilaterally with the United States, concluding in 1964, the US–Iranian Status of Force Agreement (SOFA).[22]

The White Revolution

The first reform was the agricultural one, which aimed to dismantle the feudal system then in force in the Iranian countryside. Landlords would have to sell their lands to the government, which in turn would have given them, on favourable terms, to farmers. However, the provision aroused the wrath of the country's traditionalist class (including the clergy), who lived on land rents. The reaction was harsh, but the Shah's leadership was strong enough to offset the criticism coming from the feudal barons and the clergy. In 1963, the Shah initiated a reformist turn, known as 'Enghelab-e sefid-e shah va mardom' (The White Revolution of the Shah and the people). The essential purpose of this 'revolution' was to redistribute wealth according to social justice. The White Revolution included the following structural reforms: land reform; nationalisation of forests and pastures; distribution of profits from state companies to workers; privatisation of state-owned industries; revision of the electoral law to give workers greater representation and the right to active and passive vote for women; the establishment of an 'army of knowledge.' Other reforms were added later such as the creation of a special body for the improvement of health services; the establishment of a special body for developing

172 Pejman Abdolmohammadi

courts of justice in the villages; and the reform of the administrative system and education. In January 1963, the Shah asked the electorate to approve the reform through a confirmatory referendum. According to official data, 99.9 per cent voted in favour of the reforms, but in reality a part of the population, especially the land-owners and the clergy, were against the White Revolution.[23]

The Shiite clergy was the most affected by the new reforms: in most of the villages, the clergy was in fact at the same time a religious point of reference and owner of several lands, so the agrarian reform dismantled part of their economic power. A second intolerable factor for the Shiite religious world was the granting of the right to vote to women: the clergy considered this law anti-Shariatic. As Ayatollah Kashani had said ten years earlier, 'the state must not allow women to vote, because women must remain in their respective homes and fulfill their real responsibility, which is to raise their children.' The third objective opposed by the clerical class was the establishment of the so-called 'army of knowledge.' This army, established with the White Revolution, allowed young graduates to carry out military service as primary school teachers in rural areas. The monopoly of education in the villages which for centuries, starting from the Safavid dynasty, had been held by the religious scholars would have been threatened by the arrival of educated young people willing to pass on their knowledge to the children. Knowledge and education have always been the most dangerous weapons against the clergy, who managed to maintain their socio-economic power by inculcating dogmas and superstitions. For this reason, the arrival of young teachers in the villages was not well seen by the clerical class. The fourth point of the Shah's reform that aroused the discontent of the religious was the establishment of courts in rural areas. Again, the state was invading a space dominated by the Shiite clergy. The judicial system was in fact controlled by religious scholars, who gained prestige, respect, and power within the villages; the establishment of state courts would have stripped them of much of the authority they enjoyed.[24]

These reasons were enough to mobilise the entire Shiite clerical apparatus against the Shah and his White Revolution, and it was then that Ayatollah Khomeini came out of anonymity, preparing to become the protest leader of the Iranian religious world. His speeches, starting from 1963 until 1964, when he was exiled from Iran, would make him the main protagonist of the Iranian opposition to the Pahlavi monarchy.

The Shah and the Shiite clergy in the 1960s

The White Revolution, heralding progressive laws, had improved Iran's international image. As a result, the Shah decided to continue with the reforms and, together with Prime Minister Asadollah Alam, drafted new bills. Of particular importance were the publicity profiles relating to women's civil and political rights. To undertake a progressive revision of Iranian public law, the Shah had to guarantee equal rights for women.[25]

This happened initially thanks to the outcome of the referendum, following which women acquired the right to vote actively and passively in provincial and regional councils but not in national elections. On 3 March 1963, about a month after the referendum, the government of Asadollah Alam passed a new law that gave women equal rights with men, including the right to vote in national parliamentary elections. There was then a large demonstration in which women, enthusiastic about the approval of this law, expressed their approval for the work of the Shah. The approved law granted women various rights, such as the right to vote, greater protection in family law, and the possibility of accessing careers that were previously reserved exclusively for men.[26]

Throughout the 1960s, the Shah continued to follow his reformist line while, on the foreign front, he increased relations with the United States, mitigating the historical influence of the British and the Soviets on Iranian territory. In October 1964, parliament approved a bill granting diplomatic immunity to US citizens working in Iran. This immunity also extended to their family members. The granting of these prerogatives was known in Iran with the French term 'capitolasion' and actually dated back to the capitulation regime of the Ottoman era, through which citizens of European states, residing in countries under the jurisdiction of the Ottoman Empire, had the right to evade local legislation for certain obligations and to depend on the consuls of their country of origin. To attract US external collaboration, the new Iranian law removed US citizens from national jurisdiction, thus ensuring that they were prosecutable only by US judicial authorities.[27]

This law, however, was in stark contrast to the views of the National Front and the Islamist scholars, such as Khomeini, who still found the reason and opportunity to oppose the Shah and to denounce his blind dependence on the United States.

The 1970s and the new migrants

By the realisation of its reforms, Iran started to become one of the most industrialised countries in the Middle East and one that was starting to compete with South Korea. The urbanisation became a direct consequence of this new industrialisation. Many families abandoned the countryside and moved to the cities with the hope of finding better living conditions there. In Tehran and in other large cities, such as Tabriz, Esfahan, and Shiraz, a new traditionalist and conservative social class was born: the rural population was in fact linked to religious values and had great respect for the clergy, who were considered as God's representatives on earth. The literacy process undertaken by the Shah with the White Revolution had allowed the more modest classes to access written texts. As a result, in the 1960s, various periodicals were published that dealt with the Islamic religion, especially the Shiite version. According to a survey carried out in 1976, there were 48 publishing houses dedicated exclusively to the literary production of a religious nature. Other phenomena, such as the increase in pilgrimages to Mecca and Shiite religious shrines, expressed the resurgence of the feeling of belonging to Islam among the population residing

174 Pejman Abdolmohammadi

in urban centres. This religious awareness could also be considered as a reaction to the Iranian tendencies of the Shah who, starting from the end of the 1950s, tended to marginalise Islam from the social and cultural life of the country. The population that moved into the city during the 1960s set up small religious associations, which allowed believers to socialise and integrate more easily into the urban reality. Their names are significant of the origin of the members: 'the Association of shoemakers,' 'the Association of public toilet workers,' 'the Association of the desperate,' 'the Association of Imam Hossein.' They represented some of the social groups present in the area and were mainly interested in religious issues rather than socioeconomic ones.[28] However, the importance of the formation of these associations lay in the fact that they expressed a new social reality in large cities, strongly traditionalist and contrary to the cultural modernisation of the country.[29]

The economic and social inequality between this lower-middle class of society and the richest part of the urban centres increased popular dissatisfaction with the modernisation process underway in the country. The more modest classes of society considered these inequalities as the ill-gotten fruit of Western politics and saw in Islam and in the Shiite ulama immediate and reassuring points of reference not least because the ulama denounced the wealthiest in favour of the 'disinherited' classes. The ulama, through the Islamic system of almsgiving (*zakat*) and other donations from the faithful, enjoyed considerable income, which they also used to support the needy families who frequented the mosques.[30] This strengthened their popularity with the lower middle class (mostly factory workers) while making them hostile to the policies of the Shah.[31] Another powerful social class that sided in favour of the Islamisation of the country was that of the merchants or *bazarii*. There were several factors that made the bazaar (the traditional market) very influential on the Iranian political scene: the bazaars, in all large Iranian cities, were concentrated in a specific area. This allowed merchants to communicate easily with one another and to develop a sense of mutual solidarity in times of crisis. The Shah, following his reformist political plan, had in fact prejudiced the economic interests of the *bazarii*. For example, he was promoting the establishment of supermarket chains and the introduction of new forms of commercial establishments that would break the monopoly of the *bazarii* in sectors such as food and clothing. Furthermore, in the 1960s, the government implemented a rehabilitation programme that aimed to stabilise the economy. Part of it provided for the reduction of loans and economic concessions to the *bazarii* and introduced new taxes intended to burden the merchants, causing their discontent. The economic policies of the government had further damaged the relationship between the traditional bourgeois class of the *bazarii* and the monarchy, inducing the merchants to draw ever closer to the Shiite clergy and to wait for the favourable opportunity to concretely express their hostility to the Pahlavi dynasty.[32]

The Shah's political economy did not consider this aspect. The inclusivity did not work here. The high-speed economic modernisation did not take into consideration the increasing hostility of the traditionalist *bazarii*. In addition, the industrialisation and the urbanisation created a sort of traditionalist belt around the capital and the Shah somehow managed to ignore that, contributing to the rise of Islamist forces in the heart of Iran.

The Shah on the eve of the 1970s: nationalism and foreign policy

The Shah's political role on the Middle Eastern chessboard, thanks to good relations with the United States, was becoming of fundamental importance. In the early 1970s the United States, led by President Nixon and his adviser Henry Kissinger, adopted a political strategy aimed at stabilising the Middle East. Iran and Israel were considered the 'Twin Pillars' to which the American administration would have entrusted the task of making the Middle East more stable. This strengthened the alliance between Iran and the United States and made the Shah stronger, both on the international scene and in domestic politics.[33]

The Shah thus became the 'policeman of the Gulf,' the one who was supposed to protect the area of the Persian Gulf, so that it was not influenced by Nasser's radical policies in Egypt and by the nascent Islamic fundamentalism. Iran then became very active in regional politics, supporting the United States on several occasions: in 1973, it sent troops to Oman to help the government in the suppression of rebels supported by the Marxist government of southern Yemen. In the same year, it supported the dictatorial government and pro-US Pakistan against the Baluchi rebels and provided military aid to Somalia against pro-Soviet Ethiopia during the Ogaden War (1976–1978). These interventions led Tehran to buy huge shipments of weapons from the United States. In 1972, after a visit by Nixon and Kissinger to Tehran, the United States declared that it 'must sell to the Shah all the conventional weapons that he requested for his army.'[34] Thus, starting in the 1970s, the Shah became 'the great ally' of the American administration. This unconditional alliance gave the opposition an opportunity to criticise not only domestic politics but also international politics: the Shah was considered dependent on the West and Israel and accused of enslaving the country to the United States. As the historian Ali Ansari reveals, the title 'policeman of the Gulf,' which had been attributed to him by the Pentagon was translated into Persian with the term 'Gendarme,' which had a connotation of subjection: this made the Shah in the eyes of the Iranians as subject to the power of others.

This assessment, however, as underlined by Kenneth M. Pollack, was not confirmed by the facts. According to Pollack, the Shah had well interpreted the political conditions in which the Nixon administration found itself and by offering himself as a key figure for the stability of the Middle East, he knew he could acquire greater power and independence. Pollack, in support of his thesis, explains how the Shah in 1971 without the consent of the United States had conquered three islands – Abu Musa and the two Tunbs – claimed by the Arab Emirates.[35] This military action clashed with the role of 'protector' and 'stabilizer' planned by the White House for Tehran. Furthermore, the Shah did not approve of the presence

176 Pejman Abdolmohammadi

of American military ships in the Persian Gulf, a territory in his opinion that ought to be reserved exclusively for the Persian navy. In any case, it seems that the Shah sought to escape full dependency on the Americans and this will be seen, above all, in the oil policies directed against the 'seven sisters' during the last years of his reign.[36] Evidently, the Shah was no longer prepared to be considered as a mere tool of the West. Instead, he wished to forge an alliance of equals with Washington. Overly proud and ambitious, his inflated nationalistic visions of independence were to become exceedingly problematic, not least because he did not calculate how they could damage his overall position in a bipolar world.

A first sign aimed at demonstrating the Shah's desire to exercise a predominant role in the Middle East was the organisation in October 1971, of a series of festivities in Persepolis, Shiraz, and Pasargad, to solemnise the twenty-fifth centenary of the foundation of the Persian Empire by Cyrus the Great. The Shah had invited all the world's leading heads of state to a princely ceremony. Even though President Nixon and Queen Elizabeth were not present, several prestigious representatives of the political and journalistic worlds had attended the event. During the celebration, the Shah had addressed the tomb of Cyrus the Great, pronouncing the following sentence: 'Kurosh (Cyrus in Persian) sleep in peace, because we are awake.' The main purpose of the Shah in organising this ceremony was clear: having chosen the Persian archaeological sites as the venue for the event, he wanted to demonstrate to the world the importance of Persia in history and, in some way, prepare the ground for the reconquest of the millennial lost prestige of his country.

Nonetheless, the effects of the celebrations proved less positive, both at home and abroad, than the Shah had hoped for. The ceremony had intimidated the Arab states, which saw in the commemoration of the Persian imperial past a foretelling of future expansionism and Iranian irredentist politics. These fears were confirmed when the Shah occupied the three islands near the Strait of Hormuz. These, taken from Persia by the British in the nineteenth century, were then administered by the sheikhdoms of Sharjah and Ras Al Khaimah. On the domestic front, the ceremony sparked a strong reaction from the Islamic opposition, which saw the exaltation of Iranian patriotism as a great threat to the ideology of radical Islamism and also alerted the Iranian leftists who, along with the Islamists, did not have sympathy for this kind of nationalism.

The monopartite system

In 1974, the Shah, in order to involve the population in political life, decided to create the Rastakhiz party strictly dependent on the court. In a televised message he called on all adults to join the party, stating that those who did not join would have to leave the country. The party he had created had initially generated a certain optimism and could even have grown to the point of becoming at least a functioning political machine in the likeness of the other single parties of the Middle East and the Soviet bloc; but the Shah was unsuccessful in allowing his party to assume

Mohammad Reza Shah Pahlavi **177**

a politically significant role. Thus, the Rastakhiz was quickly set aside, by both friend and foe, as one of the many elements of the imperial scenography. This was one of the first weak strategies of the Shah at the domestic level. Trying to create a monopartite system was not useful and provoked a less pluralistic trend in his policy. Somehow contradicting his first phase vision.

The fall of Nixon and the rise of carter

In 1976, the Republican administration of Gerald Ford, considered very close to the Shah, was living its last months. The polls made the Democratic candidate Jimmy Carter the favourite to win the US presidential election in November of that year. The Shah, who had not had positive experiences with presidents from the Democratic Party, feared that Carter too, like his predecessors Truman and Kennedy, would begin to put pressure on human rights and political freedoms. The fear of the Shah had found even more foundation when Carter, in a pre-election speech, had criticised Tehran for the violation of human rights, demonstrating his inclination to support a process of democratisation of the country. The Shah did everything possible to support (even financially) the Republican candidate Ford, but already in mid-1976, it could be predicted that the favourite was Carter. The Shah feared that, with the victory of the Democrats, Washington

> would withdraw its political support for Tehran and leave its regime exposed to the intrigues of both the Soviets and the British, the two colonial powers of the past, which he believed would never have recognized Iran's right to decide its own destiny.[37]

The outcome of the American elections had not only attracted the attention of the Shah; even the Iranian opposition believed that a possible victory of the Democrats would have favoured their protest movement. On the other hand, it was the Republicans who had planned the 1953 coup and the fall of Mosaddeq, while the Democrats, particularly with Kennedy, had pushed the Shah to undertake reformist policies. Consequently, the Iranian opposition, both secular and Islamic, believed that Carter's election would change the general perspective of the Iranian political arena.

To prevent the expected political pressure from Carter, the Shah, as early as mid-1976, began a policy of 'liberalisation,' attempting to decrease the political pressure exerted on the opposition and to grant greater freedom of expression to newspapers. In January 1977, when Carter took office in the White House, the Shah declared that he wanted to create 'an open political atmosphere' in Iran. In the same year, international delegations from the Red Cross, Amnesty International and the International Court of Justice were invited to examine the political and social situation in Iran.[38]

The Shah also said he wanted to reform articles of the penal code that had been found non-human rights compliant by the IGC and limit SAVAK's activities

178 Pejman Abdolmohammadi

against political opponents. Some political prisoners were also released and the climate in the country really seemed to be heading towards liberalisation. In May 1977, US Secretary of State Cyrus Vance visited Tehran, promising the Shah to continue the close collaboration between the United States and Iran; even though during his public speech, however, Vance mentioned the importance of respecting human rights.

In November 1977, the Shah, accompanied by his wife Farah Diba, visited the White House. At that time many Iranian students, thanks to the Shah's economic growth and modernising policies, had managed to obtain scholarships or government subsidies to continue their studies in the United States. Most of these students had joined a political–cultural organisation called 'The Confederation of Iranian Students.' The nucleus of this confederation was formed by the 'Islamic Student Association,' administered by one of Khomeini's closest collaborators abroad, the pharmacy student and member of the 'Liberation Movement' Ebrahim Yazdi.[39]

The news of the Shah's visit to Carter represented a good opportunity for the Iranian opposition to make public its dissent towards the government. Upon the Shah's arrival in Washington, in front of the White House, many Iranian students demonstrated against him, asking him to immediately apply Carter's directives on human rights. Nonetheless, the Shah's visit achieved great diplomatic success: Carter had shown his full support for Tehran and had appreciated the efforts made by the Shah to create greater freedoms in the country. The Shah, who had been so worried on the eve of the American elections, returned to Iran with greater confidence that he had secured the support of the United States. With this conviction, on 27 November, 29 activists formed a committee for the defence of human rights in Iran and asked for the help of the United Nations to establish democracy and freedom in Iran; a copy of the statement was sent to the office of the President of the United States. This move, again coming from the moderate liberal-nationalist wing, demonstrated the opposition's confidence in external support. The United Nations' lack of attention to this statement and Carter's visit to Iran at the end of December showed the opposition that speculation about American support was unfounded. Carter, in a statement released in Tehran, made public his esteem for the Shah and defined Iran, 'an island of stability in the stormy corner of the world,' emphasising with admiration 'the love that the (Iranian) people' felt for the Shah. Following these statements, the Shah seemed strengthened and the opposition, especially the moderate one, felt betrayed.

On 7 January 1978, with the probable approval of the Shah, the Ministry of Information had the pro-government newspaper *Ettela'at* publish an article titled 'Iran and the Red and Black Reaction') (Iran *va ertejahe sorkh va siah*). The article, signed under the false name of Ahmad Rashidi Motlagh, after explaining the good reformist intentions of the Shah's White Revolution, accused the 'black reaction' (the Shiite clergy) of having opposed the development of the country, allying themselves with communism international ('the red reaction').[40] The real target of the op-ed was Ayatollah Khomeini, who was defined as 'an adventurer without faith, linked to the colonial centers of power . . . a man with an unclear past.' The article traced Khomeini's Indian origins as 'Seyyed-e Hendi') (The Indian Seyyed), a foreigner in Persian disguise. In conclusion, Khomeini was accused of being an agent of the British and of having received a considerable sum of money (through an Arab) to oppose the Shah. The publication of this propaganda article by the government demonstrated the existing fear of Khomeini, but also the naivety of the system, because this accusation would only make Khomeini better known, placing him at the centre of attention of the population.[41] This was another false move of the Shah.

The Shah on the eve of the 1979 revolution

The starting of popular revolts had intimidated the Shah. As a result, the government tried to soften its behaviour towards the *bazarii* and the Shiite clergy.[42] Shopkeepers who had been jailed for failing to comply with government price guidelines were released; the creation of supermarket chains, contrary to the interests of the *bazarii*, was suspended. The government publicly apologised for invading the home of Ayatollah Shariatmadari, banned cinemas from showing films considered anti-Islamic, and facilitated the pilgrimage of believers to Mecca. The Shah replaced the head of SAVAK, General Nassiri, considered a violent and unscrupulous person, with General Moghaddam who, given his friendship with Shariatmadari, was well regarded by the clergy. The Shah also promised that subsequent parliamentary elections would be 'one hundred percent' free and announced the start of talks with some religious leaders. The Shah finally replaced Prime Minister Hoveyda after 13 years with a technocrat, Jamshid Amuzegar. The new premier intended to restore the economy to fight inflation and improve the standard of living of the lower and middle classes. Thus, a new economic policy based essentially on cost containment was launched. But these changes were yet another mistake made by the Shah. It showed his current difficulties and his leadership which was weakening.

It is clear that the Shah made concessions to the Islamic opposition, to the detriment of the secular side; this tactic turned out to be wrong, because in fact it took away space from secular intellectuals, the only ones who could have offered the country the prospects of freedom and democracy. Instead, those classes who demanded the complete Islamisation of society and therefore the establishment of an 'Islamic government' were favoured. It seems probable that the government was not well informed about the existence of the secret society of the fighting clergy.

The Shah had rejected his military officers' proposal to take a hard line with his opponents, and this merely encouraged the revolutionary groups. The United States sent him a message through their ambassador Sullivan, advising him to adopt a hard line against the revolutionary masses or to temporarily leave the country, subject to the appointment of a Council of Regency. The Shah, now ill and disillusioned with

180 Pejman Abdolmohammadi

the population, decided to leave the country and, following the American suggestion, appointed a Council of Regency. The Shah decided, to give confidence to the secular part of the opposition and to the American administration, by offering the leader of the National Front Sanjabi the position of Head of Government. But Sanjabi, now fully aligned with Khomeini, refused to give his support to the Shah who, among other things, had arrested him several times in recent years. Shahpur Bakhtiar, another active member of the National Front and supporter of Mosaddeqian secularism, was then appointed, but he accepted the position only on condition that the Shah leave the country. The Shah also nominated three people for the 'Regency Council' and left Iran on 16 January 1979, an hour after the parliamentary election of Bakhtiar as prime minister.

The revolutionary wave was already very strong and Ayatollah Khomeini, using his charisma and leadership, managed to lead the revolts from Paris where he remained in exile. Khomeini, supported by a wide internal coalition, composed by Islamists, leftists, and nationalists, together with the support of the Western diplomatic and political ruling elite, came back to Iran on 1 February 1979, and in the days afterwards the Islamic Revolution was fully accomplished.

In the end, the neutrality of the national army, supported by Washington, played a key role in the ending of the Shah's monarchy. Definitely, the Shah was ill and tired. Also, he did not want to repress his own people. This situation brought him to leave the country. His leadership was not strong enough to maintain the position and to adapt strategies to stop the rise of the Islamist opposition to his rule and to neutralise the Western influence for change.

Conclusions

The Shah's foreign policy, particularly the rediscovery of Iran's Persian identity from a nationalist perspective, challenged the long-established alliance with the Western bloc. From 1973 onwards, after the initial oil shock in which the Shah took the lead as the central figure in determining oil prices within the Organization of Petroleum Exporting Countries (OPEC), the alliance deteriorated further. In various interviews given to major foreign broadcasters such as the BBC and the NBC, the Shah challenged the oil companies and some Western international players, making it clear that Iran aimed to become an independent regional power. This new line of foreign policy, notably signalled by increasing independence on the international front, gradually deprived the Shah of the support of the West, until he was abandoned during the 1979 Islamic Revolution. He died in exile in Egypt in 1981.

One could contend that the Shah's international and domestic policies finally failed. Domestic policy was predicated on a meagre modernisation effort and the suppression of all alternative forces, especially secular ones, while mostly ignoring Islamic resistance. Although the rise of Persian nationalism in the final years of his rule damaged this relationship, foreign policy was primarily centred on a tight alliance with the Western countries. Some of the foreign and domestic initiatives of the Shah that were unsuccessful had the result of strengthening the alliance between internal Islamist powers and disgruntled left-wing secular factions, which had developed and strengthened under the Shah's rule.

The Shah's leadership started with rigour in the 1940s and 1950s and reached its strongest point in the late 1960s. Thereafter, his power began to wane as did his health. The fall of Nixon, the Shah's high-speed economic modernisation, his unwillingness to adopt a hard-line position against his Islamic opponents, and his own terminal illness are the main factors which brought him down and undermined the legacy he would have hoped to have left behind.

Notes

1 See Ervand Abrahamian, *Iran Between Two Revolutions* (Princeton, NJ: Princeton University Press, 1982), 152–53; N. Keddie, *Roots of Revolution: An Interpretive History of Modern Iran*, with a section by Richard Yann (New Haven, CT: Yale University Press, 2003), 116–38, 117.
2 R. M. Savory, "Social Development in Iran During the Pahlavi Era," in *Iran Under the Pahlavis*, ed. George Lenczowski (Stanford, CA: Hoover Institution Press, 1978), 99.
3 Ibid., 100.
4 R. M. Khomeini, *Kashf-easrar* [The Revelations of Secrets] (Qom: Zafar Press, 1944).
5 On the political biography of Mosaddeq, see Sepehr Zabih, *The Mosaddeq Era: The Roots of the Iranian Revolution* (Chicago: Lake View Press, 1982); Farhad Diba, *Mohammad Mosaddeq: A Political Biography* (London: Croom Helm 1989); Homa Katouzian, *Musaddiq and the Struggle for Power in Iran* (London and New York: I.B. Tauris, 1999); Gholamhossein Nejati, *Mosaddeq, Salhai-ye Mobarezeh va Moghavemat* [Mosaddeq: The Years of Struggle and Opposition], 2 vols. (Tehran: Ghazal, 1998).
6 Touraj Atabaki and Erik J. Zürcher, *Men of Order: Authoritarian Modernization Under Atatürk and Reza Shah.* (London: I.B. Tauris, 2003), 7.
7 Kurosh Za'im, *Jebhe-ye Melli Iran* [Iranian National Front], 1st ed. (Tehran, Iranmehr Edition, 1378 [1999]), 81–82.
8 Mehran Kamrava, *Revolution in Iran: The Roots of Turmoil* (London and New York: Routledge, 1990), 57; Abrahamian, *Iran Between Two Revolutions*, 229.
9 Afshin Matin-Asgari, *Both Eastern and Western: An Intellectual History of Iranian Modernity* (Cambridge: Cambridge University Press, 2018), 45.
10 The central nucleus of the National Front consisted of the National Socialist Iran Party, the socialist Zahmatkeshan Party (the laborers), the conservative Islamic party Jame'ey-e mojahedin-e Islam (the society of fighters of Islam), the patriotic party Mellat; there was also the external support of the fundamentalist movement of Fadayan-e Islam (the sacrificed for Islam). See Za'im, *Jebhe-ye Melli Iran*, 86–90.
11 See Abrahamian, *Iran Between Two Revolutions*, 233.
12 Za'im, *Jebhe-ye Melli Iran*, 149–53.
13 Mohammad Ali Movahhed, *Doctor Mosaddeq va Nehzat-e Melli-ye Iran* [Dr Mosaddeq and the National Movement of Iran], 2nd ed. (Tehran: Karnameh Edition, 1384 [2005]), 149–55.
14 Kenneth Pollack, *The Persian Puzzle*, 1st ed. (New York: Random House, 2004), 61.
15 Movahhed, *Doctor Mosaddeq va Nehzat-e Melli-ye Iran*, 172–75.
16 Pollack, *The Persian Puzzle*, 64. See also Mark J. Gasiorowski, "U.S. Perceptions of the Communist Threat in Iran During the Mossadegh Era," *Journal of Cold War Studies* (2019): 190.

182 Pejman Abdolmohammadi

17 See Stephen Kinzer, *All the Shah's Men: An American Coup and the Roots of Middle East Terror* (New York: John Wiley & Sons, 2003); Marc J. Gasiorowski and Malcolm Byrne, *Mohammad Mosaddeq and the 1953 Coup in Iran* (Syracuse, NY: Syracuse University Press, 2004); James Risen, "Secrets of History: The CIA in Iran," *New York Times*, 2000.
18 Za'im, *Jebhe-ye Melli Iran*, 301–5; see also Kinzer, *All the Shah's Men*, 5–10; Misagh Parsa, *Social Origins of the Iranian Revolution* (New Brunswick, NJ and London: Rutgers University Press, 1989), 45.
19 Roham Alvandi, *Nixon, Kissinger, and the Shah: The United States and Iran in the Cold War* (Oxford: Oxford University Press, 2014), 18.
20 For an overview of the Islamic intellectuals' political thought, see Eskandar Sadeghi-Boroujerdi, *Revolution and Its Discontents: Political Thought and Reform in Iran* (Cambridge: Cambridge University Press, 2019).
21 Nikki R. Keddie, *Modern Iran: Roots and Results of Revolution* (New Haven and London: Yale University Press, 2003), 134.
22 Alvandi, *Nixon, Kissinger, and the Shah*, 24.
23 S. A. Arjomand, *The Turban for the Crown: The Islamic Revolution in Iran* (Oxford: Oxford University Press, 1988), 72–73.
24 Pollack, *The Persian Puzzle*, 86.
25 Parvin Paidar, *Women and the Political Process in Twentieth-Century Iran* (Cambridge: Cambridge University Press, 1997), 144–46. The referendum finally took place on January 26, and women were allowed to take part in the voting. In February, the regime announced a large majority in favour of the White Revolution. Members of women's associations marched to Marmar Palace, and the Shah made a speech, stating that

> Our revolution was not complete without women's full emancipation, and with this revolution we have now made a huge leap from the terrible backwardness into the ranks of the civilised societies of the twentieth century. By granting women the right to vote, we have washed away the last stigma from our society and smashed the last chain.

26 C. Issawi, "The Iranian Economy 1925–1975: Fifty Years of Economic Development," in Lenczowski, *Iran Under the Pahlavis*, 135–46.
27 Keddie, *Roots of Revolution*, 159:

> In October 1964 the Majles passed, with an unusual number of negative votes and speeches, a bill to grant diplomatic immunity to American military personnel and advisers. Shortly afterwards the Majles agreed to a $200 million loan from the United States for the purchase of military equipment. Both the connection between the two bills and the capitulatory nature of the first were publicly and strongly denounced by Khomeini, who saw them as signs of bondage to the United States.

28 Arjomand, *The Turban for the Crown*, 91–92.
29 Kamrava, *Revolution in Iran*, 119; see also T. Skocpol, "Rentier State and Shi'a Islam in the Iranian Revolution," *Theory and Society* 11, no. 3 (May 1982): 271–72.
30 M. R. Djalili, *Diplomatie Islamique: Strategie internationale du khomeynisme* (Paris: Presses Universitaires de France, 1989), 105–6; see also R. Mottahedeh, *The Mantle of the Prophet: Religion and Politics in Iran* (Middlesex: Penguin Books, 1985), 348–50:

> Migrants to the city were not a random ingathering of Pepsi Cola lovers. Typically they were males between thirty five and thirty nine and females between twenty five and twenty nine. There were wealthy and middle class migrants, but the great numbers came from the landless poor of the villages, the farm laborers who had been the biggest losers in the wake of land reform.

31 See F. Halliday, *Iran: Dictatorship and Development* (New York: Penguin Books, 1979); H. Ladjevardi, *Labour Unions and Autocracy in Iran* (Syracuse: Syracuse University Press, 1985).

32 Savory, "Social Development in Iran During the Pahlavi Era," 125; V. Martin, *Creating an Islamic State: Khomeini and the Making of a New Iran* (London and New York: I. B. Tauris, 2003), 66.

33 William H. Forbis, *Fall of the Peacock Throne: The Story of Iran* (New York: Harper & Row, 1980), 278; E. Karsh, "From Ideological Zeal to Geopolitical Realism: The Islamic Republic and the Gulf," in *The Iran-Iraq War: Impact and Implications*, ed. E. Karsh (London: Palgrave Macmillan, 1987), 27.

34 On the Shah and relations with Nixon, see Alvandi, *Nixon, Kissinger, and the Shah*.

35 Pollack, *The Persian Puzzle*, 75–80.

36 Forbis, *Fall of the Peacock Throne*, 279; Karsh, "From Ideological Zeal to Geopolitical Realism," 27.

37 Parsa, *Social Origins of the Iranian Revolution*, 54–56.

38 T. A. Brun, *Resurgence of Popular Agitation in Iran* (Paris: LeMonde Diplomatique, 1978), 17–18.

39 Pollack, *The Persian Puzzle*, 123–24.

40 *Ettela'at*, 17Dey2536/January 7, 1978, 7.

41 Mottahedeh, *The Mantle of the Prophet*, 373.

42 Martin, *Creating an Islamic State*, 149.

CODA

Malcolm Murfett

This volume has looked at ten markedly different figures who not only became the political leaders of their respective countries but also stayed there – some for quite lengthy spells in office – at a time when the world was changing radically. It would be fatuous to imagine that anyone who gets to the top of an organisation, whatever that may be, will not have some form of personal agenda that they wish to implement once they have the power to do so. Dictators naturally seek to control all the important levers of power within the state, but even those who aren't by nature dictatorial are rarely impressed by those who thwart their policies or criticise their initiatives. Leaders, therefore, are likely to identify opposition to their policies as ingratitude on the part of their people and seek to overcome it. What opposition rarely does is to temper the leader's enthusiasm for pursuing the policy they wish to enact or have already imposed upon the people. A people's champion – a once popular and charismatic figure – can become very introverted, increasingly stubborn, and hubristically autocratic if they think that they are unappreciated by their citizens who haven't the wit to see what their leader is doing for them. We see that with the case of Julius Nyerere.

Some leaders my contributors have examined were arrogant and genuinely believed they were far brighter than those around them in the political environment and had nothing to learn from listening to them. Hendrik Verwoerd, for example, comes swiftly to mind. A university academic and ideologue, he led from the front and expected the rest of his government, let alone the white business leaders, to follow. They didn't need much convincing that it was in their best interests to do so. Verwoerd, a doctrinaire authoritarian, was so convinced that he was right about his policies that he saw no reason for turning away from them. In this regard, he reminds me of Mrs Thatcher in the 1980s.

DOI: 10.4324/9781003426165-10

Coda **185**

John Vorster was under no illusions about him being an intellectual match for his predecessor, but he was alive to the political shoals in which he was steeped and as a natural schemer could invariably fathom out a way to pass through them. He needed no tutoring on how to undermine those who obviously posed a threat to his leadership and successfully kept the others who might emerge from the shadows to challenge his authority in check through a variety of stratagems. This worked for a dozen years before age and intrigue caught up with him.

Lee Kuan Yew was not only a very talented lawyer – though perhaps not as bright as his wife in legal matters – but someone who had a remarkable vision for his island state that he was able to realise by the time he left power of his own volition 31 years after he became Prime Minister of Singapore in 1959. Hard-driven and fiercely competitive, Lee had no time for wishful thinking. His island republic was small and vulnerable. Belief in foreigners only went so far even though he couldn't do without them in some form or another. An elitist by conviction and a strategic realist by nature, he planned for the future and surrounded himself with a cadre of others who shared his outlook. He was always on the lookout for the next crisis, and complacency was something he didn't tolerate in others let alone himself. Something of a loner, his interpersonal skills and ruthlessness often left much to be desired. Aware that challenges of many kinds could be posed for his metropolitan city state, he tried to ensure that Singapore remained ahead of the economic curve by thinking out of the box and making his well-paid, cohort of officials agile and entrepreneurial enough to seize opportunities before their regional competitors responded in a similar manner. Many leaders who stay at the top for a long while as Lee did become bored and jaded, begin to perform inadequately and haphazardly, and often fall prey to patronage and corruption. On the whole, Lee bucked that trend. His accomplishments, experience, and accumulated wisdom were such that other world leaders sought his advice and opinions long after he had handed over the seals of office to his successor Goh Chok Tong.

Fidel Castro was a born survivor. Whether there were 638 assassination attempts on his life as the media claims or not, he was a figure who courted notoriety in the way he ran his island state of Cuba and dealt harshly with his opponents. Utterly ruthless and with a volcanic temperament, Castro had no time for those who didn't buy into his socialist dream for Cuba. Opponents were dispensable and could be locked up or shot, expelled, and asset stripped. It didn't matter that proof of their infidelity wasn't always provided because for Castro the revolution was everything. Nothing else mattered than to solidify the government that had replaced the despotic and corrupt autocracy of Batista. Something of a strategic ideologue, Castro revelled in leading from the front as he did in responding to the CIA-planned Bay of Pigs invasion in April 1961, and this kind of charismatic leadership went down well with the Cuban poor. While he shared power with Che Guevara for several years, Castro's competitive nature was such that he was probably highly relieved when the iconic Argentinian left Cuba for pastures new in 1965. In essence, Castro

186 Malcolm Murfett

and Cuba were synonymous with one another. Their domestic achievements were singular and unparalleled even amongst their adversaries. In rejecting neocolonialism for independence, they defied the Western world and continued to stand as exemplars of a new way forward. Pragmatic when he needed to be, Castro, as the Republic's undisputed leader, forged an evolving and nuanced identity for his country. This helped to create an aura between him and the Cuban people that was palpable and one that was never entirely dispelled.

Apart from being the world's first democratically elected woman leader of her country, Sirimavo Bandaranaike had a durability in power that few could have imagined when she first became Prime Minister of Ceylon (Sri Lanka) in July 1960. In a traditionally patriarchal country, she turned out to be a formidable adversary for her misogynistic rivals for power. Echoing her late husband Solomon's policies, she enthusiastically and divisively endorsed a populist agenda that was both racist in tone and substance favouring the majority Sinhalese at the expense of the Tamil minority. Populism may have electoral benefits for those leaders relying upon it, but the hatred and socio-economic divisions it often causes between peoples is never easily resolved. These wounds were deeply embedded in Sri Lanka as we saw in the horrific civil war that consumed the country from 1983 to 2009. Whatever else, Mrs Bandaranaike may have achieved in her nearly 18 years in power and the high international profile she rejoiced in as a result of her chairmanship of the Non-Aligned Movement, the visceral damage her populist policies did to her country cannot be overlooked or explained away as a matter of expediency let alone justification. By the same token, neither can the corruption nor the nepotism that she condoned while she was premier be expunged.

Julius Nyerere led by example. He truly believed in African Socialism and wanted to bring it about in his own country. A man of moral integrity and a staunch believer in the Catholic faith, Nyerere hated conflict but loathed white minority rule even more. A man of simplicity, referred to by some observers as the 'Gandhi of the African Continent,' he eschewed corruption and elitism in favour of egalitarianism and equity. Independent by nature, widely read, and intelligent, a thinker who was confident in his own abilities, Nyerere became a type of mentor for his fellow African leaders. Sensitive and unwilling to be dictated to by others, he could be obstinate and rigid on occasion. An unabashed nationalist, the moderate leader became more authoritarian and radical as he got older and more frustrated with the fact that *Ujamaa* and villagisation did not yield the economic progress within Tanzania that he had hoped for. Unfortunately, Tanzania under Nyerere was an experiment that in the end didn't live up to his expectations. A socialist paradise it was not.

Leonid Brezhnev represented a real change of Soviet leader from the destructive and menacing presence of Stalin and the wildly unpredictable and foul-mouthed Khrushchev. Brezhnev's leadership was not a rule of fear. His communism was more humane than those who had preceded him and reflected the fact that he loved

Coda **187**

the better things in life. He was also far more companionable and less intimidating than either of his predecessors. He didn't bully his associates but worked with them in a collective way whether in speech-writing or policy building. Demotions were also handled differently. He tried to make those whom he replaced buy into their new existence. It sounds rather utopian but it worked. Restoring trust in the Kremlin and within the CPSU was key. Consensus was his motif and peace and prosperity his ultimate goal. He had seen acute suffering and privation at close hand and wanted no more of the famines or the purges that had despoiled the Stalinist years in particular. In addition, he was far more risk-averse than the reckless Khrushchev had been. There would be no equivalent to the 'Meniscus Strategy' that had led to the Cuban Missile Crisis in October 1962. As the years passed, he found more congenial company with Willy Brandt, Georges Pompidou, and Richard Nixon than most of the leaders of the satellite states of the Warsaw Pact. Even so, his 18 years in power were not without international crises. His weary acceptance that his protégé Alexander Dubček and the 'Prague Spring' would have to be swept away caused him no end of stress and left him dependent upon sleeping tablets from 1968 onwards. His physical condition and mental acuity worsened from the mid-1970s, and by the time the Soviet invasion of Afghanistan took place in December 1979, he was not in any kind of shape to forestall the Gromyko, Andropov, and Ustinov axis that pushed for war with the Afghans.

Nicolae Ceauşescu was both a hardline communist and a fervent believer in Romanian nationalism and saw no inherent contradiction in devoting himself to both of these causes. A Stalinist of sorts, prioritising the heavy industrialisation of his country over the collectivisation of agriculture, he copied the leadership style of his former friend and mentor Gheorghiu-Dej without being either as talented or personable. Ceauşescu made up for it by astutely playing the role of the maverick statesman when it suited his purposes. Devious and unscrupulous, mercurial and contradictory, he was distrusted by Brezhnev and loathed by Gorbachev. Alert to political threats, real and imagined, and needing constant support from the cruel and vicious Securitate, he became wedded to the cult of personality which made him out to be larger than life. Living in such a bubble as this, where his virtues were constantly being aired and eulogised, may have encouraged hidden monarchical tendencies within him to come to the surface. He came to believe that he was above politics – a feeling encouraged by his wife Elena whom he trusted implicitly – and this may have contributed to a certain complacency that led to him underestimating popular rage within Romania in the wake of the fall of the Berlin Wall. As late as mid-December 1989, Ceauşescu still thought that with his country's external debts paid off, he would be able to lead Romania into the promised land. It was never to be.

Able and opportunistic, gutsy and formidable, Richard Nixon was a competitive no-holds barred political fighter with a passion to succeed against the odds in Washington. As someone who always saw himself as an outsider, Nixon had been

188   Malcolm Murfett

close to power for a long time before he finally won the presidency in November 1968. Talented and a visionary of sorts, more moderate than he had been in the 1950s, he was fascinated by the seductive intrigue of foreign affairs and relished the global spotlight that fell upon him as the leader of the free world. That he had to often share the stage with his National Security Advisor Dr Henry Kissinger was an irksome necessity, but it ensured that the first presidential term was highly successful and one that resulted in his landslide re-election in the Fall of 1972. Fascinatingly, however, the success of the 'Nixinger' duopoly didn't satisfy him as much as it should have done. He wanted more – whatever that was – and this restlessness drove him to do things he ought to have avoided. An often irascible Quaker with a short temper, Nixon sought to vanquish his political opponents by virtually any means at his disposal. Ethics went out of the window in his insatiable desire to learn what they were plotting even though this strategic intelligence was unnecessary. Where was his pragmatic idealism when he needed it most? Congress and the country were not about to bring him down until he crossed the ethical line over the Watergate break-in – whether he sanctioned it or not – and in the lying and dissembling that he indulged in to try and cover up his tracks thereafter. In the end, Nixon's battery of egregious personal flaws – his jealousy, vanity, insecurity, and a lack of moral integrity – combined to undermine his presidency. Despite being a rather unsavoury character, he was still far more adept in power than his critics would ever concede. Paradoxically, as is well known, success and failure are two sides of the same coin and so it proved in the case of the man from Yorba Linda, California.

Unlike any of the other leaders we have looked at in this volume who rose through the political ranks to assume power in their country, Mohammad Reza Shah Pahlavi inherited the Iranian monarchy at the age of 21 upon the abdication of his father on 16 September 1941. A proud and ambitious young man anxious to make his own mark upon his nation, the Shah strove to modernise Iran and make it, along with Israel, into one of the twin pillars of stability and progress in the Middle East. Seeing himself as a descendant of Cyrus the Great, the Shah's nationalism was genuine as was his desire to improve the social fabric of the country through the significant reforms he introduced under the White Revolution. Mercurial and egotistical, he was not the great strategist he imagined he was. In some senses, he was tone deaf and didn't take on board the myriad problems that his policies would stir up in the country at large. His attitude to the *bazarii* is a case in point. While the default position he adopted when dealing with any opposition to his rule was penal, the problems posed by the Shia clergy unnerved him somewhat. Although he tried to weaken their hold over teaching and acquired much of their land in the rural areas, as a loyal Muslim he could hardly ban the practice of Islam in his country and this meant, of course, that the Mosques were always a place where the opposition to both him and his reforms could flourish. Overall, the Shah's report card is a mixed bag. While his attitude to women's rights was enlightened, and many of his reforms were overdue in eliminating the feudal system of land ownership, the

Coda **189**

treachery he indulged in with the CIA over the removal of his premier Mosaddeq was culpable, and his endorsement of the SAVAK was heinous. In the end, he didn't have the charisma or loyalty necessary to carry the country with him, and as his health deteriorated so his capacity to maintain a firm hold on power in Iran eked away and left him seeking exile in Egypt from which there was no glorious return.

Looking at the leadership styles of the ten individuals my contributors have covered in this volume, it's manifestly clear that each brought something different to the top table, and the personal traits of those leaders conditioned the way that they ran their nations. Personalities matter, even at the apex of complicated structures of power and governance. This is hardly surprising and had we looked at another cast of leaders drawn from the same period, we undoubtedly would have found acute differences from those selected on this occasion. After all, the charismatic qualities of a Kwame Nkrumah or a Willy Brandt, the workaholic and micromanaging style of a Walter Ulbricht or a Jimmy Carter, the imperial haughtiness of Charles de Gaulle or the trimming opportunism of Harold Wilson were all evident in these years of change. As indeed were the uncompromising nature of a Golda Meir or the enigmatic authoritarianism of Indira Gandhi, let alone the unrivalled domination of Chairman Mao.

So what does this say about leadership? What should one expect of a good leader? Again, the list will differ according to whom one asks. For my part, I would like to see ethical people of integrity reach the top who believe in the principle of equality before the law and are capable of resisting the temptation of corruption and the acquisition of ill-gotten gains when they are in a position to make those calls. Too many have not turned a blind eye to these possibilities of personal or familial enrichment in the past. Also, I would hope that they would possess a vision for their country that wasn't animated by racism or xenophobia and only attainable through war and the defeat of neighbouring states. But as we have seen with the rise of populism and unbridled nationalism, being virtuous and moderate has not always been the golden path to the top.

Whatever else one is looking for in a leader, good communication skills surely must be of cardinal importance, and the more inspirational the speaker the greater is their chance of reaching out to a wider audience and getting buy-in to the programme they are offering to their people. If we look back at the ten leaders we have studied in this volume, not all of them were as inspirational as Castro or Nyerere, but some had an aura about them such as Lee and Verwoerd that more than made up for the way they addressed their audience.

Our volume has looked at leaders who held power for at least eight years, but the mistakes that were made by them were not always indulged in at the end of their careers, when they might have been inclined to shortcut procedures to get their own way. To prove the point, alas, witness the racial bias employed from the outset by the apartheid leaders and Mrs Bandaranaike that divided the people and made civil war more likely in both South Africa and Sri Lanka. Unfortunately, the internal security apparatus to suppress popular feeling was employed as a notorious weapon to undermine opposition in virtually every country we studied. Some leaders fell because of their personal shortcomings, Nixon and Vorster being classic examples of that trend, and others because they were complacent, took too much for granted, and refused to appreciate the rising tide of dissent within their nation, Ceauşescu and Mohammad Reza Shah being cases in point. Verwoerd and Brezhnev died in office, the former violently, the latter mercifully after a long physical decline. Age finally caught up with Castro and Bandaranaike but didn't have anything like the same effect on Lee Kuan Yew who gave up the premiership of his own free will and carried on in what technically was a subordinate capacity as a minister mentor for more than two decades afterwards.

These case studies drawn from across four continents of the world clearly reveal the yin and the yang of what high politics is all about. Control of power and the use of influence have always been seductive forces for those wielding them on the national and world stage. Personal egos have much to answer for. Lord Acton certainly thought so. In 1887, his famous aphorism about the corruption of power went on to add that 'Great men are almost always bad men.'[1] Was this still true nearly a century later? Acton's very bleak assessment of the human condition is far too sweeping a generalisation to be accepted without serious reservations. Some people who reach the 'top of the greasy pole' are notorious for one reason or another, as we have seen in this book, but not all are.

So what can we learn from these studies of leadership and what should the national leaders have done differently? A cop-out answer would be to say that these were precisely the questions that I used to ask of my excellent students at King's College London at the end of 40 hours of our classes together. Their answers were profoundly different both within the same peer group and across all five years that I ran that course on 'Political Leadership in a Time of War and Revolution.' If nothing else, this diversity of opinion suggests that effective leadership lies in the eye of the beholder. What was clear to me in the pre-Covid years and perhaps even more so now is that Leadership Studies is a fascinating discipline that is worthy of attention. It would be a comforting thought to imagine that those who study leadership and want to progress in government might avoid some of the mistakes that we have identified in this book and become better, more enlightened, leaders as a result. But will they . . .?

. . . .

Note

1 Letter to Bishop Mandell Creighton, April 5, 1887. A transcript of this letter is published in the Appendix of *Historical Essays and Studies*, ed. J. N. Figgis and R. V. Laurence (London: Palgrave Macmillan, 1907), 504.

INDEX

Abu Musa island 175–76
Acton, Baron John 190
Adevărul 142
Afghanistan 115, 187
African National Congress (ANC) 2, 6–8
African nationalism 84, 89
African Socialism 82, 85, 89, 93, 96, 186
Alam, Asadollah 172
Alegría de Pío 53–54
Allende, Salvador xviii
Amini, Ali 171
Amuzegar, Jamshid 179
Andropov, Yuri 109, 115, 187
Anglo-Iranian Oil Company (AIOC) 167
anti-colonialism 4
Antifascists Committee (*Comitetul National Antifascist*) 129–30
Antonescu, Ion 131–33
apartheid 1–2, 6–21, 73, 93, 189
Apollo 11 152–53
Apostol, Gheorghe 130
Arab-Israeli War (also known as Yom Kippur War) 1973 164
Arbatov, Georgi 107
Arusha declaration (1967) 89–90
Authentic Cuban Revolutionary Party (*los Autenticos*) 52
Ayala, Jorge Eliécer Gaitán 51

Baghdad Pact 171
Bahr, Egon 116
Baker Maurice 35, 38, 44n5

Bakhtiar, Shahpur 180
Bandaranaike, Anura 67, 76
Bandaranaike, Chandrika 67–68; *see also* Kumaratunga, Chandrika
Bandaranaike–Chelvanayakam Pact (1957) 66
Bandaranaike, Felix Dias 69–71, 76
Bandaranaike, Sirimavo xvi, 62–78, 186, 189–90
Bandaranaike, Solomon xvi, 66–71, 75–77, 186
Bantu Authorities Act 13
Bantustan strategy xiv, 14–15
Bárcenas, Rafael García 52
Basket 3 (Human Rights) 114
Batista, Fulgencio 51–55, 185
Bayamo 52
Bay of Pigs (1961) 56, 185
bazarii (merchants) 174, 179, 188
Beijing 74, 157, 159–60
Bessarabia 128–29, 131, 137, 139, 143n8
Botha, P.W 10–11
Brandt, Willy 113–14, 159, 187, 189
Brezhnev, Ilya 101–2
Brezhnev, Leonid xvii, 100–16, 186–87, 190
Brezhnev, Natalya 101–2
Brezhnev, Viktoriya 103
Brown, Pat xviii, 147
Brzezinski, Zbigniew 149, 160
Bucharest 125–26, 128–29, 131, 133, 141
Bukovina 128–29, 131

192 Index

Cambodia 158
Carter, Jimmy 114, 116, 160, 177–78, 189
Castro, Fidel xv–xvi, 50–60, 185,
    189–90
Castro, Raul 53, 60
Ceauşescu, Andruţa 127–28
Ceauşescu, Elena 125–26, 131, 133,
    142–43, 143n5, 187
Ceauşescu, Licsandra 127–28
Ceauşescu, Nicolae xvii–viii, 112, 125–43,
    187, 190
Ceauşescu, Niculuna 128
Central Committee (CPSU) 100–1, 105–9,
    111, 115–16
Ceylon *see* Sri Lanka
Chan Sun Wing 36
Chaves, Hugo 59–60
Chile xviii
China xviii, 75, 77, 85, 87, 89, 91–92,
    95, 112, 126, 138, 146, 148, 150,
    153–57, 159–60
Chin Peng 32
Churchill, Winston 168
CIA 51, 56, 168, 185, 189
Cluj 134
CMEA (Council of Mutual Economic
    Assistance) 58
Cohen, Andrew 84
Cold War i, xviii, 50, 55–56, 64–65, 73,
    77, 111, 126–27, 146–50, 154–55,
    164, 171
Colombo 67, 73–74
Common Agricultural Policy (EEC) 141
Communist Party of the Soviet Union
    (CPSU) 111, 116, 187
Conference on Security and Cooperation in
    Europe (CSCE) 114, 155
Congress (US) 148, 150–53, 155,
    157–60, 188
Cooperative Wholesale Establishment 75
Cooper-Church amendment 158
Cooray, Archbishop T.B 70
corruption xvi, 52, 75–76, 84, 90–91,
    186, 189
Council of Regency 180
Cristescu, Gheorghe 129
Cuba 50–60, 185
Cuban Missile Crisis (1962) 56, 187
Cuban People's Party (*Ortodoxos*) 52
Cult of personality xviii, 116, 134,
    138–40, 142
Cyrus the Great 176, 188
Czechoslovakia 111–13, 125, 137

Dalì, Salvador 139–40
Dar es Salaam 86–87, 90, 93
decolonisation 64–65
de Gaulle, Charles 189
de Klerk, F.W 11
democratic socialism 65
détente 16, 65, 74, 113–15, 139, 146, 148,
    150, 154–55, 157, 159–60
'developed socialism' 110
Dnepropetrovsk 100, 104–5, 109
'Dnepropetrovsk Mafia' 104
Dnieper dam 105
Dobrynin, Anatoly 155
Doftana 130
D'Oliveira, Basil 16
Draghici, Alexandru 130, 136–37
Dravida Munnetra Kazhagam (DMK) 71
Dubček, Alexander 112–13, 115, 125,
    137, 187

Egypt 146, 170, 175, 180, 189
Eisaku Satō 159
Eisenhower, President Dwight xviii,
    56, 147
Ettela'at 178

Fadayan-e Islam (those who sacrifice
    themselves for Islam) 165, 167
Fang Chuang Pi ('the Plen') 30
Federal Party 66, 69
'Fidel-Centrism' 51
Fong Swee Suan 29
Ford, Gerald 177
Fritsch, Günther 87

Gandhi, Indira 62–63, 75–76, 80n30, 189
Generation of the Centenary 52
German Democratic Republic (DDR)
    86–88, 97n19
Gheorghe Gheorghiu-Dej xvii, 129–33,
    135–36, 140, 187
Gierek, Edward 112, 138
GLBTQ+ xvi, 51
GLC (government-linked companies)
    41–43
Global South 82, 96
Goh Chok Tong 42, 185
Goh Keng Swee 30, 34–36
Goldwater, Barry xviii
Gomułka, Władysław 112, 138
González, Elián 59
Goode, Sir William 30
Gorbachev, Mikhail 115–16, 141, 187

Index **193**

Gorriarán, Camilo Cienfugos 54–55
Granma 53, 60
Gromyko, Andrei 109, 115, 187
'Guam doctrine' 153
Guantanamo Naval Base 56
Guevara, Che 50–51, 54, 57–59, 185

Haig, Alexander 156
Haldeman, H. R 154
Hallstein Doctrine 86
Havana 52–53, 55
Helsinki Final Act (1975) 114
Heng Swee Keat 37
Herstigte Nasionale Party 18
Hertzog, Albert 17
Hiss, Alger xviii
Hohenzollern-Sigmaringen, King Carol II 131
Hohenzollern-Sigmaringen, King Mihai
        131–33
'Homeland or Death' 55
Honecker, Erich 112, 116, 138
Hon Sui Sen 36
House Un-American Activities xviii
Hoveyda, Amir-Abas 179
human rights 3–6, 9, 58, 93–94, 114,
        158–59, 177–78
Hungarian Uprising (1956) 134
Hungary 110, 112, 134, 139, 144n17
Husák, Gustáv 112

Idi Amin 94
Iliescu, Ion 143
India 64, 73–77, 79n28
Indo-Ceylon Pact (1964) 74
International Monetary Fund (IMF) 94–95
Iranian National Oil Company 169
Iran xix, 142, 164–81, 188–89
Islamic intellectuals (*Roshanfekran-e
        Dini*) 169
Islamic Revolution (1979) xix, 141, 164, 180
Israel 170, 175, 188

Jain, Devaki 95
Janatha Vimukti Peramuna (People's
        Liberation Front, JVP) 73
Japan 150, 159
Jaruzelski, Wojciech 111, 115–16
Jayalalitha 70
Jeyawardene, Junius 75
Johnson, Lyndon B (LBJ) 146, 153, 155

Kádár, János 112
Kambona, Oscar 83, 86–87, 90

Kamenskoye (Kamianske) 101, 103
Karume, Abeid 86–87
Kashani, Ayatollah Abol-Ghasem 166, 172
Kazakhstan 106
Kennedy, John F xviii, 56, 84, 147, 171, 177
Kennedy School of Government, Harvard
        University 38–40
Kenyatta, Jomo 86
Khomeini, Ayatollah Ruhollah xix, 164,
        166, 169, 172–73, 178–80, 182n27
Khrushchev, Nikita xvii, 56, 100–2,
        104–10, 112–13, 127, 134, 136,
        186–87
Kim il–Sung 138
King Carol II Hohenzollern-Sigmaringen
        131; *see also* Hohenzollern-
        Sigmaringen, King Carol II
King Mihai Hohenzollern-Sigmaringen
        131–33; *see also* Hohenzollern-
        Sigmaringen, King Mihai
Kissinger, Henry xviii, 147–48, 150–53,
        155–60, 188
Komsomol 103
Kosygin, Alexander 110–11, 114
Kumaratunga, Chandrika 73, 76
Kumaratunga, Vijay 76
Kursk 101–3

Laird, Melvin 151
Laos 158
Lee Hsien Loong 37–38, 43
Lee Kuan Yew xv, 24–44, 185, 189–90
Lessing, Gottfried 86, 88
LGBTQ+ xvi, 51
Liberation Tigers of Tamil Eelam (LTTE) 72
Lim Chee Onn 37
Lim Chin Siong 29, 31–33
Lim Kim San 36
Lim Yew Hock 31
Li Peng 95
Llano 54
Luca Vasile 130

Mahathir Mohamad 38
Malayan Communist Party (MCP)
        29–33, 36
Malayan Forum 25–26
Malaysia 31, 33–35
Mandela, Nelson 73
Mao Zedong 126, 138, 156, 189
Marcovici, Smil 130
Marshall, David 31
Martí, Jose 52, 56

194 Index

Marxism-Leninism 52, 56, 59
Matos, Huber 55
Mazrui, Ali 90
Mboya, Tom 82
McCarthy, Joseph xviii
Mecca 170, 173
Medvedev, Roy 100, 107
Meir, Golda 189
Middle East 146, 171, 173, 175–76, 188
Millinga, Ntimbanjayo 89
Moghaddam, Lt. General Nasser 179
Mohamed, Bibi Titi 83
Moldova 105–6
Molotov, Vyacheslav 134
Molotov-Ribbentrop Pact (August
    1939) 131
Moncada Army Barracks (*Quartel de
    Moncada*) 51–52
Moncada veterans 54
Mondlane, Eduardo 93
Mosaddeq, Mohammad xix, 164, 166–70,
    177, 180, 189
Moscow 103, 105–6, 109, 111–16, 131,
    155, 159
*Movimiento Revolucionário 26
    de Julio – M-26–7*
    (26 July Movement) 53–55
Mwinyi, Ali Hassan 95

Nair, C.V. Devan 30, 37–38
Nassiri, General Nematolloh 179
National Front (*Jebhe-ye-Melli*) 164,
    166–69, 171, 173, 180
nationalism xviii, 64, 66, 70–72, 77, 84,
    89, 135, 140, 143, 164, 169–70,
    175–76, 180, 187–89
National Revolutionary Movement 52
National Security Council (US) 151, 156,
    158, 168
nepotism 64, 76, 78, 186
New International Economic Order (NIEO)
    93–94
'Nixon Doctrine' 153
Nixon, Richard M xviii, 113–15, 137,
    146–60, 175–77, 181, 187–88,
    190
Nkrumah, Kwame 84–85, 189
NKVD (People's Commissariat for Internal
    Affairs) 104
Non-Aligned Movement xvi, 73–75, 77,
    93, 186
North Korea 126, 138, 153
Nyerere, Julius xvi–ii, 81–96, 184,
    186, 189

Ogaden War (1976–8) 175
oil nationalization 168
Oman 175
Operation *Ajax* 168–69
Operation *Anadyr* 56
Organization of African Unity (OAU) 3,
    88, 93
Organization of American States 56, 58
Organization of Petroleum Exporting
    Countries (OPEC) 180
Organizing Department (*Secţia
    Organizatorică*) 136

Pahlavi, Mohammad Reza Shah xviii–ix,
    164–81, 188, 190
Pais, Frank 53
Pakistan 73, 77, 153, 175
pan-Africanism 83, 92–93, 96
Paris Peace Accord (1973) xviii, 154, 158
Pătrăşcanu, Lucreţiu 132–34, 136
Pauker, Ana 132–35
People's Action Party (PAP) 29–31, 35–36
People's House (*Casa Poporului*) 141
perestroika 141
Período Especial en Tiempo de Paz (Special
    Period in Time of Peace) 59
Persian Gulf 175–76
Pink Tide 60
Podgorny, Nikolai 114
Poland 110–11, 115
Politburo (CPSU) 101, 105, 107–12,
    115–16
Pompidou, Georges 113–14, 159, 187
Popescu, Dumitru 130–31
populism xvi, 32, 64, 67, 69–70, 186, 189
Prabhakaran, Vellupillai 72
Prague Spring 111–13, 115, 125, 137, 187
Presidium of the Supreme Soviet 105–7
Pyongyang 138

Qom 165, 170

Ras Al Khaimah 176
Rastakhiz 176–77
Razm Ara (also known as Haj Ali Razmara)
    167–68
Republican Party (US) 147–48
Reza Shah 165–66
Rhodesia 88, 92
Rogers, William 151–52, 157–58
Romania 125–43, 153, 187
Romanian Communist Party (RCP) 125,
    127–33, 135–36, 138–40, 142–43,
    144n21

Index **195**

Roosevelt, Eleanor 82–83
Ruvuma Development Association
(RDA) 89

Saigon 154
Sănătescu, Constantin 132
Sanjabi, Karim 180
Santiago de Cuba 52–53
SAVAK xix, 170, 177, 179, 189
Schools Takeover Act (1961) 70
Scorniceşti 127–28, 130
Securitate xviii, 126, 137, 142, 187
Senanayake, Dudley 68, 75
Senghor, Léopold 86
Sharjah 176
Shastri, Lal Bahadur 74
Shiite clergy 164–65, 170, 172, 174,
178–79, 188
Sierra Maestra 53–54, 60
Sighet prison 134
Singapore xv, 24–44
Singh, Manmohan 95–96
Sinhala Only 66–68, 70–73, 78
Sinhalese xvi, 65–66, 68, 71–72, 74–75,
77, 186
Smith, Ian 20–21
Smuts, Jan 1–2, 21
Solidarność 115
Somalia 175
Soulbury Constitution 65
South Africa 1–21, 92–93, 189
Soviet Union (USSR) xvii, 11, 33, 55–59,
65, 75, 77, 85–87, 91, 100–1, 106,
110–11, 113, 115–16, 125–26,
129, 131–37, 139, 140–41,
146–47, 151, 154–57, 159,
167–68, 171
Special Branch 29–32, 36
Sputnik 106
Sri Lanka (formerly Ceylon) xvi, 62–78,
186, 189
Sri Lanka Freedom Party (SLFP) 68–69,
71, 75–76
Stalin, Josef 100–1, 103–9, 115–16,
186–87
State Department (US) 151–52, 158
Ştei special psychiatric hospital 137
Storica, Chivu 130
Strait of Hormuz 176
Strategic Arms Limitation Talks (SALT I &
SALT II) 114, 155, 157
Sullivan, Ambassador William H 179
Suzman, Helen 18
Sverdlovsk 103

Tamil Nadu 70–71, 74
Tamils xvi, 65–66, 68, 71–72, 74–75,
79n8, 79n10, 79n28, 186
Tamil United Front 72
Tanganyika African National Union
(TANU) 81–85, 89–92
Tanganyika Rifles 87
Tanzania (United Republic of) 81, 84–85,
87–95, 97n19, 186
Târgovişte 142
Tazara Railway 91–92
Tehran 166, 173, 175, 178
Third World 93–95, 141
Third-Worldism 82, 93, 149
Time 62, 69, 138, 152
Timişoara 141–42
Toma A. Toma 130
Touré, Ahmed Sékou 86
Toynbee, Arnold 27, 33, 39
Transylvania 128–29, 134–35, 139, 143n8,
144n17
Truernicht, Andries 18
Truman, Harry 177
Tudeh Party of Iran 164, 166, 168–70
Tun Abdul Razak 34
Tunbs (Greater & Lesser) 175–76
Tunku Abdul Rahman 34–36
Twining, Edward 84

Uganda 92
Ujamaa xvii, 82, 85–86, 88–94, 186
Ukraine 101, 105–6, 109
Ulbricht, Walter 112, 189
United Kingdom 84, 88, 167–69, 173,
176–77, 179
United National Party (UNP) 68–69,
75–76
United Nations Organization (UNO) 4,
7–9, 82, 93, 168, 178
United States 40, 52, 55–56, 58–59, 65,
77, 84, 87, 111, 115, 147–50,
152–53, 155–56, 158–60, 167,
169–71, 173, 175, 178–79,
182n27
Uniunea Tineretului Comunist (communist
youth union) 128, 130, 132
US Federal Reserve 141
US-Iranian Status of Force Agreement
(SOFA) 171
Ustinov, Dmitry 115, 187

Vadu Roşca 134
Vance, Cyrus 178
verkramptes Afrikaners 16–18

196 Index

verligtes Afrikaners 10, 19
Verwoerd, Dr. Hendrik xiv, 1, 7, 11–15,
    184, 189–90
Vietnam War 146, 148–50, 152–54,
    156–58, 160
Villagisation 88, 90–92, 186
Virgin Land Campaign 106
Vittachi, Verinda Tarzie 72
Vladivostok agreement (1974) 158
Vorster, John B xiv–xv, 15–21, 185, 190

Wang Gungwu 26
War Powers Act (1973) 158
Warsaw Pact 111–13, 116, 126, 137, 187
Washington 171, 178
Watergate 146–47, 152, 158, 188
West Germany 86–88, 97n19

White House 146–47, 149, 152, 155,
    157–58, 171, 175, 177–78
White Revolution 171–73, 178, 182n25, 188
Wilson, Harold 189
Winsemius, Albert 39–40
Workers' Party 30
World Bank 86, 94

Yazdi, Ebrahim 178
Yeltsin, Boris 116

Zahedi, General Fazollah 169
Zambia 91–92
Zanzibar 81, 86–87, 92; *see also* Tanzania
Zaporozhye 105
Zhivkov, Todor 112
Zhou Enlai 156–57

Printed in the United States
by Baker & Taylor Publisher Services

PROPHESYING DESIGN

Embarking on a journey through the multifaceted world of design, one encounters an intriguing provocation: in our earnest efforts to decolonise design, do we risk inadvertently establishing a new hierarchy, one that elevates Indigenous and non-Western design philosophies to a status previously occupied by colonial aesthetics? This philosophical conundrum is not a dismissal of the vital process of decolonisation, but rather an invitation to scrutinize the complexities and potential ironies embedded within this transformative movement.

As we delve into the intricacies of design history, it becomes apparent that the narrative has been predominantly Eurocentric, often overshadowing the rich medley of global design heritage. The endeavour to rectify this skewed narrative is undoubtedly noble, yet it behoves us to ponder: in our quest to uplift Indigenous and non-Western design principles, might we risk creating a reverse hegemony? Such a scenario would see the previously marginalised design philosophies not just restored but positioned in a way that could inadvertently marginalize other design traditions. This provocation serves as a critical reflection on the journey of decolonising design. It is an acknowledgment that while reversing historical power imbalances is crucial, there lies a delicate balance in ensuring that this reversal does not morph into a new form of cultural dominance. It is a reminder that the pursuit of equity in design should aim for a harmonious coexistence of diverse design philosophies, rather than a competition for superiority.

This philosophical inquiry sets the stage for a deeper exploration and understanding of design's past, present, and future. It challenges us to envision a world of design that is truly inclusive and equitable, where diversity is not just recognised but celebrated as a source of strength and creativity. The journey of decolonising design, therefore, is as much about unlearning and relearning as it is about

Acknowledgements **vii**

To the universe
I pour libation to my life
Ye to the departed and spirits
Let the evil receive back their evil plans
To the amazing Lexi, for believing

Long life, love and kindness never depart from you
A million hugs, a million 'thank you's
You have changed my life
With watery eyes,
I cry out a thank you
To Angela, I want to thank you
You are amazing, you inspired me
The warmth you gave me
The opportunities offered me

Thank you
To Louise, our story has just begun
Yet, you have done so much
Such huge contributions
I am grateful

Finally, I thank myself for not giving up.

ACKNOWLEDGEMENTS

I dare not say I carried the burden of this book alone. The cheerful sounds I hear in the back of my head from family, friends and every other person who asked the question every PhD student is asked from day one: "What is your thesis about?" The excitement on their faces, the purity in their curiosity and their support, gave birth to this research. Three years ago, I could never have envisioned how much my life would change because of this research.

I am filled with gratitude. I am grateful for words of wisdom, inspiration, forgiveness, as well as the favours and gestures of politeness. Let me join hands with you as I channel my gratitude and express my utmost appreciation. The sensation is like gentle waves lapping at my fingers, a tangible expression of the spiritual goodness I wish to convey. If each of my words were falling rain, I would move in rhythmic dance patterns to show my feelings of gratitude and acknowledgement, an indefinable feeling of fear, respect, and the surprise of finishing the research.

To appreciate each of you
Today, I take a bow
   By drumming your names into eternity

      To my parents, I shout your praises and adoration from the heavens
   Words are not powerful enough
   The warmth of your love
   Thanks, Dad for my big head
Thanks, Mum for the endless prayers

CONTENTS

Acknowledgements	*vi*
Prophesying Design	*viii*
Prologue	*x*

1 Cultivating the Foundations: The Role of Design
  Education in Transforming the Legacy of African Education 1

2 Bridging the Divide: Culturally Relevant Pedagogy
  and Curriculum Development 42

3 Spirituality, Religion, and Artistic Practices in African
  Design Education 69

4 Politics and the Postcolonial Ideals: Use of Design to
  Fight Injustice, Racism, and Apartheid 103

Index *185*